IMAGINATION IN COLERIDGE

IMAGINATION IN COLERIDGE

Edited by
JOHN SPENCER HILL

ROWMAN AND LITTLEFIELD
Totowa, New Jersey

First published in the United States 1978
by Rowman and Littlefield, Totowa, N.J.

Printed in Hong Kong

Library of Congress Cataloging in Publication Data

Coleridge, Samuel Taylor, 1772–1834.
  Imagination in Coleridge.

  Bibliography: p.
  Includes index.
    1. Imagination – Collected works.   I.   Hill, John
Spencer.   II.   Title.
PR4472.H5   1978   821.7   77–16310
ISBN 0–8476–6026–5

for Janet

Contents

Now how to get back, having thus belabyrinthed myself in these most parenthetical parentheses? Cut thro' at once, & now say in half a dozen a Lines what half a dozen Lines would have enabled me to say at the very beginning/ but my Thoughts, my Pocket-book Thoughts at least, moved like a pregnant Polypus in sprouting Time, clung all over with young Polypi each of which is to be a thing of itself—and every motion out springs a new Twig of Jelly-Life/—

February 1805; CN II 2431

There is no way of arriving at any sciential End but by finding it at every step. The End is in the Means: or the adequacy of each Mean is already it's end. Southey once said to me: You are nosing every nettle along the Hedge, while the Greyhound (meaning himself, I presume) wants only to get sight of the Hare, & FLASH!—strait as a line!—he has it in his mouth!—Even so, I replied, might a Cannibal say to an Anatomist, whom he had watched dissecting a body. But the fact is—I do not care twopence for the *Hare*; but I value most highly the excellencies of scent, patience, discrimination, free Activity; and find a Hare in every Nettle, I make myself acquainted with. I follow the Chamois-Hunters, and seem to set out with the same Object. But I am no Hunter of *that* Chamois Goat; but avail myself of the Chace in order to [achieve] a nobler purpose— that of making a road across the Mountains, on which Common Sense may hereafter pass backward and forward, without desperate Leaps or Balloons that scar [soar?] indeed but do not improve the chance of getting onward.—

August 1820; CL v 98

Preface

Undoubtedly the most widely discussed aspect of Coleridge's literary criticism is his theory of Imagination and, principally, his distinction between Fancy and Imagination. Notwithstanding the importance and critical omnipresence of the theory both in Coleridge's own writings and in those of his commentators, however, students have been handicapped by the fact that Coleridge's pronouncements on Imagination are scattered throughout his works and cannot, in many cases, be found without a great deal of diligence on the student's part. Motivated by the desire to facilitate the study of his theory of Imagination, and hoping to bring his thought—or at least an aspect of it—within the grasp of a larger number of readers than it has hitherto had the fortune to meet, I have prepared this 'source-book' of Coleridge's statements on the nature and function of the Imagination.

The task I have set myself in the following pages is that of bringing together under one cover all of Coleridge's major, and the larger part of his 'minor' or less celebrated pronouncements on the Imagination. Such a methodology is fraught with difficulties and numerous compromises have been forced upon me. It will, for example, surprise some readers to discover that 'Kubla Khan' has been included while 'The Ancient Mariner' has not, and these readers will quite rightly complain that both poems are concerned with Imagination. I can only plead that some cut-off points were necessary and that 'Kubla Khan' seems to me more relevant to Coleridge's *theory* of Imagination than does 'The Ancient Mariner'.

More surprising, perhaps, than some of the exclusions will appear certain of the inclusions. The simple fact here is that Coleridge is an organicist, for whom Imagination is not exclusively—indeed, not even pre-eminently—a literary phenomenon. In Coleridge's scheme Imagination is one of the five central powers of the human mind, the remaining four being Reason, Understanding, Sense and Fancy. Now, while the operation of Imagination may be singled out for the purpose of argument or illustration, in actuality it forms an integral and inseparable part of the process of human cognition and thought. Imagination, that is to say, functions as an instrument of enquiry in philosophy, psychology, science and theology, as well as in literature and art; it cannot without serious distortion be abstracted and isolated on the dissecting table of the literary critic and treated *sui generis* as an aspect of artistic creativity alone. In Coleridge's writings (especially after 1815) Imagination exfoliates out and shades off into his thinking about almost everything else; indeed, divorced from the other components of his system, his theory of Imagination becomes virtually incomprehensible. For this reason it has been necessary to include Extracts and Notes explicating other seminal aspects of his thought, as (for example) his distinctions between Reason–Understanding and Imitation–Copy, his specialised use of such key terms as Symbol, 'One Life', Thought–Thing, and so forth. Coleridge is a difficult, but rewarding, author; and, since he was groping his way towards concepts for which neither a vocabulary nor a conceptual framework lay ready to hand, it is of crucial importance to meet him on his own ground, however difficult that may at times be. This book, then, while it concentrates on the theory of Imagination, may also serve as a critical Ariadne's thread to guide the reader into the labyrinth of Coleridge's thought and, I hope still clutching the thread, safely out again as well.

I considered the possibility of arranging the extracts which follow into thematic groups, but eventually rejected this notion in the belief that it would impose a rigidity on the material and a patterned artificiality foreign to the fluidity of Coleridge's thinking about Imagination. Moreover, such editorial intrusion would run the risk both of perverting Coleridge's intentions and of oversimplifying the subject. It seemed, therefore, that the only possible arrangement was a chronological one—for which, in any case, we have Coleridge's own warrant: 'All your divisions', he told his nephew and son-in-law Henry Nelson Coleridge toward the end of his life, 'are in particular instances inadequate, and they destroy the interest which arises from watching the progress, maturity, and even the decay of genius.'

I have tried throughout the book to allow Coleridge to speak for himself. This may seem a strange assertion to anyone who has glanced forward through the notes, which are numerous and often lengthy. However, since this book is intended primarily for students and non-specialists (although I hope, of course, that the Coleridge specialist will also find it useful), it has been necessary to explain a large number of terms and ideas which might otherwise be taken for granted. In general, the Notes appended to each Extract have been used for the following purposes: (a) to quote (or sometimes simply to refer the reader to) parallel or explanatory passages from elsewhere in Coleridge's writings in support or elucidation of a point under consideration; (b) to provide, occasionally, explanatory quotations from modern critics or to refer the reader to precise locations in their commentaries that bear on a point in question; (c) to give cross-references to other extracts or notes in the present volume; (d) to cite sources for and, where appropriate, to provide translations of passages which Coleridge has drawn from other authors; and (e) to give brief biographical and critical notices for important persons whom Coleridge mentions, and short explanatory statements of terms and conceptions (e.g. Baconian *idols* and Plato's theory of *recollection*) to which he alludes. These notes are intended to be helpful, but not exhaustive. I hope they will encourage the reader to explore the subject further, rather than to rest content with the hints and suggestions offered here.

I am indebted to a number of friends and colleagues who gave freely of their time and expertise to help make this a better book than I alone would have been capable of producing: *omnia non licet uni, non sperasse uni licet omnia*. I am much indebted to Dr John Beer of Peterhouse, Cambridge, who read the manuscript as it passed through the inevitable metamorphoses involved in growing from adolescence to maturity; he made many valuable suggestions and corrected me on numerous points of detail in the notes and bibliography. I owe much, too, to Professor George Whalley of Queen's University (Canada) who read the final typescript with minute attention; his depth of scholarship and familiarity with Coleridge are responsible for many corrections in the notes and I am especially in his debt for his help with the Introduction, which indeed would never have been written but for his prompting and guidance—although I suspect he may not be entirely satisfied with everything that I have said there. Dr Tony Miller and Dr Christopher Wortham, friends and colleagues at the University of Western Australia, graciously set aside their own work to read the Introduction as it was pulled, still smoking, from the typewriter. Miss Mary Alexander and her staff in the Reference Section efficiently and cheerfully filled my innumerable requests for material not available in the Reid Library. I am under a special obligation to Mrs Honoria Robertson-Dick for her scrupulous

proofreading of the final typescript, and also to her husband for so
selflessly sacrificing her company during the several weeks required
to perform this arduous task. My greatest debt is to my wife (who
survived this book still smiling) and my gratitude for her support is
acknowledged, where it ought to be, in the dedication.

Last, but by no means least, the publisher and I wish to thank the
following who have kindly given permission for the use of copyright
material. Constable & Company Ltd for the extracts from *Coleridge's
Miscellaneous Criticism*, edited by T. M. Raysor; J. M. Dent & Sons
Ltd for the extracts from *Coleridge's Shakespearean Criticism*, edited by
T. M. Raysor, and *Henry Crabb Robinson on Books and their Writers*,
edited by E. J. Morley. Oxford University Press for the extracts from
S. T. Coleridge, *Biographia Literaria*, edited by J. Shawcross; *The
Table Talk and Omniana of Samuel Taylor Coleridge*, edited by H.N.
Coleridge; *The Complete Poetical Works of Samuel Taylor Coleridge*,
edited by E. H. Coleridge; the *Collected Letters of Samuel Taylor
Coleridge*, edited by E. L. Griggs, and S. T. Coleridge, *Aids to
Reflection*, edited by H. N. Coleridge. Also Pantheon Books (Division
of Random House Inc.), for the extracts from *The Philosophical
Lectures of Samuel Taylor Coleridge*, edited by Kathleen Coburn;
Princeton University Press for the extracts from *The Collected Works
of Samuel Taylor Coleridge*, edited by Kathleen Coburn, and Routledge & Kegan Paul Ltd and Princeton University Press for the
extracts from *The Notebooks of Samuel Taylor Coleridge*, edited by
Kathleen Coburn.

Perth, Australia   J.S.H.
May 1977

List of Abbreviations

Works cited in the notes by author's surname and date of publication will be found in the Bibliography. Unless otherwise stated, quotations and page numbers in the notes refer to the most recent edition cited.

AN&Q *American Notes and Queries*

AP *Anima Poetæ, from the Unpublished Notebooks of Samuel Taylor Coleridge*, ed. E. H. Coleridge. London: Heinemann, 1895.

AR S. T. Coleridge, *Aids to Reflection*. London, 1825; 4th edition, ed. H. N. Coleridge, London, 1839.

AV Authorised Version (1611) of the Bible

BJA *British Journal of Aesthetics*

BL S. T. Coleridge, *Biographia Literaria . . . with the Aesthetical Essays*, ed. J. Shawcross. 2 vols. London and New York: O.U.P., 1907; corrected ed. 1954.

BMQ *The British Museum Quarterly*

CC *The Collected Works of Samuel Taylor Coleridge* (general editor K. Coburn). 16 vols and index (partially completed). London: Routledge & Kegan Paul, Princeton: Princeton University Press, 1967–

CE *College English*

CL *Collected Letters of Samuel Taylor Coleridge*, ed. E. L. Griggs. 6 vols. London and New York: O.U.P., 1956–71.

CN *The Notebooks of Samuel Taylor Coleridge*, ed. K. Coburn. 3 double vols so far published. London: Routledge & Kegan Paul, New York: Pantheon Books, 1957–

CPW *The Complete Poetical Works of Samuel Taylor Coleridge*, ed. E. H. Coleridge. 2 vols. London and New York: O.U.P., 1912.

CSC *Coleridge on the Seventeenth Century*, ed. R. F. Brinkley. Durham: Duke, University Press, 1955; New York: Greenwood Press, 1968.

CT	*Coleridge the Talker: A Series of Contemporary Descriptions and Comments*, ed. R. W. Armour and R. F. Howes. Ithaca: Cornell University Press, London: Milford, 1940.
C.U.P.	Cambridge University Press
DNB	*Dictionary of National Biography*
DP	*Dictionary of Philosophy*, ed. D. D. Runes. New York: Philosophical Library, 1960; Totowa, N. J.: Littlefield, Adams, 1972.
DRC	*Diary, Reminiscences, and Correspondence of Henry Crabb Robinson*, ed. T. Sadler. 3 vols. London: Macmillan, 1869.
E&S	*Essays and Studies by Members of the English Association*
EHC	Ernest Hartley Coleridge
EIC	*Essays in Criticism*
ELH	*Journal of English Literary History*
EM	*English Miscellany*
ES	*English Studies* (Amsterdam)
HCR	*Henry Crabb Robinson on Books and their Writers*, ed. E. J. Morley. 3 vols. London: Dent, 1938.
HNC	Henry Nelson Coleridge
IS	*Inquiring Spirit. A New Presentation of Coleridge from his Published and Unpublished Prose Writings*, ed. K. Coburn. London: Routledge & Kegan Paul, New York: Pantheon Books, Toronto: McClelland, 1951.
JAAC	*Journal of Aesthetics and Art Criticism*
JEGP	*Journal of English and Germanic Philology*
JHI	*Journal of the History of Ideas*
KSJ	*Keats–Shelly Journal*
LR	*The Literary Remains of Samuel Taylor Coleridge*, ed. H. N. Coleridge. 4 vols. London, 1836–9.
MC	*Coleridge's Miscellaneous Criticism*, ed. T. M. Raysor. London: Constable, 1936.
MLN	*Modern Language Notes*
MLQ	*Modern Language Quarterly*
MP	*Modern Philology*
MSP	Cardinal Mercier *et al.*, *A Manual of Modern Scholastic Philosophy*, trans. T. L. and S. A. Parker. 2 vols. London: Kegan Paul, 1915; 3rd ed. 1923, repr. 1960.
N&Q	*Notes and Queries*
NEB	*The New English Bible with the Apocrypha* (O.U.P. and C.U.P., 1961; 2nd ed. 1970).

OCD   *The Oxford Classical Dictionary*, ed. N. G. L. Hammond and H. H. Scullard. 2nd ed. corrected. Oxford: Clarendon Press, 1972.

OCCL   *The Oxford Companion to Classical Literature*, ed. Sir Paul Harvey. Oxford: Clarendon Press, 1937; corrected ed. 1940, repr. 1969.

OCEL   *The Oxford Companion to English Literature*, ed. Sir Paul Harvey and Dorothy Eagle. Oxford and New York: O.U.P., 1932; 4th ed. revised, 1967.

ODCC   *The Oxford Dictionary of the Christian Church*, ed. F. L. Cross and E. A. Livingstone. 2nd ed. London and New York: O.U.P., 1974.

OED   *The Oxford English Dictionary*
(*Note*: All word definitions cited in the Notes which are NOT marked '*OED*' are quoted or adapted from *The Shorter Oxford English Dictionary*, 3rd ed. corrected, 2 vols, 1975.)

O.U.P. Oxford University Press

PL   *The Philosophical Lectures of Samuel Taylor Coleridge*, ed. K. Coburn. London: Pilot Press, New York: Philosophical Library, 1949.

PMLA *Publications of the Modern Language Association*

PQ   *Philological Quarterly*

REL   *Review of English Literature*

RES   *Review of English Studies*

SC   *Coleridge's Shakespearean Criticism*, ed. T. M. Raysor. 2 vols. London: Constable, Cambridge, Mass.: Harvard University Press, 1930; London: Dent, 1960 (slightly abridged).

SEL   *Studies in English Literature* (Rice University)

SIR   *Studies in Romanticism*

SP   *Studies in Philology*

SR   *Sewanee Review*

STC   Samuel Taylor Coleridge

TLS   *The Times Literary Supplement*

TT   *The Table Talk and Omniana of Samuel Taylor Coleridge*, ed. H. N. Coleridge. London and New York: O.U.P., 1917.

TWC   *The Wordsworth Circle*

UTQ   *University of Toronto Quarterly*

List of Extracts

Introduction

The prevailing concept of 'mind' in eighteenth-century England was that advanced by empirical philosophers like Hobbes, Locke, Hume, and Hartley. In their systems the mind is represented as a *tabula rasa* or as a sheet of 'white paper void of all characters, without any *ideas*' on which external impressions conveyed through the five senses are printed. 'Whence has [the mind] all the materials of reason and knowledge? To this I answer, in one word, from *experience*; in that all our knowledge is founded, and from that it ultimately derives itself'. [1] The mind, then, functions merely as the passive recorder of sense impressions, especially those originating in sight. These mental 'images' or replicas of original sense impressions are stored in the memory, and in the acts of thinking or reflection they are recalled and combined with other stored-up images by the faculty of association. William Godwin has left the following summary of empirical epistemology:

> The human mind, so far as we are acquainted with it, is nothing else but a faculty of perception. All our knowledge, all our ideas, every thing we possess as intelligent beings, comes from impression. All the minds that exist, set out from absolute ignorance. They received first one impression, then a second. As the impressions became more numerous, and were stored up by the help of memory, and combined by the faculty of association, so the experience increased, and with the experience the knowledge, the wisdom, every thing that distinguishes man from what we understand by a 'clod of the valley'. [2]

In such empiricist systems and in the aesthetic theories derived from them, the role of Imagination is severely restricted and its operation regarded with suspicion. Functioning only as a mode or aspect of Memory, it is an illusion-making, 'castle-building' faculty diametrically opposed to the sovereign faculty of Reason; its concern is with fiction rather than fact, and it takes as its object not truth but intentional falsehood. (It may be added that, although there are some exceptions,[3] neoclassical criticism generally did not discriminate between the terms Imagination and Fancy.) The orthodox eighteenth-century theory is stated concisely in Samuel Johnson's *Dictionary of the English Language* (1755), where *Imagination* is defined as 'Fancy; the power of forming ideal pictures; the power of representing things absent to one's self or others'. One or two examples will make his meaning clearer. In the first place, Imagination is an aspect of Memory and its function is to reproduce past sensory experience (tastes, smells, objects of vision, &c.) in the form of mental images recalled and constructed out of materials stored in the Memory. Thomas Hobbes, for example, holds that 'Imagination and Memory are but one thing [namely, 'decaying sense'], which for divers considerations hath divers names'; and John Dryden develops the same point in an image, likening 'the faculty of imagination' to 'a nimble spaniel, [that] beats over and ranges through the field of memory, till it springs the quarry it hunted after. . . . It is some lively and apt description, dressed in such colours of speech, that it sets before your eyes the absent object, as perfectly, and more delightfully than nature'.[4] But Imagination is more than simply a mode of Memory; it is also the power by which originally distinct impressions are welded together – but *not* fused or blended – to form images that have no existence or counterpart in sense experience: for example, the image of a horse combined with that of a man yields a hybrid known as a centaur. The production of such mythological grotesques was often adduced by neoclassical aestheticians as an illustration of the way in which Imagination combines originally discrete images in its fabrications. In these terms, however, Imagination is a *combining and associative* but not a truly *creative* faculty; and it is therefore with a heavily qualified definition of 'creativity' that one must approach such statements as William Duff's assertion that the Imagination, 'by its plastic power of inventing new associations of ideas, and of combining them with infinite variety, is enabled to present a creation of its own'.[5] The same limitation applies to Dugald Stewart's description: 'The province of Imagination is to select qualities and circumstances from a variety of different objects; and, by combining and disposing these, to form a new creation of its own. In this appropriated sense of the word, it coincides with what some authors have called *Creative* or *Poetical Imagination*'.[6]

It is in opposition to these theories and the mechanical faculty psychology on which they depend that Coleridge gradually develops his conviction that Imagination is a more truly creative power. Rather than being simply a faculty for rearranging materials fed to it by the senses and the memory, the Imagination is a shaping and ordering power, a 'modifying' power which colours objects of sense with the mind's own light:

> Ah! from the Soul itself must issue forth
> A Light, a Glory, and a luminous Cloud
>   Enveloping the Earth!
> And from the Soul itself must there be sent
> A sweet & potent Voice, of it's own Birth,
> Of all sweet Sounds the Life & Element. [7]

The mind is not the passive recorder of sense impression; it is not (as for the empiricist) like an inert block of wax on which external objects imprint themselves. On the contrary, for Coleridge as for Wordsworth, perception is a bilateral rather than a unilateral activity; sense experience is a stimulus that evokes a response and involves (to borrow a phrase from Wordsworth) 'A balance, an ennobling interchange Of action from within and from without'. [8] Thus the product in any given act of perception is a modified combination of the percipient and the thing-perceived and is, as Coleridge asserts in *Biographia* Chap xii, neither a subject (perceiver) nor an object (thing-perceived) exclusively, but rather the most original union of both. In and through the act of blending 'thoughts' and 'things', the (primary) Imagination functions as a fusing, synthesising power—an *esemplastic* power whose operation generates a new reality by shaping parts into wholes, by reconciling opposites and drawing unity from diversity. It is not, as for the neoclassical critic, a mechanical faculty ('aggregative and associative'); it is, rather, a vital and organic *power* common to all men, which permits the mind to penetrate beneath the transitory surface of the material world, that is, to see into the life of things and experience the intimate relationship between the perceiving mind and the objects of its contemplation. The germinal potency of Coleridge's theory of Imagination lies in his rejection of passive perception, his recognition of perception as integrative, poietic, and necessarily correlative with feeling, and his understanding that the poetic Imagination grows out of a seamless bond between perception, memory, association, feeling, intellect, and a sense of language as being in some way autonomous. But this is to anticipate. Before we come to his mature theory, we must travel a little way along the path that led him to its formulation.

It is not surprising that initially Coleridge's understanding of the word Imagination should be determined by neoclassical usage; accordingly, in the years 1790–1801 he uses the terms Imagination and Fancy interchangeably to denote the mental faculty opposed to Reason and characterised by the ability either of recalling past images or of creating illusions of its own. Thus he writes of 'the wanderings of my castle building Imagination', inveighs with mock gravity against 'Truth, that Poisoner of Imagination', and in a more serious vein observes that 'this bodily frame is an imitative Thing, and touched by the imagination gives the hour that is past, as faithfully as a repeating watch' (CL I 48–9, 478 and VI 1012). Similar examples might easily be multiplied from the letters of this period and from the early poetry.[9]

Occasionally, however, there are hints in these early writings of a departure from normal neoclassical usage. In a letter of March 1798 to John Wicksteed, for example, the Imagination shows signs of emerging from its subordination to the Memory and is hesitantly invested with a mimetic function of its own: 'People in general are not sufficiently aware how often the imagination creeps in and counterfeits the memory—perhaps to a certain degree it does always blend with our supposed recollections' (CL I 394). In November 1800 the Imagination is more confidently disengaged from its associative, purely mnemonic role in empiricist theory: 'she appears to me to have been injured by going out of the common way without any of that Imagination, which if it be a Jack o'Lanthorn to lead us out of that way is however at the same time a Torch to light us whither we are going. A whole Essay might be written on the Danger of *thinking* without Images' (CL I 646). Here, the Imagination is an autonomous faculty and, instead of being the antagonist of Reason (as in neoclassical theory), is a complementary power functioning as its correlate in rational inquiry. Perhaps more remarkable than the two passages just quoted in terms of Coleridge's mature position are the adumbration of the later theory of 'primary' Imagination in the Slave-Trade lecture of 1795 (Extract 1) and the description in 'The Destiny of Nations' (1796) of how Fancy–Imagination 'unsensualises the dark mind' (Extract 2). But such early statements must be approached with a degree of caution. Interesting though they may be, it is dangerous to assign to them a greater conceptual or theoretic sophistication than they deserve or require. Because these passages include details that, with hindsight, we recognise to be part of the mature formulation, there is a temptation to construe them as premonitions and make them more important than they really are. But hindsight must not be confounded with prescience. In the final analysis the early deviations from the empiricist view of Imagination cannot be seen as material anticipations of the later theory. What they represent, in fact, are emergent occasions which did not come to fruition; many of the apparent correspondences with later theoretic developments are verbal rather than in any sense substantive, are merely echoes of ideas that were in the air at the time.

Although largely extrinsic to Coleridge's mature theory, these early statements nevertheless provide valuable evidence of his inherent dissatisfaction with the purely materialistic explanation of perception and the role of Imagination, and they imply a quality of mind that will lead him inevitably to reject the empirical hypothesis and to greet his later discovery of Kant's epistemology with the enthusiasm of a homecoming. According to Coleridge's own account in one of the autobiographical letters (16 October 1797) written at the request of Thomas Poole, he had longed in childhood and youth for 'the Vast' and a unified view of life which lay beyond the testimony of the senses and (consequently) outside the grasp of an empirical psychology:

I remember, that at eight years old I walked with my father one winter evening from a farmer's house, a mile from Ottery—& he told me the names of the stars—and how Jupiter was a thousand times larger than our world—and that the other twinkling stars were Suns that had worlds rolling round them—& when I came home, he shewed me how they rolled round—/. I heard him with a profound delight & admiration; but without the least mixture of wonder or incredulity. For from my early reading of Faery Tales, & Genii &c &c—my mind had been habituated *to the Vast*—& I never regarded *my senses* in any way as the criteria of my belief. I regulated all my creeds by my conceptions not by my *sight*—even at that age. Should children be permitted to read Romances, & Relations of Giants & Magicians, & Genii?—I know all that has been said against it; but I have formed my faith in the affirmative.—I know no other way of giving the mind a love of 'the Great', & 'the Whole'.—Those who have been led to the same truths step by step thro' the constant testimony of their senses, seem to me to want a sense which I possess—They contemplate nothing but *parts*—and all *parts* are necessarily little—and the Universe to them is but a mass of *little things*.—It is true, that the mind *may* become credulous & prone to superstition by the former method—but are not the Experimentalists credulous even to madness in believing any absurdity, rather than believe the grandest truths, if they have not the testimony of their own senses in their favor?—I have known some who have been *rationally* educated, as it is styled. They were marked by a microscopic acuteness; but when they looked at great things, all became a blank & they saw nothing—and denied (very illogically) that any thing could be seen; and uniformly put the negation of a power for the possession of a power—& called the want of imagination Judgment, & the never being moved to Rapture Philosophy!—

(*CL* I 354–5)

Here is the seed, the special quality of mind, whose growth and divarication must eventually choke the materialistic epistemology and lead to a rejection of the 'mechanical' psychology that treats the Imagination as no more than an 'aggregative and associative' faculty. Here too, although it is not yet endowed with any systematic depth or precision, is the germ of Coleridge's life-long campaign against what he called in *Biographia* Chap vi the 'despotism of the eye', that is, the natural inclination to reduce all thought to visual terms: 'under this strong sensuous influence, we are restless because invisible things are not the objects of vision; and metaphysical systems, for the most part, become popular, not for their truth, but in proportion as they attribute to causes a susceptibility of being *seen*, if only our visual organs were sufficiently powerful' (*BL* I 74). [10] But the full working out of these ideas lies still in the future. In 1797 they bespeak only a quality and habit of mind that has been neither fully articulated nor integrated into any meaningful conceptual framework; indeed, there is a passage in a letter to John Thelwall analogous to that quoted above from the autobiographical letter to Poole and written only two days before it, which shows clearly that while he yearned for 'the Vast' and a unified view he had not yet discovered it:

I can *at times* feel strongly the beauties, you describe, in themselves, & for themselves—but more frequently *all things* appear little—all the knowledge, that can be acquired, child's play—the universe itself—what but an immense heap of *little* things?—I can contemplate nothing but parts, & parts are all *little*—!—My mind feels

as if it ached to behold & know something *great*—something *one &*
indivisible—and it is only in the faith of this that rocks or waterfalls,
mountains or caverns give me the sense of sublimity or majesty!—
But in this faith *all things* counterfeit infinity!—

(*CL* 1 349)

Coleridge recognised that discovery comes as a *saltus*, with a leap,
and involves an irrevocable change of state. (Keats's formulation of
Negative Capability in a letter provides a fine dramatic instance of
how this happens: he was having 'not a dispute but a disquisition with
Dilke, on various subjects' when suddenly 'several things dovetailed
in my mind, & at once it struck me, what quality went to form a Man
of Achievement especially in Literature. . . .'[11]) Fortunately, in the
case of Coleridge's initial insight into the nature and role of
Imagination we have a record of the leap, although we cannot date it
accurately. It occurs in *Biographia* Chap iv where, having observed
that 'genius produces the strongest impressions of novelty, while it
rescues the most admitted truths from the impotence caused by the
very circumstance of their universal admission', he continues: 'This
excellence, which in all Mr. Wordsworth's writings is more or less
predominant, and which constitutes the character of his mind, I no
sooner felt, than I sought to understand. Repeated meditations led me
first to suspect, (and a more intimate analysis of the human faculties,
their appropriate marks, functions, and effects matured my conjecture into full conviction,) that fancy and imagination were two
distinct and widely different faculties, instead of being, according to
the general belief, either two names with one meaning, or, at furthest,
the lower and higher degree of one and the same power' (*BL* 1 60–1;
Extract 33–C). Since this passage appears within the context of
Coleridge's first meeting with Wordsworth and the latter's recitation
of 'Guilt and Sorrow', the probable date of the initial insight and
consequent determination to investigate the seminal principles of
Wordsworth's art is the autumn of 1795.[12] But the original leap was
not final; it pointed the path but did not immediately bring him to the
goal. The overthrow of Hartleian psychology and the concomitant
desynonymisation of Fancy and Imagination required 'repeated
meditations' and 'a more intimate analysis of the human faculties'
before the initial 'conjecture' was finally matured into a 'full
conviction'. The precise length of this maturative process cannot with
certainty be determined; however, the first clear formulations of the
nature of Imagination appear in a series of letters to William Sotheby

dating from mid-1802 (Extracts 7–9) which culminate in the earliest direct statement of the Imagination–Fancy distinction: 'At best, it is but Fancy, or the aggregating Faculty of the mind—not *Imagination*, or the *modifying*, and *co-adunating* Faculty'. There are compelling reasons (which I shall examine presently) for believing that July–September 1802–the period when the letters to Sotheby were written–were crucial months in the shaping of the theory of Imagination. Although it is an exaggeration to say that the literary aspects of the theory had been fully developed by mid-1802, it is nevertheless true that earlier statements are fragmentary and inchoate and that later statements, while they refine and give theoretic precision to the 1802 formulation, do not substantially alter its terms or character. If Coleridge plunged impulsively into the Rubicon in 1795, it is equally clear that he emerged on the further shore in the late summer of 1802 and advanced directly on Rome with confidence and a firmly defined sense of mission.

The formulation of 1802 was made possible by three cardinal factors. First, the innate platonising quality of Coleridge's mind bred a natural distrust of purely materialistic explanations and led him eventually to reject the 'mechanical' faculty psychology and passive perception of the rationalist school. Second, there is the inductive leap occasioned by the recognition of Wordsworth's genius and the implications for Coleridge's criticism of his puzzling over the nature and special characteristics of Wordsworth's art. Third, there is the fecundating relationship between Coleridge's own experience of poetic creativity and the growth of his critical faculty. I shall take these points in turn.

In December 1794 Coleridge bluntly declared to Southey that he was 'a compleat Necessitarian—and understand the subject as well almost as Hartley himself—but I go farther than Hartley and believe in the corporeality of *thought*' (*CL* 1 137), and in May 1796 he made a similar assertion in a letter to John Thelwall (ibid., 213). However, despite his obvious debt to empiricism and to Hartley in particular, there is as I mentioned earlier a constitutive transcendental strain in Coleridge's thought that precludes his resting at ease within the materialistic framework of empiricism. According to his own retrospective account in the autobiographical letters to Poole, the yearning for truths beyond the grasp of sense experience originated in his reading fairy tales and 'all the gilt-cover little books' that were to be had either in the Ottery vicarage or in his aunt's '*every-thing* Shop' at Credition (*CL* 1 347–8). This early reading prepared a fertile seed-bed for his introduction to the writings of Plato and the Neoplatonists during his years (1782–1791) at Christ's Hospital School. There, he steeped himself in the works of philosophers like Proclus, probably with the aid of Thomas Taylor's recent translations; by 1787 he had himself apparently translated into anacreontics eight hymns of Synesius, 'the hyper-platonic Jargonist' as he later called him (*CN* I 200); and many years afterwards Charles Lamb recalled how 'the young Mirandula' had unfolded to fellow-students and entranced passers-by 'the mysteries of Jamblichus, or Plotinus' in the school cloisters.[13] Later, he discovered the Cambridge Neoplatonists, and in May 1795 and again in November 1796 he borrowed the 1743 edition of Ralph Cudworth's *True Intellectual System of the Universe* from the Bristol Library.[14] Such reading established a dissonant counterpoint to the ideas gathered from Hume, Hartley, and Priestley. So, too, did the diffused Christian figuration (itself deeply tinged with Platonism) that he absorbed from sources as diverse as the sermons of Jeremy Taylor, Thomas Burnet's *Telluris Theoria Sacra*, and George Berkeley's *Treatise on the Principles of Human Knowledge*.

In terms of Coleridge's intellectual development, his discovery in 1795 of Cudworth's *True Intellectual System* was an event of great importance. Cudworth had challenged the rising tide of empiricism in his day by asserting that the universe was not (as Hobbes and others believed) composed merely of inert material atoms governed by mechanical laws; rather, the natural world was symbolic of a transcendent reality that lay beyond material appearances. The explanation of organic life, that is, the explanation of the inter-relations of the corporeal and the incorporeal, Cudworth finds in what he calls the 'spermatic reason or plastic nature' which is held to be the life-force and principle of growth in the universe.[15] Cudworth's doctrine of nature as an adumbration of deity, a second book of Scripture through which God continuously reveals himself, was promptly appropriated by Coleridge in his lectures on revealed religion of May–June 1795; he borrowed *The True Intellectual System* on May 15 and in the first lecture, delivered only four days later, we find him asserting that 'The Omnipotent has unfolded to us the Volume of the World, that there we may read the Transcript of himself' (*CC* I 94; cf also Lecture 3, ibid., 158). Hereafter, the theme becomes a commonplace in his writings, particularly in his poetry. In August 1795, for example, it turns up linked with the principle of 'plastic nature' in lines 44–8 of 'The Eolian Harp'.

Or what if all of animated nature
Be but organic Harps diversely fram'd,
That tremble into thought, as o'er them sweeps
Plastic and vast, one intellectual breeze,
At once the Soul of each, and God of all?

Perhaps about this same time it was incorporated into 'Religious
Musings' (lines 126–31); in 1796 it resurfaces in lines 13–26 of 'The
Destiny of Nations' (Extract 2), and in 1798 it is given its finest
expression in lines 58–62 of 'Frost at Midnight':

so shalt thou see and hear
The lovely shapes and sounds intelligible
Of that eternal language, which thy God
Utters, who from eternity doth teach
Himself in all, and all things in himself.

The relevance of this neoplatonic pantheism to Coleridge's theory of
the Imagination is made clear in his lecture on the slave-trade of June
1795 (Extract 1): 'The noblest gift of Imagination is the power of
discerning the *Cause* in the *Effect* [,] a power which when employed
on the works of the Creator elevates and by the variety of its pleasures
almost monopolizes the Soul. We see our God everywhere—the
Universe in the most literal Sense is his written Language.' Imagination, then, is the mental faculty that allows man to interpret the
symbolic language in which God has written himself into the *natura
naturata* and to discover an all-embracing unity extending through
the multiform appearances of the material universe.

The nature and extent of Coleridge's debt to Cudworth's *True
Intellectual System* is difficult to assess with any precision. On the one
hand, the work clearly pleased him and in some way spoke to his
condition; he borrowed it twice from the Bristol Library, read it with
enthusiastic attention, and drew on it immediately and repeatedly for
lectures, poems, and notebook entries (cf *CN* I 200–5, 244–7, and
nn). On the other hand, however, there is nothing particularly
remarkable in the ideas which he took from Cudworth; they are by
and large the staples of second- and third-hand Platonism and he
knew many of them already from other sources (particularly the
Enneads of Plotinus which he read long before he came to Cudworth)
and would meet them shortly again in works like Henry More's
Enthusiasmus triumphatus and *An Antidote against Atheism*. Neverthe-

less Cudworth seems to occupy a special place. The most reasonable explanation is simply that Coleridge stumbled upon *The True Intellectual System* at an opportune moment, that the innate platonising strain in his faith and thought had grown too acute to remain tranquil for long within the enclosure of Priestley and Hartley, and that Cudworth's book was the lens which focused this dissatisfaction and so was instrumental in releasing him from the confines of their narrow mechanistic rationalism and materialism. If this is indeed what happened, it is not surprising that he should call Imagination a 'restless faculty' (Extract 1).

However, it is important to recognise that although Coleridge appropriated the neoplatonic pantheism of Cudworth and others he did not immediately succeed in assimilating it and stamping it with his own personality. In the form in which we have it the 'One Life' theme (beloved of recent critics because it is 'portable') is so unremarkable and pervasive as to be almost banal. The 'Volume of the World' and nature as 'one mighty alphabet For infant minds' is a widely dispersed notion, current certainly among the Cambridge Platonists (especially Cudworth and Henry More) but still very much in the air in the 1790s. Moreover, the dreamy versified philosophy of poems like 'Religious Musings' or 'The Destiny of Nations' philosophising which offers sonorous short-cuts at the very points where speculative clarity is demanded, does less than justice to the acuity and power of Coleridge's mind. And it may be added that what is true of Coleridge's early adoption of Neoplatonism is also true of his attitude to Christianity. Although his faith was certainly sincere by the mid-1790s, it was not 'carried alive' into his heart but was rather manipulated with an almost secular enthusiasm as it swam up in response to the threat of materialism. 'But tho' all my doubts are done away,' he confessed to J. P. Estlin in 1798, 'tho' Christianity is my *Passion*, it is too much my *intellectual* Passion: and therefore will do me but little good in the hour of temptation & calamity' (*CL* 1 407).[16]

Despite these reservations, however, the fact remains that Cudworth's *True Intellectual System*, encountered in May 1795, sparked a reaction—given Coleridge's inherent Platonic cast of mind, an inevitable reaction—against the Hartleian epistemology; and at the same time it supplied him, for the moment, both with a systematic vision and a terminology with which to combat the doctrine of mechanical necessity. It also, as we know from the Slave-Trade lecture of June 1795, prompted him to see the Imagination as an interpretative rather than merely an associative faculty of the mind. But the symbol-reading power assigned here to Imagination is still a long way from the dynamic, integrative, poietic energy ascribed to it in the mature formulation. In the final analysis, Cudworth's system was no more Coleridge's own than Hartley's had been; but by extricating him from necessitarianism, it prepared the soil and left it tilled and fertilised, ready for the sowing of new seed. That seed was planted, as Coleridge tells us in *Biographia* Chap iv (above, p. 7), by the sudden revelation of Wordsworth's genius in the autumn of 1795; it germinated in a 'conjecture' of the difference in kind between Fancy and Imagination, broke into bud with the desynonymisation of these two powers in the letters of 1802 to Sotheby, and achieved fruition in 1815 in a literary autobiography culminating in a mature assessment of Wordsworth's art and genius. From there, releasing the new seed that had been ripening for some time in the pods of the parent stalk, the plant began to spread growth into the neighbouring fields of philosophy, psychology, science and theology.

In experiential terms, the 'leap' occasioned by the insight of 1795 into the nature of Wordsworth's art (and the subsequent desire to isolate and define its characteristic genius) led first to a recognition of the difference between himself and Southey, with whom he lodged and worked in Bristol in 1795–6. In his own case, as he told Thelwall in December 1796, thought and feeling are inextricably linked, and in some vague way Imagination (which he still calls Fancy) is bound up with both:

> I feel strongly, and I think strongly; but I seldom feel without thinking, or think without feeling. Hence tho' my poetry has in general a *hue* of tenderness, or Passion over it, yet it seldom exhibits unmixed & simple tenderness or Passion. My philosophical opinions are blended with, or deduced from, my feelings: & this, I think, peculiarizes my style of Writing. And like every thing else, it is sometimes a beauty, and sometimes a fault. But do not let us introduce an act of Uniformity against Poets—I have room enough in *my* brain to admire, aye & almost equally, the *head* and fancy of Akenside, and the *heart* and fancy of Bowles, the solemn Lordliness of Milton, & the divine Chit chat of Cowper: and whatever a man's excellence is, that will be likewise his fault.
>
> (*CL* I 279)

Southey, on the other hand, as he told Thelwall a fortnight later, possessed fluency but wanted Imagination: 'In language at once natural, perspicuous, & dignified, in manly pathos, in soothing & sonnet-like description, and above all, in character, & *dramatic* dialogue, Southey is unrivalled; but as certainly he does not possess opulence of Imagination, lofty-paced Harmony, or that *toil* of thinking, which is necessary in order to plan *a Whole*' (CL 1 293–4). Here again Imagination is connected with thinking; and the nature of that relationship is made somewhat clearer four months later in a letter to Joseph Cottle, where Southey is contrasted with Milton:

> Wordsworth complains, with justice, that Southey writes *too much at his ease*—that he seldom 'feels his burthened breast
> Heaving beneath th' incumbent Deity.'[17]
> He certainly will make literature more *profitable to him* from the fluency with which he writes, and the facility with which he pleases himself. But I fear, that to posterity his wreath will look unseemly—here an ever living amaranth, and close by its side some weed of an hour, sere, yellow, and shapeless—his exquisite beauties will lose half their effect from the bad company they keep. Besides I am fearful that he will begin to rely too much on *story* and *event* in his poems, to the neglect of those *lofty imaginings*, that are peculiar to, and definitive of, the poet. The *story* of Milton might be told in two pages—it is this which distinguishes an *Epic Poem* from a *Romance in metre*. Observe the march of Milton—his severe application, his laborious polish, his deep metaphysical researches, his prayers to God before he began his great poem, all that could lift and swell his intellect, became his daily food.
>
> (CL 1 320)

The precise relation between thought and Imagination is by no means clear to Coleridge here, but he senses that in some way they are connected and correlative. Looking ahead, we can see where this line of thought will ultimately lead, for from the security of his mature formulation he will assign to Southey 'great fancy but no imagination' (Extract 18).

The second stage of development is marked by the association with Wordsworth and especially by the events of the *annus mirabilis*, 1797–8. In his retrospective account in *Biographia* Chap iv of the sudden revelation produced by the recitation of Wordsworth's 'Guilt and Sorrow' in 1795, Coleridge remembered that what had 'made so unusual an impression on my feelings immediately, and subsequently on my judgement . . . was the union of deep feeling with profound thought; the fine balance of truth in observing, with the imaginative faculty in modifying the objects observed; and above all the original gift of spreading the tone, the *atmosphere*, and with it the depth and height of the ideal world around forms, incidents, and situations, of which, for the common view, custom had bedimmed all the lustre, had dried up the sparkle and the dew drops' (Extract 33–C). As we have just seen, he was soon led to the recognition that Southey lacked the requisite 'union of deep feeling with profound thought' that Wordsworth (and Milton) possessed and that he believed himself to possess, though in a less developed state than Wordsworth. And the perception of the differences between his own ideas and Southey's poetic practice drove him to consolidate his original insight, to attempt to understand and explain the 'unusual impression' made on his feelings by the strange and powerful impact of Wordsworth's genius.

Although Coleridge apparently did not see Wordsworth again until over a year after their first meeting in late 1795, the two men did carry on a correspondence, either directly or through Cottle, the Bristol publisher. In March 1796 Cottle transmitted a copy of 'Guilt and Sorrow' to Coleridge, who (according to Azariah Pinney) read the poem 'with considerable attention' and 'interleaved it with white paper to mark down whatever may strike him as worthy your [i.e. Wordsworth's] notice'.[18] In fact, Coleridge kept the manuscript for over a month, and his careful study of the text more than confirmed the opinion of original genius formed when the poem had been read to him the previous autumn, for on May 13 he described Wordsworth as 'a very dear friend of mine, who is in my opinion the best poet of age' (*CL* I 215). Coleridge moved to Nether Stowey at the end of December 1796; the following March Wordsworth paid him a visit and Coleridge reciprocated by spending three weeks with the Wordsworths at Racedown in June. The effect of renewed personal contact deepened further Coleridge's estimate of his friend's abilities: 'I speak with heart-felt sincerity & (I think) unblinded judgement,' he wrote to Cottle from Racedown, 'when I tell you, that I feel myself a *little man by his* side; & yet do not think myself the less man, than I formerly thought myself' (*CL* I 325).[19] By the middle of July the Wordsworths had settled at Alfoxden, some three miles from Stowey, and the two men were together almost daily. They discussed poetry and poetic theory in rambles over the Quantocks and on sheltered hill-sides overlooking the Bristol Channel and the low

purple outline of the Welsh coast ten miles distant. These talks led to
the composition of such poems as 'Kubla Khan', 'Frost at Midnight',
'The Nightingale', and Part I of 'Christabel'. A walking tour to the
Valley of Stones near Lynmouth in November 1797 resulted in the
composition of 'The Ancient Mariner', although the poem was not
finally completed until the following March.[20] 'The Ancient
Mariner' was originally conceived as a joint-production, but Wordsworth, realising that he 'could only have been a clog' upon it,
withdrew at an early stage. Nevertheless, the poem and the literary
discussions surrounding it did lead in the spring of 1798 to the plan of
the *Lyrical Ballads*: see Extract 33–G and n 2.

The effect of the collaboration with Wordsworth on the development of Coleridge's thought is too complex and extensive a subject to
admit detailed exposition here. It will, I hope, be enough for the
moment simply to point out that their intimate association found an
immediate outlet not so much in poetic theory as in practice, not in
philosophic elaboration of a theory of Imagination so much as in its
actual application in the writing of poetry. And what characterises his
verse in this *annus mirabilis* and sharply distinguishes it from that
composed before mid-1797 is its heightened rendering of perceptual
experience:

> The Frost performs its secret ministry,
> Unhelped by any wind. The owlet's cry
> Came loud—and hark, again! loud as before.
> The inmates of my cottage, all at rest,
> Have left me to that solitude, which suits
> Abstruser musings: save that at my side
> My cradled infant slumbers peacefully.
> 'Tis calm indeed! so calm, that it disturbs
> And vexes meditation with its strange
> And extreme silentness. Sea, hill, and wood,
> This populous village! Sea, and hill, and wood,
> With all the numberless goings-on of life,
> Inaudible as dreams! the thin blue flame
> Lies on my low-burnt fire, and quivers not;
> Only that film, which fluttered on the grate,
> Still flutters there, the sole unquiet thing.
> Methinks, its motion in this hush of nature
> Gives it dim sympathies with me who live,
> Making it a companionable form,

Whose puny flaps and freaks the idling Spirit
By its own moods interprets, every where
Echo or mirror seeking of itself,
And makes a toy of Thought.

'Frost at Midnight', 1–23

Here, in fact, in practice rather than in theory, illustrated rather than expounded, are the very elements which first drew his attention to Wordsworth's genius: the fusion of thought and feeling, the blending of sight and insight, and 'above all the original gift of spreading the tone, the *atmosphere*, and with it the depth and height of the ideal world around forms, incidents, and situations, of which, for the common view, custom had bedimmed all the lustre, had dried up the sparkle and the dew drops'. The theory would follow in due course; and when it came, when it was finally articulated, it would owe its birth as much to experience as to observation, as much to the action of his own poetic genius as to his meditations on the operation of Wordsworth's.

Although the theory itself lay still in the future, the association with 'the Giant Wordsworth' and the intense experience of the exercise of Imagination in his own poetry were quickly guiding him toward its formulation. The answer, he now saw clearly, was rooted in the doctrine of perception. What precisely was the relationship between the percipient and the perceived? To answer that question he would need to explore more fully and philosophically the connections between man and nature, and the investigation would centre on a close study of the functions and potential of the human mind: 'I have for some time past,' he told his brother George in March 1798,

withdrawn myself almost totally from the consideration of *immediate* causes, which are infinitely complex & uncertain, to muse on fundamental & general causes—the 'causae causarum.'—I devote myself to such works as encroach not on the antisocial passions—in poetry, to elevate the imagination & set the affections in right tune by the beauty of the inanimate impregnated, as with a living soul, by the presence of Life—in prose, to the seeking with patience & a slow, very slow mind 'Quid sumus, et quidnam victuri gignimur'—What our faculties are & what they are capable of becoming.—I love fields & woods & mountains with almost a visionary fondness—and because I have found benevolence & quietness growing within me as that fondness has increased, therefore I should wish to be the means of implanting it in others—& to destroy the bad passions not by combating them, but by keeping them in inaction.

(CL 1 397)[21]

The third stage of Coleridge's developing theory of Imagination opens with his trip to Germany in 1798–9 and closes with the letters to Sotheby in 1802. The search for 'fundamental & general causes' prompted him to devote most of his energies while he was in Germany to compiling materials for a biography of Lessing, which he believed would give him 'an opportunity of conveying under a better name, than my own ever will be, opinions, which I deem of the highest importance' (CL 1 519). But the Life of Lessing was never completed. The main reason for the failure to write the work was that, as he read and thought and gathered materials, Coleridge was developing his own theories; what he wanted increasingly to do was to state not Lessing's views but his own, and his interest shifted from the biography proper to the general essay on poetry planned originally as an introduction to the work: 'The works which I gird myself up to attack as soon as money-concerns will permit me, are the Life of Lessing—& the Essay on Poetry. The latter is still more at my heart than the former—it's Title would be an Essay on the Elements of Poetry/ it would in reality be a *disguised* System of Morals & Politics—' (CL 1 632).

The desire to establish the general principles of poetry is reflected also in the preface which was added to the second edition of the *Lyrical Ballads* which appeared in January 1801 (although the title-page bore the date 1800). According to Wordsworth's marginal note in Barron Field's *Memoirs of the Life and Poetry of William Wordsworth*, it was an accident that the preface had been written by him instead of by Coleridge: 'In the foregoing there is frequent reference to what is called Mr W's theory, & his Preface. I will mention that I never cared a straw about the theory—& the Preface was written at the request of Mr Coleridge out of sheer good nature. I recollect the very spot, a deserted Quarry in the Vale of Grasmere where he pressed the thing upon me, & but for that it would never been thought of.'[22] This is confirmed by Coleridge's statement that the 'Preface arose from the heads of our mutual Conversations &c—& the first passages were indeed partly taken from notes of mine/ for it was at first intended, that the Preface should be written by me—' (CL 11 811).

At first there was, Coleridge believed, a perfect agreement in their theoretical views, and he informed Daniel Stuart in September 1800 that the 'Preface contains our joint opinions on Poetry' (*CL* I 627). However, by the time the third edition (1802) of *Lyrical Ballads* was published with a revised preface and an appendix on poetic diction, the situation had changed and he found it necessary to set Sotheby right 'with regard to my perfect coincidence with his poetic Creed':

> In my opinion every phrase, every metaphor, every personification, should have it's justifying cause in some *passion* either of the Poet's mind, or of the Characters described by the poet—But *metre itself* implies a *passion*, i.e. a state of excitement, both in the Poet's mind, & is expected in that of the Reader—and tho' I stated this to Wordsworth, & he has in some sort stated it in his preface, yet he has not done justice to it, nor has he in my opinion sufficiently answered it. In my opinion, Poetry justifies, as *Poetry* independent of any other Passion, some new combinations of Language, & *commands* the omission of many others allowable in other compositions/ Now Wordsworth, me saltem judice, has in his system not sufficiently admitted the former, & in his practice has too frequently sinned against the latter.—Indeed, we have had lately some little controversy on this subject—& we begin to suspect, that there is, somewhere or other, a *radical* Difference in our opinions. . . .
>
> (*CL* II 812)

And writing to Southey a fortnight later (29 July 1802) he indicates that this '*radical* Difference' has made it necessary that he should set down his own theoretical opinions on poetry:

> I exceedingly like the Job of Amadis de Gaul²³—I wish, you may half as well like the Job, in which I shall very shortly appear. Of it's sale I have no doubt; but of it's prudence?—There's the Rub.—Concerning Poetry, & the characteristic Merits of the Poets, our Contemporaries—one Volume Essays, the second Selections/ the Essays are on Bloomfield, Burns, Bowles, Cowper, Campbell, [Erasmus] Darwin, Hayley, Rogers, C. Smith, Southey, Woolcot, Wordsworth—the Selections from every one, who has written at all, any way above the rank of mere Scribblers—Pye & his Dative Case Plural, Pybus, Cottle &c &c—The object is not to examine what is good in each writer, but what has ipso facto pleased, & to what faculties or passions or habits

of the mind they may be supposed to have given pleasure/ Of course, Darwin & Wordsworth having given each a defence of *their* mode of Poetry, & a disquisition on the nature & essence of Poetry in general, I shall necessarily be led rather deeper—and these I shall treat of either first or last/ But I will apprize you of one thing, that altho' Wordsworth's Preface is half a child of my own Brain/ & so arose out of Conversations, so frequent, that with few exceptions we could scarcely either of us perhaps positively say, which first started any particular Thought—I am speaking of the Preface as it stood in the second Volume [i.e. the second edition of 1800]—yet I am far from going all lengths with Wordsworth/ He has written lately a number of Poems (32 in all) some of them of considerable Length/ (the longest 160 lines) the greater number of these to my feelings very excellent Compositions/ but here & there a daring Humbleness of Language & Versification, and a strict adherence to matter of fact, even to prolixity, that startled me/ his alterations likewise in Ruth perplexed me/ and I have thought & thought again/ & have not had my doubts solved by Wordsworth/ On the contrary, I rather suspect that some where or other there is a radical Difference in our theoretical opinions respecting Poetry—/ this I shall endeavor to go to the Botton of—and acting the arbitrator between the old School & the New School hope to lay down some plain, & perspicuous, tho' not superficial, Canons of Criticism respecting Poetry.

(*CL* II 829–30)

Southey's less than charitable response was to say, 'You spawn plans like a herring; I only wish as many of the seed were to vivify in proportion'.[24] However, as George Whalley has pointed out, the 'various modifications of the Lessing scheme, the talks with Wordsworth that produced the 1800 Preface, and the attempts to resolve the "radical difference" that he mentioned to Southey in July 1802, made the need for a personal statement imperative';[25] and in fact the first crystal of this personal statement, destined to appear finally as the *Biographia Literaria* over a decade later, is to be found in a notebook entry dating from September–October 1803: 'Seem to have made up my mind to write my metaphysical works, as *my Life*, & *in* my Life—intermixed with all the other events/ or history of the mind & fortunes of S. T. Coleridge' (*CN* I 1515).

But what exactly were these radical differences that he felt to exist between his views and those of Wordsworth? The foundation on which Wordsworth raised his poetic theories in the 1800 preface to *Lyrical Ballads* was the mechanistic faculty psychology of David Hartley's *Observations on Man* (1749), and at the heart of Hartley's system lay the doctrine of the association of ideas.[26] Wordsworth made his debt to Hartley clear enough in the 1800 preface (italics mine):

> The principal object, then, proposed in these Poems was to choose incidents and situations from common life, and to relate or describe them, throughout, as far as was possible in a selection of language really used by men, and, at the same time, to throw over them a certain colouring of imagination, whereby ordinary things should be presented to the mind in an unusual aspect; and, further, and above all, to make these incidents and situations interesting by tracing in them, truly though not ostentatiously, the primary laws of our nature: *chiefly, as far as regards the manner in which we associate ideas in a state of excitement*. . . . For all good poetry is the spontaneous overflow of powerful feelings: and though this be true, Poems to which any value can be attached were never produced on any variety of subjects but by a man who, being possessed of more than usual organic sensibility, had also thought long and deeply. *For our continued influxes of feeling are modified and directed by our thoughts, which are indeed the representatives of all our past feelings*; and, as by contemplating the relation of these general representatives to each other, we discover what is really important to men, so, by the repetition and continuance of this act, our feelings will be connected with important subjects, till at length, if we be originally possessed of much sensibility, such habits of mind will be produced, that, *by obeying blindly and mechanically the impulses of those habits*, we shall describe objects, and utter sentiments, of such a nature, and in such connection with each other, that the understanding of the Reader must necessarily be in some degree enlightened, and his affections strengthened and purified.

Here was what dissatisfied Coleridge. Wordsworth's poetry was the product of a shaping power, a power which fused and blended past and present impressions with thought and feeling, not simply of an associative faculty governed by blind, mechanical laws.

When Coleridge settled at Keswick in July 1800, he spent the first six months of his residence in the North penning enthusiastic descriptions of the view from Greta Hall for his friends in Bristol and London, pushing on with his plans for the biography of Lessing, trying to finish 'Christabel' — and transcribing Wordsworth's *Lyrical Ballads* for the press. However, early in 1801 he embarked on a thorough and serious study of philosophy. In the chest of 'metaphysical books' he had sent from Germany were copies of the works of the great German philosophers of the preceding century, and he devoured them with a passion that brooked little interruption: 'Change of Ministry interests *me* not', he wrote to Poole in February; 'I turn at times half reluctantly from Leibnitz or Kant even to read a smoking new newspaper/ such a purus putus Metaphysicus am I become' (*CL* II 676). From 1800, when he began to absorb Kant's theory of knowing, he found in it both a recognition and a liberation, although full understanding and appreciation came only later. Nevertheless, the experience of German transcendentalism and especially of Kant who, as he said later (*BL* I 99), 'took possession of me as with a giant's hand' prompted a detailed reconsideration of empirical epistemology; and in a series of philosophical letters addressed to Josiah Wedgwood he succeeded (in Wedgwood's phrase) in plucking 'the principal feathers out of Locke's wings' (*CL* II 677). Inextricably linked to his philosophical researches was a growing interest in psychology: he watched the operation of his own mind, struggled to discover the relation between 'thoughts' and 'things', studied the phenomena of dreams and of what he called *ocular spectra*,[27] tried to define the connections between thought and feeling, and explored the noumenal function of language.[28] Increasingly, he began to understand that the operations of the mind were determined not by discrete, compartmentalised *faculties* but by interrelated *powers*; he became aware that the mind was essentially synthesising rather than passive and associative, and he saw that in the doctrine of perception, rightly interpreted, lay the key to the poetic Imagination.

As I suggested earlier, the germinal potency of the theory of Imagination lies in Coleridge's rejection of passive perception. The mind, he told Poole in 1801, is made in 'the Image of the *Creator*'; it is not, as materialists maintain, 'a lazy Looker-on on an external world' and there is, therefore, 'ground for suspicion, that any system built on the passiveness of the mind must be false, as a system' (Extract 4). Perception — or 'Primary Imagination' as he later called it (Extract 33–F) — is integrative, poetic, and necessarily correlate with feeling; it is a creative activity in which images, ideas and feelings are fused and blended by the mind. This power is supremely human and is a part of every man's birthright, and it makes each of us in a way a poet: 'We all have obscure feelings that must be connected with some thing or other—the Miser with a guinea—Lord Nelson with a blue Ribbon—Wordsworth's old Molly with her washing Tub—Wordsworth with the Hills, Lakes, & Trees—/ all men are poets in their way, tho' for the most part their ways are *damned bad ones*' (*CL* II 768). Related to this activity and differing from it in degree but not in kind is the operation of the poetic (or Secondary) Imagination, a power which is latent but not equally developed in all men. This power works, by breaking down and then refashioning original perceptions, to re-present the common universe in such a way that we see it as if for the first time.

Hartley's rigid empiricism and doctrine of mechanistic association could not long survive in this atmosphere, and it is not surprising that Coleridge began to suspect that somewhere or other there existed a '*radical* Difference' between his poetic theory and the Hartleian-based views that Wordsworth had propounded in the 1800 preface to *Lyrical Ballads*. And when Wordsworth revised and reissued the preface without altering its conceptual foundation in the third edition (1802) of the *Lyrical Ballads*, Coleridge was immediately prompted to 'go to the botton' of their theoretical differences. The new publication was the spur that drove him to set down his own views, the catalyst that brought together the various elements of his thought over the preceding two years and resulted, in September 1802, in the initial formulation of the Fancy–Imagination distinction in the letter to William Sotheby. Wordsworth's theory did not explain his own poetry; mechanical association could produce only works of Fancy, and Wordsworth's poetry was the product of the shaping power of Imagination. Coleridge proposed to establish the discrepancy between his friend's theory and practice, as he told Southey, by 'acting the arbitrator between the old School & the New School' and laying down 'some plain, & perspicuous, tho' not superficial, Canons of Criticism respecting Poetry'. This statement is important. Hartley's system is not to be absolutely rejected; rather, Coleridge is to *arbitrate* between Wordsworth's associationist theory of poetry (based on Hartley) and his actual poiétic activity in the making of poetry. And it is to this mediation between 'the old School & the New School' that we owe the Fancy–Imagination distinction. There are indeed moods in which the mind merely aggregates and associates ideas and impressions, holding them in a loose mixture where the separate elements remain discrete and discontinuous: this is the operation of Fancy, which in poetry is indicated pre-eminently in formal similes. But this is not the highest and most characteristic form of association and it does not describe Wordsworth's poetic achievement. There is another higher mood in which feeling, intellect, memory, and sense experience are fused and blended in such a way that the components are modified and coadunated: this is the operation of Imagination, the distinctive quality of Wordsworth's poetry. Here is Coleridge's own statement to Sotheby in September 1802: 'A Poet's *Heart & Intellect* should be *combined, intimately* combined & *unified*, with the great appearances in Nature—& not merely held in solution & loose mixture with them, in the shape of formal Similes. I do not mean to *exclude* these formal Similies—there are moods of mind, in which they are natural—pleasing moods of mind, & such as a Poet will often have, & sometimes express; but they are not his highest, & most appropriate moods. They are "Sermoni propiora" which I once translated—"Properer for a Sermon" ' (Extract 9; cf Extract 12). The theory of Imagination, then, is rooted in the *qualitative* nature of association as a function of perception.

One of the most significant features of Coleridge's statements to Sotheby and Southey in 1802 is his emphasis on the underlying *principles* of poetic activity. While Wordsworth's purpose in the various prefaces to *Lyrical Ballads* had been to examine the manifestations of poetic Imagination, Coleridge proposed to explore the seminal principle and to lay down general 'Canons of Criticism respecting Poetry'. As he later expressed it in *Biographia* Chap iv (Extract 33–C): 'My friend has drawn a masterly sketch of the branches with their *poetic* fruitage. I wish to add the trunk, and even the roots as far as they lift themselves above ground, and are visible to the naked eye of our common consciousness.' However, the 'abstruse metaphysical researches' undertaken in the search for this seminal principle led, he believed, to the impairment of his imaginative power: see Extract 5 and n 3. These reiterated declarations of the 'loss of Imagination' must be handled with caution, and they must not be permitted to reinforce the uncritical notion that he ceased being a poet whenever he stopped writing poetry. Coleridge's theory of Imagination is important (and germinal) not because he was a theorist but because he was a *poet* of great technical refinement who knew what it felt like to compose 'The Ancient Mariner', 'Kubla Khan' and 'Christabel', and who used that experience as a constant test for his theorising about poetry. It is significant, for example, that his first clear formulations of the nature of Imagination and its function in the poetic process should have been written to William Sotheby, a poet whose intelligence and critical acumen he greatly respected. Moreover, it may be added that Coleridge's protestations of a 'loss of Imagination'—in 'Dejection: An Ode', for example—often have much that is positive to tell us about Imagination.[29]

The purpose of an Introduction is to introduce. This is Coleridge's book, and he is his own best advocate. I have no desire to produce another discursive account of his theory of Imagination; we have enough of these already and, while many of them are extremely helpful, there needs now to be some purifying of the wells in a return to the primary materials themselves. The sole object of this Introduction is to establish a context, to shape the early materials so that the reader comes to the first entries with some measure of recognition. For the rest, Coleridge shall speak for himself; and for the careful reader the modernity and originality of his thought will be a voyage of self-discovery:

> Some one said: 'The dead writers are remote from us because we *know* so much more than they did.' Precisely, and they are that which we know.[30]

Notes

1. Locke, *Essay Concerning Human Understanding* (1690) ii i 2.
2. *Enquiry Concerning Political Justice* (1793) i v.
3. See Bibliography entries under Bate and Bullitt, and Wasserman.
4. Hobbes, *Leviathan* (1651) i ii; Dryden, 'Annus Mirabilis' (1667) Preface.
5. *Essay on Original Genius* (1767) 6–7.
6. *Outlines of Moral Philosophy* (1793) i viii.
7. Lines 302–7 of Coleridge's verse letter to Sara Hutchinson (Extract 6). Cf also Wordsworth, *The Prelude* (1805) ii 387–93:

>   An auxiliar light
> Came from my mind which on the setting sun
> Bestow'd new splendor, the melodious birds,
> The gentle breezes, fountains that ran on,
> Murmuring so sweetly in themselves, obey'd
> A like dominion; and the midnight storm
> Grew darker in the presence of my eye.

8. *The Prelude* (1805) XII 376–7.
9. For other statements of this kind in the letters of 1791–9, see *CL* I 7, 67, 71, 93, 103, 204, 249–50, 378, 409, 459, 506. Similar formulations appear frequently in the early poetry: 'Monody on the Death of Chatterton' (1790) 29–31; 'To the Evening Star' (1790?) 10–12; 'Inside the Coach' (1791) 23–7; 'Happiness' (1791) 7–16; 'An Effusion at Evening' (1792) 1–22 and *passim*; 'Apologia Pro Vita Sua' (1800).
10. Cf Extract 42–A and n 8.
11. Letter to George and Tom Keats, 21 December 1817.
12. Coleridge almost certainly met Wordsworth for the first time in September–October 1795 when Wordsworth was in Bristol discussing the possible publication of 'Guilt and Sorrow' with Cottle: see L. Hanson, *The Life of S. T. Coleridge: The Early Years* (London: Allen & Unwin, 1938) 84–5.
13. Elia, 'Christ's Hospital Five-and-Thirty Years Ago'.
14. George Whalley, 'The Bristol Library Borrowings of Southey and Coleridge', *Library* 4 (1949) 120, 124.
15. For an elucidation of these ideas, see R. L. Brett, 'Coleridge's Theory of the Imagination', *ES* 20 (1949) 80–1, and W. Schrickx, 'Coleridge and the Cambridge Platonists', *REL* 7 (1966) 77–9.
16. For much in this paragraph I am indebted to personal correspondence with George Whalley.
17. This quotation has a pointed touch of irony, since it is from Southey's own *Joan of Arc* (1796) i 461–2:

> From that night I could feel my burthen'd soul
> Heaving beneath incumbent Deity.

18. See E. L. Griggs's note: *CL* I 216, n 2.
19. There is a similar statement in a letter to Southey a month later: 'Wordsworth is a very great man—the only man, to whom *at all times* & in *all modes of excellence* I feel myself inferior' (*CL* I 334).
20. Coleridge's references to 'The Ancient Mariner' in his letters begin on 20 November 1797 when he tells Cottle that he has written 'a ballad of about 300 lines' (*CL* I 357); on 18 February 1798 he wrote again to say, 'I have finished my ballad—it is 340 lines' (ibid., 387). There must have been extensive revision over the next few weeks, for the poem eventually ran to 658 lines.
21. The anticipations in this letter of Wordsworth's 'Tintern Abbey' (composed four months later) have often been pointed out. What has not before been noticed (so far as I am aware) is the echo of Milton's elevated conception of the poetic office in the preface to Book Two of *The Reason of Church-Government* (1642): '[Poetic] abilities, wheresoever they be found, are the inspired guift of God rarely bestow'd, but

yet to some (though most abuse) in every Nation: and are of power beside the office of a pulpit, to imbreed and cherish in a great people the seeds of vertu, and publick civility, to allay the perturbations of the mind, and set the affections in right tune, to celebrate in glorious and lofty Hymns the throne and equipage of Gods Almightinesse, and what he works, and what he suffers to be wrought with high providence in his Church . . .' (*Complete Prose Works*, Yale edition I 816–17).

22. Barron Field, *Memoirs of Wordsworth*, ed. Geoffrey Little (Sydney: Sydney University Press, 1975) 62 n.

23. Southey's *Amadis of Gaul* was published in 1803.

24. The Life and Correspondence of the late Robert Southey, ed. C. C. Southey, 6 vols. (London, 1849–50) II 190.

25. 'The Integrity of *Biographia Literaria*', *ES* n.s. 6 (1953) 92. This seminal article should be read in full.

26. For a helpful introduction to Hartley's thought, see Chap 8 of Basil Willey's *Eighteenth-Century Background* (London: Chatto & Windus, 1940; Penguin Books, 1962) 133–49.

27. 'My eyes have been inflamed to a degree, that rendered reading & writing scarcely possible; and strange as it seems, the act of poetic composition, as I lay in bed, perceptibly affected them, and my voluntary ideas were every minute passing, more or less transformed into vivid spectra' (*CL* I 649; 2 December 1800). Cf also ibid., II 737, 961.

28. For Coleridge, *words* are not mere denotative cyphers: 'Is *thinking* impossible without arbitrary signs? &—how far is the word "arbitrary" a misnomer? Are not words &c parts & germinations of the Plant? And what is the Law of their Growth?—In something of this order I would endeavor to destroy the old antithesis of *Words & Things*, elevating, as it were, words into Things, & living Things too' (*CL* I 625–6; 22 September 1800).

29. George Whalley (to whom this paragraph owes a good deal) has pointed out to me that it is in the verse letter to Sara Hutchinson (Extract 6) that Coleridge, perhaps for the first time, describes Imagination not as a 'faculty' but as a state or condition of the person and as inseparable from the *quality* of perception. The poem is, then, an important landmark in Coleridge's rejection of faculty psychology.

30. T. S. Eliot, 'Tradition and the Individual Talent' (1919).

Extracts and Notes

1. from 'LECTURE ON THE SLAVE-TRADE' (June 1795)[1]

But we were not made to find Happiness in the complete gratification of our bodily wants—the mind must enlarge the sphere of its activity, and busy itself in the acquisition of intellectual aliment. To develope the powers of the Creator is our proper employment—and to imitate Creativeness by combination our most exalted and self-satisfying Delight.[2] But we are progressive and must not rest content with present Blessings. Our Almighty Parent hath therefore given to us Imagination[3] that stimulates to the attainment of *real* excellence by the contemplation of splendid Possibilities that still revivifies the dying motive within us, and fixing our eye on the glittering Summits that rise one above the other in Alpine endlessness still urges us up the ascent of Being, amusing the ruggedness of the road with the beauty and grandeur of the ever-widening Prospect.[4] [The noblest gift of Imagination is the power of discerning the *Cause* in the *Effect* a power which when employed on the works of the Creator elevates and by the variety of its pleasures almost monopolizes the Soul. We see our God everywhere—the Universe in the most literal Sense is his written Language.][5] Such and so noble are the ends for which this restless faculty was given us—but horrible has been its misapplication. Hence the Savage eagerly seizes every opportunity of intoxication—and hence the polished Citizen lies framing unreal Wants, and diverts the pains of Vacancy by the pestilent inventions of Luxury.

(*CC* I 235–6)

Notes

1. The lecture was delivered at Bristol on 16 June 1795.
2. Although the imitation of 'Creativeness by combination' looks back to neoclassical theory, this sentence is an adumbration of STC's later definition of the 'primary Imagination' which is 'a repetition in the finite

mind of the eternal act of creation in the infinite I AM' (*Biographia* Chap xiii; Extract 33–F). Cf also *The Watchman* of 25 March 1796: 'Man, a vicious and discontented *Animal*, by his vices and his discontent is urged to develop the powers of the Creator, and by new combinations of those powers to imitate his creativeness' (*CC* II 132).

3. Cf *The Watchman* (25 March 1796): 'What Nature demands, she will supply, asking for it that portion only of *Toil*, which would otherwise have been necessary as *Exercise*. But Providence, which has distinguished Man from the lower orders of Being by the progressiveness of his nature, forbids him to be contented. It has given us the restless faculty of *Imagination*' (*CC* II 131). Cf also Extract 40–B.

4. Cf STC's extended metaphor on the ascent of knowledge in *Biographia* Chap xii (Extract 33–E). The inspiration for this Alpine image may have come from Mark Akenside's *Pleasures of the Imagination* (1757) I 177–8; or from Alexander Pope's 'Essay on Criticism' (1711) 219–32:

> Fir'd at first Sight with what the *Muse* imparts,
> In *fearless Youth* we tempt the Heights of Arts,
> While from the bounded *Level* of our Mind,
> *Short Views* we take, nor see the *Lengths behind*,
> But *more advanc'd*, behold with strange Surprize
> New, distant Scenes of *endless* Science rise!
> So pleas'd at first, the towring *Alps* we try,
> Mount o'er the Vales, and seem to tread the Sky;
> Th' Eternal Snows appear already past,
> And the first *Clouds* and *Mountains* seem the last:
> But *those attain'd*, we tremble to survey
> The growing Labours of the lengthen'd Way,
> Th' *increasing* Prospect *tires* our wandring Eyes,
> Hills peep o'er Hills, and *Alps* on *Alps* arise!

5. These two sentences, not included in the 'Lecture on the Slave-Trade', appear at this point in a fragment which seems to be a missing leaf from that lecture: cf *CC* I 338–9. For an assessment of the significance of these sentences, see introduction, p. 10.

2. from 'THE DESTINY OF NATIONS' (1796)

> For what is Freedom, but the unfettered use
> Of all the powers which God for use had given?

But chiefly this, him First, him Last to view   15
Through meaner powers and secondary things
Effulgent, as through clouds that veil his blaze.
For all that meets the bodily sense I deem
Symbolical, one mighty alphabet[1]
For infant minds; and we in this low world   20
Placed with our backs to bright Reality,[2]
That we may learn with young unwounded ken
The substance from its shadow. Infinite Love,
Whose latence is the plenitude of All,
Thou with retracted beams, and self-eclipse   25
Veiling, revealest thine eternal Sun.

    . . . . .

As ere from Lieule-Oaive's vapoury head[3]
The Laplander beholds the far-off Sun   65
Dart his slant beam on unobeying snows,
While yet the stern and solitary Night
Brooks no alternate sway, the Boreal Morn[4]
With mimic lustre substitutes its gleam,
Guiding his course or by Niemi lake   70
Or Balda Zhiok,[5] or the mossy stone
Of Solfar-kapper, while the snowy blast ·
Drifts arrowy by, or eddies round his sledge,
Making the poor babe at its mother's back[6]
Scream in its scanty cradle: he the while   75
Wins gentle solace as with upward eye
He marks the streamy banners of the North,
Thinking himself those happy spirits shall join
Who there in floating robes of rosy light
Dance sportively. For Fancy is the power   80
That first unsensualises the dark mind.[7]
Giving it new delights; and bids it swell
With wild activity; and peopling air,
By obscure fears of Beings invisible,
Emancipates it from the grosser thrall   85
Of the present impulse, teaching Self-control,
Till Superstition with unconscious hand
Seat Reason on her throne. Wherefore not vain,
Nor yet without permitted power impressed,
I deem those legends terrible, with which   90
The polar ancient[8] thrills his uncouth throng:

Whether of pitying Spirits that make their moan
O'er slaughter'd infants, or that Giant Bird
Vuokho, of whose rushing wings the noise
Is Tempest, when the unutterable Shape   95
Speeds from the mother of Death, and utters once
That shriek, which never murderer heard, and lived.

(*CPW* I 132—4)

Notes

1. Cf Extracts 13–H and 50.
2. Alludes to Plato's Simile of the Cave in *The Republic* VII 514–17c.
3. *Lieule-Oaive*, like *Balda Zhiok* and *Solfar-kapper* (lines 71–2), are mountains in northern Scandinavia. The imagery in these lines treating the Laplander and his family is much influenced by STC's reading of M. de Maupertuis, *The Figure of the Earth . . . at the Polar Circle* (London, 1738); Knud Leems (= Leemius), *De Lapponibus Finmarchiae* (Copenhagen, 1767); and David Crantz, *The History of Greenland* (London, 1767). Lowes (1930, 96—102) examines these lines from 'The Destiny of Nations' in some detail and demonstrates STC's manner of 'dovetailing and interweaving' reminiscences from Maupertuis, Leemius and Crantz into his imagery. Lowes also points out that the 'great stanzas in "The Ancient Mariner" which depict the terrors of the polar ice were not put together from material got up for the occasion. There had been, on the contrary, a long, slow charging of the cells before the final release of creative energy. And that gradual storing of Coleridge's mind with images, and those tentative feelings after adequate expression, throw curious and interesting light upon the genesis of the masterpiece itself, and on the operations of the power which begot it' (93—4).
4. *Boreal Morn*, i.e., the *aurora borealis* or Northern Lights, which are bands of light seen in high latitudes. In line 77 he calls them 'the streamy banners of the North'. Cf also STC's sonnet 'To William Godwin', 3—4: 'In Finland's wintry skies the Mimic Morn/ Electric pours a stream of rosy light'.
5. *STC's note*: 'Balda-Zhiok, i.e. mons altitudinus, the highest mountain in Lapland.'
6. *STC's note*: 'The Lapland women carry their infants at their backs in a piece of excavated wood which serves them for a cradle: opposite to the infant's mouth there is a hole for it to breathe through.'
7. Cf Extract 22.
8. The *polar ancient* is the Scandinavian bard, who is pictured reciting terrifying tales from popular mythology to his 'uncouth' audience.

3. 'KUBLA KHAN' (Autumn 1797)[1]

In Xanadu did Kubla Khan[2]
A stately pleasure-dome decree:
Where Alph, the sacred river, ran
Through caverns measureless to man
    Down to a sunless sea.   5
So twice five[3] miles of fertile ground
With walls and towers were girdled round:[4]
And there[5] were gardens bright with sinuous rills,
Where blossomed many an incense-bearing tree;
And here were forests ancient as the hills,   10
Enfolding sunny spots of greenery.[6]

But oh! that deep romantic chasm which slanted[7]
Down the green hill athwart a cedarn cover!
A savage place! as holy and enchanted
As e'er beneath a waning moon was haunted   15
By woman wailing for her demon-lover!
And from this chasm, with ceaseless turmoil seething,[8]
As if this earth in fast thick pants were breathing,
A mighty fountain momently was forced:
Amid whose swift half-intermitted burst   20
Huge fragments vaulted like rebounding hail,
Or chaffy grain beneath the thresher's flail:
And 'mid these dancing rocks at once and ever
It flung up momently the sacred river.
Five miles meandering with a mazy motion   25
Through wood and dale the sacred river ran,
Then reached the caverns measureless to man,
And sank in tumult to a lifeless ocean:[9]
And 'mid this tumult Kubla[10] heard from far
Ancestral voices prophesying war!   30
    The shadow of the dome of pleasure
    Floated midway on the waves;
    Where was heard the mingled measure
    From the fountain and the caves.
It was a miracle of rare device,   35
A sunny pleasure-dome with caves of ice.[11]

    A damsel with a dulcimer
    In a vision once I saw:

It was an Abyssinian maid,
And on her dulcimer she played,   40
Singing of Mount Abora.[12]
Could I revive within me
Her symphony and song,
To such a deep delight 'twould win me,
That with music loud and long,   45
I would build that dome in air,
That sunny dome! those caves of ice!
And all who heard should see them there,
And all should cry, Beware! Beware!
His flashing eyes, his floating hair!   50
Weave a circle round him thrice,
And close your eyes with holy dread,[13]
For he on honey-dew hath fed,
And drunk[14] the milk of Paradise.[15]

(*CPW* I 297–8)

Notes

1. The version of the poem here reprinted is the *textus receptus*, i.e., with three alterations (listed below in the notes) the text of the first edition (1816). I have also listed in the notes the more important variants in the Crewe Manuscript text. (For the Crewe Manuscript, see Extract 34, n 1.) 'Kubla Khan' is the one great poem that STC wrote *directly* on the nature of poetry and the power of Imagination.

   The date of composition of 'Kubla Khan' has been widely disputed. In the 1816 Preface STC says it was written in 'the summer of the year 1797', but the Crewe Manuscript gives the date as 'the fall of the year, 1797'. E. K. Chambers after a careful examination of the question settled on a date in October 1797: 'The Date of Coleridge's *Kubla Khan*' RES 11 (1935) 78–80, and *Samuel Taylor Coleridge: A Biographical Study* (Oxford: Clarendon Press, 1938) 100–3. EHC assigns the poem to the summer of 1798: *CPW* I 295, n 2; L. Hanson argues for May 1798: *The Life of S. T. Coleridge: The Early Years* (London: Allen & Unwin, 1938) 259–60; and E. Schneider (after an exhaustive review) pushes the date to October 1799 or sometime in the spring of 1800: *Coleridge, Opium and 'Kubla Khan'* (1953) 153–237. In general, however, scholarly opinion now seems to lean toward a date in the autumn of 1797.

   In 1963 Richard Gerber suggested that 'It is fairly safe to say that no poem in the English language has provided more pages of comment per line than "Kubla Khan"'. The intervening thirteen years serve to confirm this guess yet further. See, for example, the Bibliography entries under Lowes (1930), Bodkin (1934), House (1953), Beer (1959), Chayes (1966), Watson (1966) and Brisman (1975). Other recent studies (less directly concerned with STC's theory of Imagination in the poem) include the following: S. K. Heninger, Jr, 'A Jungian Reading of "Kubla Khan"' *JAAC* 18 (1959–60) 358–67; R. H. Fogle, 'The Romantic Unity of "Kubla Khan"' *CE* 22 (1960–1) 112–16; G. Watson, 'The Meaning of "Kubla Khan"' *REL* 2 (1961) 21–9; A. C. Purves, 'Formal Structure in "Kubla Khan"' *SIR* 1 (1962) 187–91; E. E. Bostetter, *The Romantic Ventriloquists* (Seattle: University of Washington Press, 1963) 84–91; R. Gerber, 'Keys to "Kubla Khan"' *ES* 44 (1963) 321–41; M. F. Schulz (1963) 114–24; K. Raine, 'Traditional Symbolism in *Kubla Khan*' *SR* 72 (1964) 626–42; R. Gerber, 'Cybele, Kubla Khan, and Keats' *ES* 46 (1965) 369–89; Bate (1968) 75–84; Fruman (1971) 334–49 and 392–402; H. W. Piper, 'The Two Paradises in *Kubla Khan*' *RES* n.s. 27 (1976) 148–58.

A number of scholars have engaged in tracking down the sources of STC's imagery in 'Kubla Khan': see especially Lowes (1930), Beer (1959) and W. W. Beyer, *The Enchanted Forest* (Oxford: Blackwell, 1963) 118–43. I have cited one or two of the better known (and generally accepted) instances in the notes below.

2. *Crewe MS*: 'In Xannadù did Cubla Khan'. The changes in spelling are discussed by Beer (1959) 216–17.

3. *Crewe MS*: 'six'.

4. *Crewe MS*: 'compass'd round'. The imagery of these opening lines was inspired, as STC notes in his 1816 Preface (Extract 34), by a sentence in Samuel Purchas's *Purchas his Pilgrimage* (1617): 'In Xamdu did Cublai Can build a stately Palace, encompassing sixteene miles of plaine ground with a wall, wherein are fertile Meddowes, pleasant Springs, delightfull Streames, and all sorts of beasts of chase and game, and in the middest thereof a sumptuous house of pleasure, which may be removed from place to place.'

5. *Crewe MS* and *1816 edition*: 'And here'.

6. *Crewe MS*: 'Enfolding'. *1816 edition*: 'And folding'. For similar imagery, see Extract 47–B and n 10.

7. The Crewe MS does not begin a new verse paragraph with this line. In the Crewe MS there are only two stanzas in the poem: lines 1–36 and lines 37–54.

8. *Crewe MS*: 'From forth this Chasm with hideous Turmoil seething'.

9. With lines 25–9 compare the opening stanzas of STC's early poem 'A Wish' (1792):

> Lo! through the dusky silence of the groves,
> Thro' vales irriguous, and thro' green retreats,

> With languid murmur creeps the placid stream
> And works its secret way.
>
> Awhile meand'ring round its native fields
> It rolls the playful wave and winds its flight:
> Then downward flowing with awaken'd speed
> Embosoms in the Deep!
>
> (*CPW* I 33)

10. *Crewe MS*: 'Cubla'.
11. It was probably sometime in 1796 or early 1797 when STC jotted the following sentence down in his Gutch Memorandum Note Book: 'In a cave in the mountains of Cashmere an Image of Ice, which makes its appearance thus— ["] two days before the new *moon* there appears a bubble of Ice which increases in size every day till the 15th day, at which it is an ell or more in height: then as the moon decreases, the Image ["] does also till it vanishes' (*CN* I 240). The section in quotation marks ["] is transcribed from Thomas Maurice's *The History of Hindostan* (1795); for STC's use of Maurice, see Lowes (1930) 379–83 and Beer (1959) 224–5, 246–7.

    On the 'reconciliation of opposites', see Extract 33–G and n 11. A number of critics have examined the reconciliation of opposites in the imagery of 'Kubla Khan': e.g., C. Moorman, 'The Imagery of "Kubla Khan"' *N&Q* 204 (1959) 321–4; R. H. Fogle, 'The Romantic Unity of "Kubla Khan"' *CE* 22 (1960–1) 112–16; D. B. Schneider, 'The Structure of "Kubla Khan"' *AN&Q* 1 (1963) 68–70.
12. *Crewe MS*: 'Amora' altered to 'Amara'. Cf Milton, *Paradise Lost* IV 280–4:

> Nor where Abassin kings their issue guard,
> Mount Amara, though this by some supposed
> True Paradise under the Ethiop line
> By Nilus' head, enclosed with shining rock,
> A whole day's journey high . . .

    For the significance of STC's alterations (Amora–Amara–Abora), see Beer (1959) 256; Gerber, 'Keys to "Kubla Khan"' (n 1 above), 323; Brisman (1975) 472–4; H. W. Piper, 'Mount Abora' *N&Q* n.s. 20 (1973) 286–9.
13. *Crewe MS*: 'in holy Dread'.
14. *Crewe MS* and *1816 edition*: 'drank'.
15. While there are a number of literary echoes in the last seven lines (e.g. Exodus 3:8 and Ovid, *Metamorphoses* I 111–2), the most striking parallel occurs in Plato's description of the inspired poet in *Ion* 533e–34.

4. from a LETTER TO THOMAS POOLE (23 March 1801)

My opinion is this—that deep Thinking is attainable only by a man of deep Feeling, [1] and that all Truth is a species of Revelation. The more I understand of Sir Isaac Newton's works, the more boldly I dare utter to my own mind & therefore to *you*, that I believe the Souls of 500 Sir Isaac Newtons would go to the making up of a Shakspere or a Milton. [. . .] Newton was a mere materialist—*Mind* in his system is always passive—a lazy Looker-on on an external World. If the mind be not *passive*, if it be indeed made in God's Image, & that too in the sublimest sense—the Image of the *Creator*—there is ground for suspicion, that any system built on the passiveness of the mind must be false, as a system. [2]

(*CL* II 709)

Notes

1. Two years later (7 August 1803) STC wrote as follows to Southey: 'I hold, that association depends in a much greater degree on the recurrence of resembling states of Feeling, than on Trains of Idea/ [. . .] Believe me, Southey! a metaphysical Solution, that does not instantly *tell* for something in the Heart, is grievously to be suspected as apocryphal. I almost think, that Ideas *never* recall Ideas, as far as they are Ideas—any more than Leaves in a forest create each other's motion— The Breeze it is that runs thro' them/ it is the Soul, the state of Feeling—' (*CL* II 961).

2. Early in 1801 STC began a serious study of philosophy, beginning with an examination of Locke's system. In three letters of February 1801 he attacked Locke's philosophical views, and these letters are important evidence of STC's disaffection with British empirical philosophy: cf *CL* II 678ff.

5 from a LETTER TO WILLIAM GODWIN (25 March 1801)

I fear, your Tragedy [1] will find me in a very unfit state of mind to sit in Judgement on it. I have been, during the last 3 months, undergoing a process of intellectual *exsiccation*. [2] In my long Illness I had compelled into hours of Delight many a sleepless, painful hour of Darkness by chasing down metaphysical Game—and since then I have continued the Hunt, till I found myself unaware at the Root of Pure Mathematics—and up that tall smooth Tree, whose few poor Branches are all at it's very summit, am I climbing by pure adhesive strength of arms and thighs—still slipping down, still renewing my ascent.—You would not know me—! all sounds of similitude keep at such a distance from each other in my mind, that I have *forgotten* how to make a rhyme—I look at the Mountains (that visible God Almighty that looks in at all my windows) I look at the Mountains only for the Curves of their outlines; the Stars, as I behold them, form themselves into Triangles—and my hands are scarred with scratches from a Cat, whose back I was rubbing in the Dark in order to see whether the sparks from it were refrangible by a Prism. The Poet is dead in me[3]—my imagination (or rather the Somewhat that had been imaginative) lies, like a Cold Snuff on the circular Rim of a Brass Candle-stick, without even a stink of Tallow to remind you that it was once cloathed & mitred with Flame.[4] That is past by!—I was once a Volume of Gold Leaf, rising & riding on every breath of Fancy—but I have beaten myself back into weight & density, & now I sink in quick-silver, yea, remain squat and square on the earth amid the hurricane, that makes Oaks and Straws join in one Dance, fifty yards high in the Element. However, I will do what I can—Taste & Feeling have I none, but what I have, give I unto thee.— But I repeat, that I am unfit to decide on any but works of severe Logic.[5] [. . .] Have you seen the second Volume of the Lyrical Ballads,[6] & the Preface prefixed to the First?— I should judge of a man's Heart, and Intellect precisely according to the degree & intensity of the admiration, with which he read those poems. . . . If I die, and the Booksellers will give you any thing for my Life, be sure to say—'Wordsworth descended on him, like the Γνῶθι σεαυτόν[7] from Heaven; by shewing to him what true Poetry was, he made him know, that he himself was no Poet.'

(*CL* II 713–4)

Notes

1. Godwin's *Abbas, King of Persia* (1801).
2. *exsiccation*: 'made absolutely dry or arid'.
3. Loss of Imagination (which STC ascribed to illness and to his abstruse metaphysical researches) is a recurring theme in the letters of 1800–3. (Cf also Extracts 6, 8, 48 and n 14, and 50.) The following passages will make clear the nature of the case as STC apprehended it:

(a) *To J. W. Tobin, 17 September 1800*: 'The delay in Copy has been owing in part to me, as the writer of Christabel—Every line has been produced by me with labor-pangs. I abandon Poetry altogether—I leave the higher & deeper Kinds to Wordsworth, the delightful, popular & simply dignified to Southey; & reserve for myself the honorable attempt to make others feel and understand their writings, as they deserve to be felt & understood.' (*CL* 1 623)

(b) *To John Thelwall, 17 December 1800*: 'As to Poetry, I have altogether abandoned it, being convinced that I never had the essentials of poetic Genius, & that I mistook a strong desire for original power.' (Ibid. 656)

(c) *To Francis Wrangham, 19 December 1800*: 'As to our literary occupations they are still more distant than our residences—He [Wordsworth] is a great, a true Poet—I am only a kind of a Metaphysician.' (Ibid. 658)

(d) *To Robert Southey, 29 July 1802*: 'As to myself, all my poetic Genius, if ever I really possessed any *Genius*, & it was not rather a mere general *aptitude* of Talent, & quickness in Imitation/ is gone—and I have been fool enough to suffer deeply in my mind, regretting the loss—which I attribute to my long & exceedingly severe Metaphysical Investigations—& these partly to Ill-health, and partly to private afflictions [i.e., the unhappy relations with his wife and his hopeless love for Sara Hutchinson] which rendered any subject, immediately connected with Feeling, a source of pain & disquiet to me/'. (Ibid. 11 831)

(e) *To William Godwin, 10 June 1803*: 'It seemed a Dream, that I had ever *thought* on Poetry—or had ever written it—so remote were my Trains of Ideas from Composition, or Criticism on Composition.' (Ibid. 950)

Although the desertion of the Muse is certainly a recurring motif in the letters of these years, it is also true that at the same time STC harboured poetic hopes and aspirations. Thus, on 1 February 1801 we find him writing to Poole in these terms: 'I hope, that shortly I shall look back on my long & painful Illness only as a Storehouse of wild Dreams for Poems, or intellectual Facts for metaphysical Speculation. Davy in the kindness of his heart calls me the Poet-philosopher—I hope, Philosophy & Poetry will not neutralize each other, & leave me an inert mass. But I talk idly—I feel, that I have power within me: and I humbly pray to the Great Being, the God & Father who has bidden me "rise & walk" that he will grant me a steady mind to employ the health of my youth and manhood in the manifestation of that power' (*CL* 11 668—9). And, again to Poole, he wrote on 7 May 1802: 'I can venture to promise you that by the end of the year I shall have disburthened myself of all my metaphysics, &c—& that the next year I shall, if I am alive & in possession of my present faculties, devote to a long poem' (Ibid. 799). For an interesting assessment of STC's sense of 'lost' poetic ability, see Whalley (1974).

4. The phrase 'mitred with Flame' recalls the Pentecostal gift of tongues in Acts 2:3 – 'And there appeared unto them cloven tongues like as of fire, and it sat upon each of them.'

5. A month later (28 April 1801) STC wrote again to Godwin in the same vein: 'I will give your manuscript my best attention, & what I think, I will communicate—but indeed, indeed, I am not dissembling when I express my exceeding scepticism respecting the sanity of my own Feelings and Tone of Intellect, relatively to a work of Sentiment & Imagination.— I have been compelled, (wakeful thro' the night, & seldom able, for my eyes, to read in the Day) to seek resources in austerest reasonings—& have thereby so denaturalized my mind, that I can scarcely convey to you the disgust with which I look over any of my own compositions . . .' (CL II 725).

6. STC refers to the second edition (1800) of the Lyrical Ballads, enlarged and with a Preface by Wordsworth.

7. Γνῶθι σεαυτόν : 'Know thyself' This famous precept, which was carved on the temple at Delphi, is an often-quoted Socratic maxim (e.g., Charmides 164d–165b, Phaedrus 230a, Protagoras 343b) and was later used by Juvenal (Satires xi 27). STC employs it frequently: in|Biographia Chap xii, this maxim is described as the 'postulate of philosophy and at the same time the test of philosophic capacity' (BL 1 173); and later in the same chapter he writes that 'as long as there are men in the world to whom the Γνῶθι σεαυτόν is an instinct and a command from|their own nature, so long will there be metaphysicians and metaphysical speculations' (ibid. 192), and then in Chap xxiv the phrase is made the prime rule of metaphysics (ibid. II 212 n). In Appendix C of The Statesman's Manual (1816) and again in the 'Essays on the Principles of Method' in the 1818 Friend the phrase is applied to scientific analysis (cf CC VI 79 and IV i 509); and in 1832 STC used Juvenal's formulation E coelo descendit γνῶθι σεαυτόν ('From heaven it descends, the "know thyself"') both as motto and theme of his poem 'Self-Knowledge' (CPW 1 487).

6. from a VERSE LETTER TO SARA HUTCHINSON (4 April 1802)[1]

> O dearest Sara! in this heartless Mood   30
> All this long Eve, so balmy & serene,
> Have I been gazing on the western Sky
> And it's peculiar Tint of Yellow Green—

And still I gaze—& with how blank an eye!
And those thin Clouds above, in flakes & bars,   35
That give away their Motion to the Stars;
Those Stars, that glide behind them, or between,
Now sparkling, now bedimm'd, but always seen;
Yon crescent Moon, as fix'd as if it grew
In it's own cloudless, starless Lake of Blue—   40
A boat becalm'd! dear William's Sky Canoe![2]
 —I see them all, so excellently fair!
 I see, not feel, how beautiful they are![3]

   [. . . . . .]

  Yes, dearest Sara! yes!   231
There *was* a time when tho' my path was rough,[4]
The Joy within me dallied with Distress;
And all Misfortunes were but as the Stuff
Whence Fancy made me Dreams of Happiness: 235
For Hope grew round me, like the climbing Vine,
And Leaves & Fruitage, not my own, seem'd mine!
But now Ill Tidings bow me down to earth/
Nor care I, that they rob me of my Mirth/
  But oh! each Visitation   240
Suspends what Nature gave me at my Birth,
  My shaping Spirit of Imagination![5]

   [. . . .]

O Sara! we receive but what we give,   296
And in *our* Life alone does Nature live.
Our's is her Wedding Garment, our's her Shroud—
And would we aught behold of higher Worth
Than that inanimate cold World allow'd   300
To the poor loveless ever-anxious Crowd,
Ah! from the Soul itself must issue forth
A Light, a Glory, and a luminous Cloud
  Enveloping the Earth!
And from the Soul itself must there be sent   305
A sweet & potent Voice, of it's own Birth,
Of all sweet Sounds the Life & Element.
O pure of Heart! thou need'st not ask of me
What this strong music in the Soul may be,
  What, & wherein it doth exist,   310

This Light, this Glory, this fair luminous Mist,
This beautiful & beauty-making Power!
Joy, innocent Sara! Joy, that ne'er was given
Save to the Pure, & in their purest Hour,
[Life, and Life's effluence, cloud at once and shower,]⁶
Joy,⁷ Sara! is the Spirit & the Power,   315
That wedding Nature to us gives in Dower
     A new Earth & new Heaven
Undreamt of by the Sensual & the Proud!
Joy is that strong Voice, Joy that luminous Cloud—
    We, we ourselves rejoice!   320
And thence flows all that charms or ear or sight,
All melodies the Echoes of that Voice,
All Colours a Suffusion of that Light.

                     (*CL* II 791, 796–8)

Notes

1. This letter (340 lines in length) is the earliest version of what later became 'Dejection: An Ode' (139 lines in length); the lines quoted here appear—with numerous changes—as lines 25–38, 76–86, and 47–75 respectively in the received version of 'Dejection'.

2. See Wordsworth's 'Peter Bell' (composed 1798, published 1819) lines 1–190. This line is omitted in the published version of 'Dejection'.

3. Cf STC's letter of 1 November 1800 to Josiah Wedgwood: 'Often when in a deep Study I have walked to the window & remained there *looking without seeing . . .*' (*CL* I 644; the remainder of the sentence is quoted below in Extract 33–C, n 6). On STC's loss of Imagination, see Extracts 5 and n 3; 8, 48 and 50.

4. For the starting-point of lines 232ff, see STC's 'The Mad Monk' (1800) 9–16: *CPW* I 348.

5. For recent discussions of Imagination in 'Dejection: An Ode', see Fogle (1950), Schulz (1963), Bouslog (1963) and Simmons (1966–7).

6. This line, not in the verse letter of 1802, was added when 'Dejection' was published in *Sibylline Leaves* (1817). For an account of the various drafts of 'Dejection', see E. de Selincourt, 'Coleridge's *Dejection: An Ode*' *E&S* 22 (1936) 7–25.

7. Coleridge's *joy*, as Dorothy Emmet (1952) remarks, is not simply 'a reading of our own feelings into nature. It is rather the possibility of entering into a deep *rapport* with something in the world beyond us, seeing it with such loving sympathy that we make, as Coleridge says, the "external internal, the internal external" and out of this comes the possibility of the creation of imaginative symbolism. But the first

condition of such creation is that we should be able not only to look, but to love as we look' (173). Cf also Extract 45.

7. from a LETTER TO WILLIAM SOTHEBY (13 July 1802)

On my return to Keswick I reperused the erste Schiffer[1] with great attention; & the result was an increasing Disinclination to the business of translating it/ tho' my fancy was not a little flattered by the idea of seeing my Rhymes in such a gay Livery. . . . But the Poem was too silly. The first conception is noble—so very good, that I am spiteful enough to hope that I shall discover it not to have been original in Gesner—he has so abominably maltreated it.—First, the story is very inartificially constructed—we should have been let into the existence of the Girl & her Mother thro' the young Man, & after *his* appearance/ this however is comparatively a trifle.—But the machinery is so superlatively contemptible & common-place—as if a young man could not dream of a Tale which had deeply impressed him without Cupid, or have a fair wind all the way to an Island within sight of the Shore, he quitted, without Æolus. Æolus himself is a God devoted & dedicated, I should have thought, to the Muse of Travestie/ his Speech in Gesner is not deficient in Fancy—but it is a Girlish Fancy—& the God of the winds exceedingly disquieted with *animal* Love/ ind[uces?] a very ridiculous Figure in my Imagination.—Besides, it was ill taste to introduce Cupid and Æolus at a time which we positive[ly] know to have been anterior to the invention & establishment of the Grecian Mythology—and the speech of Æolus reminds me perpetually of little Engravings from the Cut Stones of the Ancients, Seals, & whatever else they call them.—Again, the Girl's yearnings & conversations with [her] Mother are something between the Nursery and the Veneris Volgivagae Templa—et libidinem spirat et subsusurrat, dum innocentiae loquelam, et virgineae cogitationis dulciter offensantis luctamina simulat.[2]—It is not the Thoughts that a lonely Girl *could* have; but exactly such as a Boarding School Miss whose *Imagination*, to say no worse, had been somewhat stirred & heated by the perusal of French or German Pastorals, would suppose her to say. But this is indeed general in the German & French Poets. It is easy to cloathe Imaginary Beings with our own Thoughts & Feelings; but to send ourselves out of ourselves, to *think* ourselves in to the Thoughts and Feelings of Beings in circumstances wholly & strangely different from our own/ hoc labor, hoc opus[3]/ and who has atchieved it? Perhaps only Shakespere.[4] Metaphisics is a word, that you, my dear Sir! are no great Friend to/ but yet you will agree, that a great Poet must be, implicitè if not explicitè, a profound Metaphysician. He may not have it in logical coherence, in his Brain & Tongue; but he must have it by *Tact*/ for all sounds, & forms of human nature he must have the *ear* of a wild Arab listening in the silent Desert, the eye of a North American Indian tracing the footsteps of an Enemy upon the Leaves that strew the Forest—; the *Touch* of a Blind Man feeling the face of a darling Child—/ and do not think me a Bigot, if I say, that I have read no French or German Writer, who appears to me to have had a *heart* sufficiently pure & simple to be capable of this or any thing like it./ I could say a great deal more in abuse of poor Gesner's Poem; but I have said more than, I fear, will be creditable in your opinion to my good nature.

(*CL* II 809–11)

Notes

1. Salomon Gessner's prose romance 'Der erste Schiffer' (The First Sailor) is the tale of Melida, a young maiden domiciled with her mother on an otherwise deserted island in the sea. Melida dreams of other human beings, but her mother (devoted to her daughter's purity) discourages all such speculation. However, a young man on the mainland is given a vision of Melida, and fashioning a log into a boat, he sets out to find her—thereby becoming 'der erste Schiffer' to come to the island. 'Der erste Schiffer' was first published in Gessner's *Gedichte* (Zurich, 1762).
2. *Veneris . . . simulat*: 'the Temple of Erotic Passion—and she breathes and murmurs-low her desire, while simulating the speech of innocence and the struggles of virginal meditation, which she finds sweetly offensive'.
3. *hoc labor, hoc opus*: 'this is the task, this the toil'. Variant of Virgil, *Aeneid* VI 1802: *hoc opus, hic labor est*.
4. Cf Keats's doctrine of 'Negative Capability' as expounded in the letter of 22 December 1817 to his brothers George and Tom. Cf also STC's *Biographia* Chap XV (Extract 33–H), and the Notebook entries in Extracts 13–B, 13–M, 13–N and 17–B.

8. from a LETTER TO WILLIAM SOTHEBY (19 July 1802)

I trouble you with another Letter, to inform you that I have finished the first Book of the Erste Schiffer. [1] [. . .] I was probably too severe on the *morals* of the Poem—uncharitably perhaps, but I am a homebrewed Englishman, and tolerate downright grossness more patiently than this coy and distant Dallying with the Appetites. [. . .] Now I avow, that the grossness & vulgar plain Sense of Theocritus's[2] Shepherd Lads, bad as it is, is in my opinion less objectionable than Gesner's Refinement—which necessarily leads the imagination to Ideas without *expressing them*—Shaped & cloathed—the mind of a pure Being would turn away from them, from natural delicacy of Taste/ but in that shadowy half-being, that state of nascent Existence in the Twilight of Imagination, and just on the vestibule of Consciousness, they are far more incendiary, stir up a more lasting commotion, & leave a deeper stain. The Suppression & obscurity arrays the simple Truth in a veil of something like Guilt, that is altogether *meretricious*, as opposed to the *matronly majesty*—of our Scriptures, for instance—/—and the Conceptions, as they *recede* from distinctness of *Idea, approximate* to the nature of *Feeling*, & gain thereby a closer & more immediate affinity with the appetites. [. . .] I translated the Poem, partly, because I could not endure to appear *irresolute & capricious* to you, in the first undertaking which I had connected in any way with your person . . . & partly too, because I wished to force myself out of metaphysical trains of Thought—which, when I trusted myself to my own Ideas, came upon me uncalled—& when I wished to write a poem, beat up Game of far other kind—instead of a Covey of poetic Partridges with whirring wings of music, or wild Ducks *shaping* their rapid flight in forms always regular (a still better image of Verse) up came a metaphysical Bustard,[3] urging it's slow, heavy, laborious, earth-skimming Flight, over dreary & level Wastes. To have done with poetical Prose (which is a very vile Olio[4]) Sickness & some other & worse afflictions, first forced me into *downright metaphysics*/ for I believe that by nature I have more of the Poet in me/ [. . .]

(*CL* II 813–14)

Notes

1. Cf Extract 7, n 1. STC's translation has not come to light.
2. Theocritus (*fl. c.* 270 BC) is regarded as the 'father' of pastoral poetry; his

Idylls, usually in the form of a dialogue between rustics, present an idealised view of his native Sicily. Gessner, who imitated this mode in his *Idyllen* (1756 and 1772), was called 'the Swiss Theocritus'.

3. Fruman (1971) points out that this image seems to derive from Wordsworth's 'Guilt and Sorrow' in its earliest form: *Coleridge, The Damaged Archangel* 496 n 43.

4. Olio: 'a hotchpotch; *lit.* a dish of various meats and vegetables which have been highly spiced'. House (1953) comments on this passage as follows: 'though the letter jokingly repudiates what it calls "poetical prose", it has achieved, in the three kinds of bird and their three kinds of flight, clear, precise, fully realised images for the mental moods of which he is speaking. The paragraph is working (as so much of the best prose is) through the mind's processes from the less full to the fuller expression of its purpose. But the clarity of physical vision, and the expression of that vision, is what needs to be stressed' (47). Cf Introduction, pp. 23 – 4, and Extract 48 and n 14.

9. from a LETTER TO WILLIAM SOTHEBY (10 September 1802)

Bowles's Stanzas on Navigation[1] are among the best in that second Volume/ but the whole volume is woefully inferior to it's Predecessor. There reigns thro' all the blank verse poems such a perpetual trick of *moralizing* every thing—which is very well, occasionally—but never to see or describe any interesting appearance in nature, without connecting it by dim analogies with the moral world, proves faintness of Impression. Nature has her proper interest; & he will know what it is, who believes & feels, that every Thing has a Life of it's own, & that we are all *one Life*.[2] A Poet's *Heart & Intellect* should be *combined, intimately* combined & *unified*, with the great appearances in Nature—& not merely held in solution & loose mixture with them, in the shape of formal Similies.[3] I do not mean to *exclude* these formal Similies—there are moods of mind, in which they are natural—pleasing moods of mind, & such as a Poet will often have, & sometimes express; but they are not his highest, & most appropriate moods. They are 'Sermoni propiora' which I once translated—'*Properer for a Sermon.*'[4] The truth is—Bowles has indeed the *sensibility* of a poet; but he has not the *Passion* of a great Poet. His latter Writings all want *native* Passion—Milton here & there supplies him with an appearance of it—but he has no native Passion, because he is not a Thinker—& has probably weakened his Intellect by the haunting Fear of becoming extravagant/ Young[5] somewhere in one of his prose works remarks that there is as profound a Logic in the most daring & dithyrambic parts of Pindar, as in the 'Οργανον[6] of Aristotle—the remark is a valuable one/

> Poetic Feelings, like the flexuous Boughs
> Of mighty Oaks, yield homage to the Gale,
> Toss in the strong winds, drive before the Gust,
> Themselves one Giddy storm of fluttering Leaves;
> Yet all the while, self-limited, remain
> Equally near the fix'd and parent Trunk
> Of Truth & Nature, in the howling Blast
> As in the Calm that stills the Aspen Grove.—[7]

That this is deep in our Nature, I felt when I was on Sca' fell—.[8] I involuntarily poured fourth a Hymn in the manner of the *Psalms,* tho' afterwards I thought the Ideas &c disproportionate to our humble mountains—& accidentally lighting on a short Note in some swiss Poems, concerning the Vale of Chamouny, & it's Mountain, I transferred myself thither, in the Spirit, & adapted my former feelings to these grander external objects. You will soon see it in the Morning Post[9]—& I should be glad to know whether & how far it pleased you.— It has struck [me] with great force lately, that the Psalms afford a most compleat answer to those, who state the Jehovah of the Jews, as a personal & national God—& the Jews, as differing from the Greeks, only in calling the minor Gods, Cherubim & Seraphim—& confining the word God to their Jupiter. It must occur to every Reader that the Greeks in their religious poems address always the Numina Loci,[10] the Genii, the Dryads, the Naiads, &c &c—All natural Objects were *dead*—mere hollow Statues—but there was a Godkin or Goddessling *included* in each[11]— In the Hebrew Poetry you find nothing of this poor Stuff—as poor in genuine Imagination, as it is mean in Intellect—/ At best, it is but Fancy, or the aggregating Faculty of the mind—not *Imagination*, or the *modifying*, and *co-adunating* Faculty.[12] This the Hebrew Poets appear to me to have possessed beyond all others—& next to them the English. In the Hebrew Poets each Thing has a Life of it's own, & yet they are all one Life.[13] In God they move & live, & *have* their Being—not *had*, as the cold System of Newtonian[14] Theology represents/ but *have*.[15]

(*CL* II 864–6)

Notes

1. Bowles's 'The Spirit of Navigation', a poem of twenty 10-line stanzas in rhymed pentameter. William Lisle Bowles, *Poems* (1802).
2. Cf Extract 13–A, n 2.
3. Cf STC's later remarks: 'a simile is not expected *to go on all fours*' (*BL* II 219); 'It is but a simile, and no Simile is expected to be compleat in all points—' (*CN* III 4378). The necessary conjunction of poet and philosopher is one of STC's most cherished beliefs: e.g. Introduction, pp. 12–13 and also Extracts 4, 12 and 33–H.
4. *Sermoni propiora*: 'nearer to prose'. Cf Horace, *Satires* I iv 41–2: *neque, si qui scribat uti nos/sermoni propiora, putes hunc esse poetam*, 'nor would you account anyone a poet who writes, as I do, lines nearer to prose'. The witty rendering 'Properer for a Sermon' is in fact Charles Lamb's, not STC's.
5. Edward Young (1683–1765). Cf Young's *A Discourse on Lyric Poetry* (1728): 'It is the genuine character and true merit of the Ode, a little to startle some apprehensions. Men of cold complexions are very apt to mistake a want of vigour in their imaginations for a delicacy of taste in their judgements; and, like persons of a tender sight, they look on bright objects in their natural lustre as too glaring; what is most delightful to a stronger eye, is painful to them. Thus Pindar, who has as much logic at the bottom as Aristotle or Euclid, to some critics has appeared as mad; and must appear so to all who enjoy no portion of his own divine spirit. Dwarf understandings, measuring others by their own standard, are apt to think they see a monster, when they see a man.' Cf also Extract 33–A where a similar remark is ascribed to James Boyer rather than to Young.
6. Οργανον: *the Organon* ('instrument'), a generic term for Aristotle's six treatises on formal logic.

   Pindar (518–443 B.C.), Greek writer of choral lyrics. 'His poetry is marked by elevation of thought and grandeur of style, and the constant use of bold metaphors and a highly coloured language' (*OCCL* 328); 'Pindar's language is an elaborate poetical creation, made of several dialects, with many echoes and variations from Homer. His poems are written in regular stanzas . . . [but] no two poems are the same metrically' (*OCD* 834).

   Cf STC's early reference to 'the boldness of *Pindaric* Daring' in a letter to George Coleridge: 31 March 1791; *CL* I 7. While there is a tradition of (not-very-Pindaric) 'Pindaricks' running from Cowley to Gray which influenced both 'Dejection: An Ode' and Wordsworth's 'Immortality Ode', the original strain is purer in 'Kubla Khan' which is perhaps the closest thing in English to a true Pindaric ode. In 1806 STC became very interested in Pindar's elaborate prosody (which he studied in the most authoritative German editions): cf *CN* II 2835, 2881–7, and nn.

7. Lines 34–41 of STC's 'To Matilda Betham from a Stranger': cf *CPW* I 375–6.

8. Scafell Pike (Cumberland), which STC climbed on a solitary walking-tour of Cumberland (1–9 August 1802) and described in a letter to Sara Hutchinson: cf *CL* II 834–41. STC says nothing in the letter about composing a poem on Scafell; nor is there anything in the Notebooks: cf *CN* I 1212–18.

9. 'Chamouny; The Hour Before Sunrise' appeared in *The Morning Post* on 11 September 1802. Cf Extract 10.

10. *Numina Loci*: 'spirits of the place'. A *numen* is 'the power or spirit dwelling in each natural object—a tree, a fountain, the earth—and also in each man, controlling the phenomena of nature and the actions of man' (*OCCL* 289). A *genius* (plural: *genii*) is the indwelling spirit or *numen* of Man; *dryads* are the indwelling spirits (nymphs) of trees, *naiads* those of springs, rivers and lakes, and *oreads* those of mountains.

11. The connection between polytheism and pantheism formed part of Lecture xi (cf Extract 40–B) in the series of 1818: 'A confounding of God with Nature, and an incapacity of finding unity in the manifold and infinity in the individual,—these are the origin of polytheism. The most perfect instance of this kind of theism is that of early Greece . . .' (*MC* 191). Earlier, in Lecture x (27 February 1818) of the same lecture series, STC had contrasted Christianity with 'the spirit of pagan Greece, which receiving the very names of its gods from Egypt, soon deprived them of all that was universal. The Greeks changed the ideas into finites, and these finites into *anthropomorphi*, or forms of men. Hence their religion, their poetry, nay, their very pictures, became statuesque. With them the form was the end. The reverse of this was the natural effect of Christianity; in which finites, even the human form, must, in order to satisfy the mind, be brought into connexion with, and be in fact symbolical of, the infinite; and must be considered in some enduring, however shadowy and indistinct, point of view, as the vehicle or representative of moral truth' (*MC* 148). Cf also *CL* I 280.

12. *co-adunating*: 'joining together into one, combining, uniting'.

13. Cf Extract 13–A, n 2.

14. Cf Extract 4.

15. Appleyard (1965) argues that STC's Fancy–Imagination distinction is 'fully stated' in this letter to Sotheby. His comments bear repetition: 'It is to be noted that in this statement [i.e., the concluding four sentences of the letter] the operation by which the imagination modifies and coadunates is posterior to and by virtue of the real existence of things in a

unified way. Thus, both knowing and being are involved, and the latter is prior to and the source of the possibility of the former. It may be asked what exactly the imagination unifies. [The earlier part of the letter] would suggest that the main work of the imagination is to fuse thought and feeling. Though this is true, it does not go far enough in specifying how the imagination operates as a mode of expression or communication, or even of knowing. In other words we must add making to the concepts of being and knowing. An important passage in a letter of 1804 clarifies this. [Summarises and quotes from STC's letter to R. Sharp (15 January 1804): cf Extract 12.] The elements therefore which the imagination works on are thought, feeling, and poetic forms. Prior to the imaginative act, there is the world of objects, not dead, as the Greeks conceived them, but possessing a being that actively (they *have* life, not *had*) participates in some way in the divine being. Our reaction to this world involves thought and feeling and, if artistic externalization is our aim, poetic form. When the mind merely aggregates these elements in a loose mixture, or a solution, so that the expression of our awareness of the external world is made in formal similes, Coleridge says the fancy is at work. The imagination, on the other hand, matches thought and feeling and arrays them in forms, the whole process being distinguished by a modification and coadunation of the elements. What this is precisely Coleridge does not really say here. He suggests [in the letter to Sharp: Extract 12] that the operation of imagination is dimly analogous to divine creation (actually, though dim, the best analogue we have). What is at least implied is a totally new kind of existence which cannot conceivably be the result of the mere unity of the pre-existing elements, but rather connotes an informing act of the imagination' (96–7).

10. from 'CHAMOUNY; THE HOUR BEFORE SUNRISE' (1802)[1]

> O dread and silent form! I gaz'd upon thee,
> Till thou, still present to my bodily eye,
> Did'st vanish from my thought.[2] Entranc'd in pray'r,   15
> I worshipp'd the INVISIBLE alone.
> Yet thou, meantime, wast working on my soul,
> E'en like some deep enchanting melody,
> So sweet, we know not, we are list'ning to it.
> But I awoke, and with a busier mind,   20

And active will self-conscious, offer now
Not, as before, involuntary pray'r
And passive adoration!—
                    Hand and voice,
Awáke, awake! and thou, my heart, awake!
Awake ye rocks! Ye forest pines, awake!   25
Green fields, and icy cliffs! All join my hymn![3]

(CPW 1 572)

Notes

1. As published in *The Morning Post*, 11 September 1802. Cf Extract 9 for STC's comment to Sotheby on these lines.
2. This seems to draw on STC's records of *ocular spectra*: cf Introduction, n 27, and also lines 43–76 of 'This Lime-Tree Bower' (CPW 1 180–1). Cf also Keats, 'Ode on a Grecian Urn', 44–5:

   Thou, silent form, dost tease us out of thought
   As doth eternity.

   Cf also the 'boat episode' in Wordsworth's *The Prelude* (1805) 1 372–427.
3. For a later version of these lines and STC's attitude to them nearly twenty years later, see Extract 44 and n 2.

11. from the *NOTEBOOKS* (15 August 1803)

Out of the little parlour window looking across the market place & over the market House, a group of Ashes, of which the hithermost hath its topmost Twig exactly like a Rook or Magpie perching on the topmost Twig. N.B. The manifest magnitude which this Twig attained by its assimilation to a familiar Form, the size of which had been exempted by its old acquaintance, Queen Imagination, from all changes of perspective.[1]

(CN 1 1426)

Note

1. Cf also *CN* 1 1350 (February–March 1803): 'Perfect Symmetry,

diminishes the sense of magnitude. St Peter's Church & the Apollo Belvedere in perfect symmetry?' Cf also 'Apologia Pro Vita Sua': *CPW* I 345. On Memory and Imagination, see Introduction, p. 4.

12. from a LETTER TO RICHARD SHARP (15 January 1804)

Wordsworth is a Poet, a most original Poet—he no more resembles Milton than Milton resembles Shakespere—no more resembles Shakespere than Shakespere resembles Milton—he is himself: and I dare affirm that he will hereafter be admitted as the first & greatest philosophical Poet—the only man who has effected a compleat and constant synthesis of Thought & Feeling and combined them with Poetic Forms,[1] with the music of pleasurable passion and with Imagination or the *modifying* Power in that highest sense of the word in which I have ventured to oppose it to Fancy, or the *aggregating* power—in that sense in which it is a dim Analogue of Creation, not all that we can *believe* but all that we can *conceive* of creation.[2] Wordsworth is a Poet, and I feel myself a better Poet, in knowing how to honour *him*, than in all my own poetic Compositions, all I have done or hope to do[3]—and I prophesy immortality to his *Recluse*,[4] as the first & finest philosophical Poem, if only it be (as it undoubtedly will be) a Faithful Transcript of his own most august & innocent Life, of his own habitual Feelings & Modes of seeing and hearing.[5]

(*CL* II 1034)

Notes

1. Cf Extract 33–C.
2. Cf Extract 1, n 2.
3. Cf Extract 5.
4. *The Recluse*, a poem in three parts which was planned in 1798 when Wordsworth was living at Alfoxden near STC, was never completed. *The Excursion*, the second part of the projected tripartite *Recluse* and the only part of that poem to be completed, was eventually published in 1814.
5. For Appleyard's (1965) comments on this letter, see Extract 9, n 15.

13. from the *NOTEBOOKS*

(A) 14 April 1804
Every one of these sails[1] is *known* by the Intellect to have a strict & necessary action & reaction on all the rest, & that the whole is made up of parts, each part referring at once to each & to the whole[2]/ —and nothing more administers to the Picturesque than this phantom of complete visual wholeness in an object, which visually does not form a whole, by the influence ab intra[3] of the sense of its perfect Intellectual Beauty or Wholeness.— To all these must be added the Lights & Shades, sometimes *sunshiny*, sometimes *snowy*: sometimes shade-coloured, sometimes dingy—whatever effect distance, air tints, reflected Light, and the feeling connected with *the* Object (for all Passion unifies as it were by natural Fusion) have in bringing out, and in melting down, differences & contrast, accordingly as the mind finds it necessary to the completion of the idea of Beauty, to prevent sameness or discrepancy.[4]

(*CN* II from Entry 2012)

Notes

1. In this passage STC is analysing the elements of the 'picturesque effect of a ship/ a man of war, for instance'.
2. Cf STC's later statement that a Shakespearean 'play is a *syngenesia**— each [character] has indeed a life of its own and is an *individuum* [*'individual thing'*] of itself, but yet an organ to the whole' (*MC* 95). [**syngenesia*: 'plants having stamens coherent by the anthers, and flowers (florets) in close heads or *capitula*' (*OED*).] As an organicist in his criticism, STC stresses both the parts and the whole, both the unity itself and the things unified. On STC as an organicist in literary theory, see McKenzie (1939) and Fogle (1962); J. Benziger traces the development of the idea in his paper 'Organic Unity: Leibniz to Coleridge' *PMLA* 66 (1951) 24–48; McFarland (1969) examines the philosophic, rather than the aesthetic, implications of STC's theory of organic unity; Barfield (1972, especially 41–68) examines STC's *Theory of Life* and points out that 'it can be inaccurate and misleading to adduce Coleridge's thought as an example of "organicism"'. For STC's later organic views, see Extract 28 and n 2.
3. *ab intra*: 'from within'.
4. For STC on *beauty*, see Extracts 26 and 40–C.

(B) 2 May 1804
A really important Hint suggested itself to me, as I was falling into my

first Sleep—the effect of the posture of the Body, *open mouth* for instance, on first Dreams—& perhaps on all. White Teeth in behind open mouth of a dim face—/ My mind is not vigorous enough to pursue it—but I see, that it leads to a developement of the effects of continued Indistinctness of *Impressions* on the Imagination[1] according to laws of Likeness & what ever that may solve itself into.

(CN II from Entry 2064)

Note

1. In her note on this passage Miss Coburn points out that 'semi- or preconscious states and their relation to Imagination were of constantly recurring interest [to STC], without a precise vocabulary for them'; and she directs the reader to Notebook entries 1718, 2073, 2080, and 2915. Cf also *CN* II 2086 (10 May 1804) where STC connects artistic creativity with the subconscious mind: 'Poetry a rationalized dream dealing [?about] to manifold Forms our own Feelings, that never perhaps were attached by us consciously to our own personal Selves.—What is the Lear, the Othello, but a divine Dream/ all Shakespere, & nothing Shakespere.—O there are Truths below the Surface in the subject of Sympathy, & how we *become* that which we understandly behold & hear, having, how much God perhaps only knows, created part even of the Form.—[?and so] good night—'. Cf also Extract 14.

(C) 5 June 1804

In the men of continuous and discontinuous minds explain & demonstrate the vast difference between the disjunction conjunctive of the sudden Images *seized* on from external Contingents by Passion & Imagination (which is Passion eagle-eyed) —The Breeze I see, is in the Tree— It comes to cool my Babe and me.[1]—which is the property & prerogative of continuous minds of the highest order, & the conjunction disjunctive of Wit—

> And like a lobster boil'd the Morn
> From black to red began to turn,[2]

which is the excellence of men of discontinuous minds—

Arrange and classify the men of continuous minds—the pseudo-continuous, or *juxta-ponent* mind/ metaphysician not a poet—poet not a metaphysician?—poet+metaphysician[3]/ —*the faithful* in Love &c—

(CN II Entry 2112)

Notes

1. Wordsworth, 'Her Eyes Are Wild' (1798) 39−40; in *Lyrical Ballads* this same poem is entitled 'The Mad Mother'. In *Biographia* Chap xxii, STC cites these same two lines as an instance of 'the blending, *fusing* power of Imagination and Passion' (cf Extract 33−J).

2. Samuel Butler, *Hudibras* (1663−78) II ii 31−2. In *TT* STC cites these lines as an instance of Fancy, which 'brings together images which have no connexion natural or moral, but are yoked together by the poet by means of some accidental coincidence': cf Extract 51−E.

3. The conjunction of *poet* and *metaphysician* here is a succinct reassertion of STC's desire to reconcile poetry and philosophy: cf also *CN* I 383; ibid. II 3158 (Extract 13−K); and ibid. I 1541: 'Mix up Truth & Imagination, so that the Imag. may spread its own indefiniteness over that which really happened, & Reality its sense of substance & distinctness to Imagination/'. Cf also Extracts 4, 9, 12 and 33−H.

(D) December 1804

Idly talk they[1] who speak of Poets as mere Indulgers of Fancy, Imagination, Superstition, &c— They are the Bridlers by Delight,[2] the Purifiers, they that combine them with *reason* & order, the true Protoplasts,[3] Gods of Love who tame the Chaos.[4]

(*CN* II Entry 2355)

Notes

1. John Locke (STC's *bête noire*), for example, asserts in his *Essay Concerning Human Understanding* (1690) that 'we must allow that all the art of rhetoric . . . all the artificial and figurative application of words eloquence hath invented, are for nothing else but to insinuate wrong *ideas*, move the passions, and thereby mislead the judgment' (III x 34). Much earlier Plato had advanced the same argument against poetry in Book x of *The Republic* (esp. 606d).

2. Renaissance apologists in answering Plato's charges against poetry (and unconsciously anticipating those of Locke *et al.*) had stressed that the function of poetry is to teach delightfully (*docere cum delectatione*): cf for example J. C. Scaliger's *Poetics* (1561) and A. S. Minturno's *De Poeta* (1559). Sir Philip Sidney summarises this position happily in his *Apologie for Poetrie* (1595): 'Poesie therefore is . . . a speaking picture: with this end, to teach and delight. . . . [And] if it be, as I affirme, that no learning is so good as that which teacheth and mooueth to vertue, and that none can both teach and moue thereto so much as Poetry, then is the conclusion manifest that Incke and Paper cannot be to a more

profitable purpose employed.' Cf Extract 28, n 4; Extract 40–B, n 7, and especially Extract 33–G and n 7.

3. *Protoplast*: 'that which is first formed, fashioned, or created; the first-made thing or being of its kind; the original, archetype' (*OED*). Cf STC's 'Destiny of Nations' 288–91:

> Night
> An heavy unimaginable moan
> Sent forth, when she the Protoplast beheld
> Stand beauteous on Confusion's charméd wave.

STC's MS note (written late in life) to these lines reads, 'These are very fine Lines, tho' I say it, that should not; but, hang me, if I know or ever did know the meaning of them, tho' my own composition' (*CPW* 1 140 n).

4. The notion (derived from classical sources like Plato's *Symposium* and *Timaeus*) that the Creation was effected by the god of Love imposing order on a chaos of warring elements was common in Florentine Neoplatonism and in Renaissance poetry drawing on it—for example, Spenser's 'Hymn in Honour of Love' (1596) 78–87:

> The earth, the ayre, the water, and the fyre,
> Then gan to raunge them selues in huge array,
> And with contrary forces to conspyre
> Each against other, by all meanes they may,
> Threatning their owne confusion and decay:
> Ayre hated earth, and water hated fyre,
> Till Loue relented their rebellious yre.
>
> He then them tooke, and tempering goodly well
> Their contrary dislikes with loued meanes,
> Did place them all in order . . .

(E) December 1804

One of the most noticeable and fruitful facts in Psychology is the modification of the same feeling by difference of form/ The Heavens lift up my soul, the sight of the Ocean seems to widen it. We feel the same Force at work, but the difference from Body & Mind both that we should feel in actual travelling horizontally or in direct ascent, that we feel in fancy—for what are our feelings of this kind but a motion imagined? with the feelings that would accompany that motion less distinguished more blended, rapid, confused, & thereby co-adunated—as white is the very emblem of one in being the confusion of all.

(*CN* II Entry 2357)

(F) December 1804

In the Preface of my Metaphys. Works I should say—Once & all read Tetens, Kant, Fichte, &c—& there you will trace or if you are on the hunt, track me. Why then not acknowledge your obligations step by step? Because, I could not do in a multitude of glaring resemblances without a lie/ for they had been mine, formed, & full formed in my own mind, before I had ever heard of these Writers, because to have fixed on the partic. instances in which I have really been indebted to these Writers would have [been] very hard, if possible, to me who read for truth & self-satisfaction, not to make a book, & who always rejoiced & was jubilant when I found my own ideas well expressed already by others, [& would have looked like a *trick*, to skulk there not quoted,]¹ & lastly, let me say, because (I am proud perhaps but) I seem to know, that much of the matter remains my own, and that the Soul is *mine*. I fear not him for a Critic who can confound a Fellow-thinker with a Compiler.²

(*CN* II Entry 2375)

Notes

1. The parenthesised section is a later addition by STC.
2. S. Prickett (1970) comments on this passage: 'Like Wordsworth, [STC] was constantly struggling to articulate what he already knew, existentially, in his own experience. . . . Here, as so often elsewhere, there seems to be a semi-Platonic "recognition" theory underlying his method of reading and acquiring knowledge. He does not seem to be reading Kant and Fichte to understand what *they* have to say, but to understand what he already (in some sense) *knows*. He scythes through abstruse German philosophy in search of himself' (78–9). Cf also *Biographia* Chap ix: 'I regard truth as a divine ventriloquist: I care not from whose mouth the sounds are supposed to proceed, if only the words are audible and intelligible' (*BL* I 105). On Tetens, see McFarland (1972).

(G) February 1805

. . . the English [language]¹ not by accidental Production of Genius, but by its natural constitution stands unequalled for all kinds of Poetry, in which the more complex and profounder Passions are united with deep Thought, for the Drama, whether Comedy or Tragedy, so that it is *Poetry* (for in modern Comedies that professedly *copy* elegant conversation I am disposed to believe that the French are our Superiors) for dramatic poetry, for impassioned and *particularized*

Description, (see Burns' description of a Brook,[2] and Wordsworth's Poetry in a hundred places) for rapid associations of sensuous Images and that species of Delight (from unexpected combinations of them) which when it excites a disposition to laughter or even to a smile is usually called wit, and fancy in other cases (this tho' the common distinction, I perceive to be deficient/ a better & perhaps the true & only tenable distinction would be, (that where the manifest intention of the passage is to direct the attention chiefly to the combination for its own sake, for the sake of the pleasure derived from the Surprize, it is properly called *wit*/ but where the combination is introduced either for the sake of Some Reasoning or Fact to be illustrated by it (even tho' the illustration should bedazzle the res illustrate[3] into obscurity by error of judgment in the writer) or if introduced for its own sake, yet for the pleasure produced by the picture as gratifying the mental eye either by its colours, or its picturesque combination or both, and not chiefly for the electric sensation derived from the surprize, then it is properly called Fancy/ the difference is indeed only in the Tone of mind of the writer or speaker, & in the intention of the sentence or sentences/ but these two dispositions are according to the *predominance* of the one or the other characteristic of two very very different sorts of intellectual power/ the first belongs to the men of Cleverness and Talent, the latter tho' by no means essentially constitutive of Genius, has yet a close affinity to it, and is most often an effect and attendent of it/) (end.)[4] Now how to get back, having thus belabyrinthed myself in these most parenthetical parentheses?

(*CN* II from Entry 2431)

Notes

1. The earlier part of this Notebook entry is devoted to showing that 'one language may have advantages, which another has not'; English, for example, is distinguished from other modern European languages 'in the immense number of its practical words' *and* 'by its monosyllabic, naturalizing, and marvellously metaphorical Spirit' which 'can express more meaning, image, and passion *tri-unely* in a given number of articulate sounds than any other in the world, not excepting even the ancient Greek'.

2. It is uncertain to which of Burns's poems STC is referring—perhaps 'Afton Water' or 'The Banks o' Doon'.

3. *res illustrate*: presumably *res illustrata*, 'the thing illustrated'.

4. *end*: i.e., the end of the 'parenthetical parentheses'.

(H) 14 April 1805

Saturday Night, April 14, 1805—In looking at objects of Nature while I am thinking, as at yonder moon dim-glimmering thro' the dewy window-pane, I seem rather to be seeking, as it were *asking*, a symbolical language for something within me that already and forever exists, than observing any thing new. Even when that latter is the case, yet still I have always an obscure feeling as if that new phænomenon were the dim Awaking of a forgotten or hidden Truth of my inner Nature/ It is still interesting as a Word, a Symbol! It is Λογος,[1] the Creator! [and the Evolver!][2]

(*CN* II from Entry 2546)

Notes

1. Λογος : 'Logos', i.e., the Word or Second Person of the Trinity: cf John I: 1–5. In *CN* II 2445 (February 1805) STC develops the idea of the creative and mediative Logos in Platonic terms: 'Reason, Proportion, communicable Intelligibility intelligent and communicant, the WORD—which last expression strikes me as the profoundest and most comprehensive Energy of the human Mind, if indeed it be not in some distinct sense ενεργημα θεοπαραδοτον [energy given by God]'. For a later expansion of this idea, see *CN* II 3159 (September 1807), where STC argues by etymological analogy that the creative Logos permeates the material universe as a unifying or coadunating principle.

2. The square brackets indicate a later insertion by STC. Coburn (1974) comments on this Notebook entry as follows: 'A Word, a Symbol, Logos, the Creator, the Evolver. The newly observed phenomenon is intuitively recognized as a relationship, a mysterious truth of communication between the single mortal human being and the universal eternally creative principle under whatever name' (64). Cf also House (1953) 27–9.

(I) November–December 1805

A man's Imagination fitfully awaking & sleeping = the odd metaphors & no metaphors of modern poetry/ Language in its first state without the *inventive* passion.

(*CN* II Entry 2723)

(J) February 1807

As when the Taper's white cone of Flame is seen double, till the eye moving brings them into one space; & there they become one—so did the Idea in my imagination coadunate with your present Form/ soon after I first gazed on you with love.[1]

(CN II Entry 2994)

Note

1. Cf *CN* III 4158 (May 1812): 'Quære—the *Echo* in the mind which makes the reflection on a form present, if the reflection be sudden & vivid, pass into a *feeling* of memory with a sense of *Presence*—thence perplexity—& a seeking—which if the Object be desirable & the preconceptions & sensations most important, will needs impress it very deeply—applied to Love in a moment. I cannot conceive any thing more lovely, more divine, more deserving of our admiration, than that identification or coadunation of the two lovers, Amatus Amata [the Lover and his Love], in which each retains its individualizing contra-distinguishing qualities, and yet *eminenter*, in a certain transcendent mode,[1] acquires the virtues of the other—the rich tenderness, the woman elevation &c—the Sublime & the Beautiful—'.

   George Whalley has supplied me with the following note: '*eminenter*—"in a certain transcendent mode" is a rather special rendering of this scholastic term, the companion to which is *formaliter*. Coleridge's most striking illustration of the two terms is in a marginal note on Hobbes: " . . . *formaliter*, i.e. as a dog impresses reflection on a mirror . . . *eminenter*, as the painter's brush impresses the figure of the dog on a canvass... .." The usual definition is that a thing is related to its cause *formaliter* if the defining characteristics inhere in it: *eminenter* if its defining characteristics are an inferior version of those found in the cause (as man in God).'

(K) September 1807

Form is factitious[1] *Being*, and Thinking is the Process. Imagination the Laboratory, in which Thought elaborates Essence into Existence.[2] A Psilosopher,[3] i.e. a nominal Ph[ilosopher] without Imagination,[4] is a *Coiner*—Vanity, the *Froth* of the molten Mass, is his *Stuff*—and Verbiage the Stamp & Impression. This is but a *deaf* Metaphor—better say, that he is guilty of Forgery—he presents the same [sort of][5] *Paper* as the honest Barterer, but when you carry it to the *Bank*, it is found to be drawn on—Outis,[6] *Esq*^{re}. His words had deposited no Forms there, payable at Sight—or even at any imaginable Time from the Date of the Draft/

(CN II Entry 3158)

Notes

1. *factitious*: 'made by or resulting from art; artificial'.
2. In *Biographia* Chap xviii STC defines the terms *essence* and *existence* as follows: 'Essence, in its primary signification, means the principle of *individuation*, the inmost principle of the possibility of any thing, as that particular thing. It is equivalent to the *idea* of a thing, when ever we use the word, idea, with philosophic precision. Existence, on the other hand, is distinguished from essence, by the superinduction of *reality*. Thus we speak of the essence, and essential properties of a circle; but we do not therefore assert, that any thing, which really exists, is mathematically circular. Thus too, without any tautology we contend for the *existence* of the Supreme Being; that is, for a reality correspondent to the idea. There is, next, a *secondary* use of the word essence, in which it signifies the point or ground of contradistinction between two modifications of the same substance or subject. Thus we should be allowed to say, that the style of architecture of Westminster Abbey is *essentially* different from that of St Paul's, even though both had been built with blocks cut into the same form, and from the same quarry' (*BL* II 47–8).
3. *Psilosopher*: 'mere thinker' (a Coleridgean neologism). The Greek adjective ψιλός means 'mere, simple, unsupported' – e.g., ψιλοὶ λόγοι (Plato, *Theaetetus*, 165a) = 'mere argumentation unsupported by evidence'. *OED* gives 'psilosophy' as 'shallow philosophy'.

    Cf *CN* II 3121 (May–September 1807): 'Pseudo-philosophus quidam, vel ut accuratius loquar, ψιλοσοφος — Psilosophia Gallica// philosophia Teutonica' (*translation*: 'Pseudo-philosopher, or rather, to speak accurately, psilosopher—French Psilosophy// German philosophy'). Miss Coburn's note to *CN* II 3121 states that 'Coleridge used the term [psilosophy] frequently to distinguish mere cerebration from a full and complex appraisal of philosophical problems. In his view it usually implies a rejection of idealism in any form, and a refusal to recognize the legitimacy and importance of the imagination in the intellectual process.'
4. Cf Extract 13–C and n 3.
5. A later insertion by STC.
6. *Outis*: Greek for 'Nobody'. Cf the famous story of Odysseus (Κύκλωψ, εἰρωτᾷς μ' ὄνομα κλυτόν; ... οὖτις ἐμοί γ' ὄνομα: 'Cyclops, do you ask me my famous name? ... My name is Noman') and Polyphemus in Homer, *Odyssey* ix 364–414.

(L) [*Venus and Adonis*] January 1808 (?)[1]
6.7.8.[2]—Instances of the poetic Power of making every thing present to the Imagination/ both the forms, & the passions that modify these forms either actually, as in the representation of Love or Anger or other human affections; or imaginatively by the different manner, in

which inanimate objects, or objects unimpassioned themselves, are seen by the mind in moments of strong excitement, and according to the kind of the excitement—whether of Jealousy, or Rage, or Love, in its only appropriate sense of the word, or of the lower Impulses of our nature, [or finally of the poetic feeling/]³—It is perhaps chiefly in the power of producing or reproducing the latter,⁴ that the poet stands distinct.

(*CN* III from Entry 3246)

Notes

1. While this and the following extract probably belong to January 1808 when STC was planning his first series of lectures on literature, it is possible that they may be notes made for the lecture series of 1811–12.
2. I.e., stanzas 6–8 (lines 31–48) of Shakespeare's *Venus and Adonis*. Extracts 13–L to N, 17–B and 33–H centre on this poem.
3. A later insertion by STC.
4. *the latter*: 'Presumably *the poetic feeling*, i.e. the *strong excitement of Imagination*' (Coburn's note).

(M) January 1808 (?)

1. Sense of Beauty—this thro' the whole poem,¹ even to almost effeminacy of sweetness—good sign/ painter who begins with old men's and old women's faces, a bad sign²—coarse & strong is easily done so as to *strike*—

2. With things remote from his own feelings—and in which the romanticity³ gives a vividness to the naturalness of the sentiments & feelings—

3. Love of natural Objects—quote the Hare, p. 23⁴—there is indeed a far more admirable description precedent,⁵ but less fitted for public recitation/

4. Fancy, or the aggregative Power—13ᵗʰ· p[age]—Full gently now &c⁶—the bringing together Images dissimilar in the main by some .one point or more of Likeness—distinguished—read from Pocket book⁷—/ both common in the writers of Shakspere's time/⁸

5.—That power of & energy of what a living poet⁹ has grandly & appropriately. To flash upon that inward Eye Which is the Bliss of Solitude—& to make every thing present by a Series of Images—This an absolute Essential of Poetry, & of itself would form a poet, tho' not of the highest Class—It is however a most hopeful Symptom, & the V[enus] & A[donis] is one continued Specimen/

6. Imagination/ power of modifying one image or feeling by the

precedent or following ones—.—So often after afterwards to be illustrated that at present I shall speak only of—one of its effects—namely, that of combining many circumstances into one moment of thought to produce that ultimate end of human Thought, and human Feeling, Unity and thereby the reduction of the Spirit to its Principle & Fountain, who alone is truly *one*. (Quote the passage p. 28.[10] *before this* observation.)—& p. 29.[11]—for

7. [The describing natural objects by cloathing them appropriately with human passions/ Lo, here the gentle Lark/][12]

8. Energy, depth, and activity of Thought without which a man may be a pleasing and affecting Poet; but never a great one. Here introduce Dennis's[13]—enthus: & vulgar pass:—& from the excess of this in Shakespere be grateful that circumstances probably originating in choice led him to the Drama, the subject of my next lecture—& end with Chapman's[14]—

Previous to 1.[15]—notice the unpleasing nature of the Subject—which would not be introduced but that this very reason makes it so illustrative of Shakespere's character—There are men who can write most eloquently, and passages of deepest pathos & even Sublimity, on circumstances personal & deeply exciting their own passions; but not therefore poets—Mothers—Deborah's Song[16]—Nature is the Poet here—but to become by power of Imagination another Thing[17]—Proteus, a river, a lion, yet still the God felt to be there/—Then his thinking faculty & thereby perfect abstraction from himself—he writes exactly as if of an other planet, or as describing the movement of two Butterflies—

(*CN* III Entry 3247)

Notes

1. Shakespeare's *Venus and Adonis*: see Extract 13–L, nn 1 and 2.
2. Cf letter to Sir George Beaumont (7 December 1811): 'The longer I live, the more deeply am I convinced of the high importance, as a *symptom*, of the Love of *Beauty* in a young Painter— It is neither honorable to a young man's Heart or Head to attach himself year after year to old or deformed Objects, comparatively too so easy, especially if bad Drawing & worse Colouring leaves the Spectator's Imagination at lawless Liberty— & he cries out "How very like!" just as he would at a coal in the centre of the Fire, or at a Frost-figure on a Window-pane' (*CL* III 352).
3. *romanticity*: 'romantic quality or character'. Earliest usage cited in *OED*

is 1782, but the word was rare even in STC's time.

4. *Venus and Adonis*, 679–708: Venus's affecting account of the 'purblind hare' pursued by hounds and hunter.

5. The *admirable description precedent* is doubtless that of the 'high desire' of Adonis' 'trampling courser' for a lusty young breeding-jennet: lines 259–318.

6. *Venus and Adonis*, 361–6:

> Full gently now she takes him by the hand,
> A lily prison'd in a gaol of snow,
> Or ivory in an alabaster band;
> So white a friend engirts so white a foe:
>   This beauteous combat, wilful and unwilling,
>   Show'd like two silver doves that sit a-billing.

7. It is uncertain which of STC's Notebooks this refers to.

8. The reference is to the conceits of the Metaphysical poets: cf Extract 16, n 13.

9. Wordsworth. 'To flash upon . . . Bliss of Solitude': lines 21–2 of Wordsworth's 'I wandered lonely as a cloud'.

10. *Venus and Adonis*, 815–22:

> Look how a bright star shooteth from the sky,
> So glides he in the night from Venus' eye;
>
> Which after him she darts, as one on shore
> Gazing upon a late-embarked friend,
> Till the wild waves will have him seen no more,
> Whose ridges with the meeting clouds contend.
>   So did the merciless and pitchy night
>   Fold in the object that did feed her sight.

11. Ibid., 853–8:

> Lo, here the gentle lark, weary of rest,
> From his moist cabinet mounts up on high,
> And wakes the morning, from whose silver breast
> The sun ariseth in his majesty;
>   Who doth the world so gloriously behold
>   That cedar-tops and hills seem burnish'd gold.

12. A later insertion by STC.

13. John Dennis, *The Grounds of Criticism in Poetry* (1704). The distinction between the 'Vulgar and Enthusiastick Passions rais'd in Poetry' appears in Chap iv: relevant section quoted in *CN* III 3247 n.

14. George Chapman (1559?–1634?), remembered chiefly for his translations of Homer. The quotation from Chapman with which STC proposed to close this lecture is unknown.

15. *Previous to 1*: 'i.e. previous to the discussion of Shakespeare's humanizing imagery and circumstance at the beginning of the lecture?' (Coburn's note).

16. Judges 5. STC elsewhere cites the Song of Deborah as a striking instance of effective pleonasm: cf *CN* III 4113, where he argues that the 'passionate repetition of a sublime Tautology (as in the Song of Debora)' is justified by the 'Law of Passion which inducing in the mind an unusual activity seeks for means to waste its superfluity'; the same notion appears in *Biographia* Chap XVII: 'Nothing assuredly can differ either in origin or in mode more widely from the *apparent* tautologies of intense and turbulent feeling, in which the passion is greater and of longer endurance than to be exhausted or satisfied by a single representation of the image or incident exciting it. Such repetitions I admit to be a beauty of the highest kind; as illustrated by Mr Wordsworth himself from the song of Deborah. "*At her feet he bowed, he fell, he lay down; at her feet he bowed, he fell; where he bowed, there he fell down dead.*" ' (Judges 5: 27). Cf also *CN* III 4116.

17. Cf Extracts 7, 13–N and 33–H. For Proteus, a sea-god with the power of assuming any given shape, see Homer, *Odyssey* IV 351ff.

(N) March 1808

I have endeavored to prove that he[1] had shewn himself a *poet*, previously to his appearance, [as] a dramatic poet—& that had no Lear, No Othello, no Henry the Fourth, no Twelfth Night, appeared, we must have admitted that Shakespere possessed the chief if not all the requisites of a Poet—namely, deep Feeling & exquisite sense of Beauty, both as exhibited to the eye in combinations of form, & to the ear in sweet and appropriate melody (with the except: of Spenser, he is &c[2])—. That these feelings were under the command of *his own Will*—that in his very first productions[3] he projected his mind out of his own particular being, & felt and made others feel, on subjects no way connected with himself, except by force of Contemplation—& that sublime faculty, by which a great mind becomes that which it meditates on.[4]— To this we are to add the affectionate Love of Nature & Natural Objects, without which no man could have observed so steadily, or painted so truly & passionately the very minutest beauties of the external world—

Next, we have shewn that he possessed Fancy, considered as the faculty of bringing together &c &c.—"Full gently now she" &c[5]/ Still mounting, we find undoubted proof in his mind of Imagination or the power by which one image or feeling is made to modify many others, & by a sort of *fusion to force many into one*—that which after shewed itself in such might & energy in Lear, where the deep anguish of a Father spreads the feeling of Ingratitude & Cruelty over the very Elements of Heaven—.[6] Various are the workings of this greatest faculty of the human mind—both passionate & tranquil—in its tranquil & purely pleasurable operation it acts chiefly by producing out of many things, as it would have appeared in the description of an ordinary mind, described slowly & in unimpassioned succession, a oneness/ even as Nature, the greatest of Poets, acts upon us when we open our eyes upon an extended prospect— Thus the flight of Adonis from the enamoured Goddess in the dusk of the Evening—

> Look! how a bright star shooteth from the Sky,
> So glides he in the night from Venus' Eye—.[7]

How many Images & feelings are here brought together without effort & without discord—the beauty of Adonis—the rapidity of his flight—the yearning yet hopelessness of the enamoured gazer—and a shadowy ideal character thrown over the whole—/ or it acts by impressing the stamp of humanity, of human feeling, over inanimate Objects—The Pines shorn by the Sea wind & seen in twilight/[8] Then

> Lo! here the gentle Lark—[9]

and lastly, which belongs only to a great poet, the power of so carrying on the Eye of the Reader as to make him almost lose the consciousness of words—to make him *see* every thing—& this without exciting any painful or laborious attention, without any *anatomy* of description, (a fault not uncommon in descriptive poetry) but with the sweetness & easy movement of nature—

Lastly, he—previously to his Drama—gave proof of a most profound, energetic & philosophical mind, without which he might have been a very delightful Poet, but not the great dramatic Poet/ but this he possessed in so eminent a degree that it is to be feared &c &c[10]—if—

But Chance & his powerful Instinct combined to lead him to his proper province—in the conquest of which we are to consider both the difficulties that opposed him, & the advantages—

(*CN* III from Entry 3290)

Notes

1. Shakespeare. This extract, like the two preceding it, forms part of STC's notes for his lectures on literature of 1808.
2. 'The conclusion of the sentence was probably some such phrase as "the most musical of English poets"' (Coburn's note).
3. 'We are certain indeed, that the Venus & Adonis, and the Rape of Lucrece were his two earliest Poems': *CN* III 4115.
4. Cf STC's letter of 21 October 1794 to Southey: 'It is not enough, that we have once swallowed it—The *Heart* should have *fed* upon the *truth*, as Insects on a Leaf—till it be tinged with the colour, and shew it's food in every the minutest fibre' (*CL* I 115). This image is repeated in *Conciones ad Populum* (1795): cf *CC* I 49; also ibid. IV i 338.
5. *Venus and Adonis* 361ff: quoted in Extract 13—M, n 6.
6. Cf *King Lear* III ii 14–24.
7. *Venus Venus and Adonis* 815–16: quoted in Extract 13–M, n 10.
8. For the same image, see Extract 33–H and n 12.
9. *Venus and Adonis* 853: quoted in Extract 13–M, n 11.
10. Cf *Biographia* Chap xv: 'No man was ever yet a great poet, without being at the same time a profound philosopher. For poetry is the blossom and the fragrancy of all human knowledge, human thoughts, human passions, emotions, language. In Shakespeare's *poems* the creative power and the intellectual energy wrestle as in a war embrace' (cf Extract 33–H). See also Extract 13–C.

14. from *THE FRIEND* (5 October 1809)[1]

As I shall devote some future Numbers[2] to the Subject of Dreams, Visions, Ghosts, Witchcraft, &c. in which I shall first give, and then endeavour to explain the most interesting and best attested fact of each, which has come within my knowledge, either from Books or from personal Testimony, I defer till then the explanation of the mode in which our Thoughts, in states of morbid Slumber, become at times perfectly *dramatic* (for in certain sorts of dreams the dullest Wight becomes a Shakespeare) and by what Law the form of the Vision appears to talk to us its own thoughts in a voice as audible as the shape is visible;[3] and this too oftentimes in connected trains, and sometimes even with a concentration of Power which may easily impose on the soundest judgements, uninstructed in the *Optics* and *Acoustics* of the inner sense, for Revelations and gifts of Prescience. I will only remark, in aid of the present case, that it would appear incredible to Persons not accustomed to these subtle notices of self observation, what small and remote resemblances, what mere *hints* of likeness from some real external object, (especially if the shape be aided by colour) will suffice to make a vivid thought consubstantiate with the real object, and derive from it an outward perceptibility.[4] Even when we are broad awake, if we are in anxious expectation, how often will not the most confused sounds of nature be heard by us as articulate sounds? for instance, the babbling of a brook will appear, for a moment, the voice of a Friend, for whom we are waiting, calling out our own names, &c. A short meditation, therefore, on this Law of the imagination, that a Likeness in part tends to become a likeness of the whole, will make it not only conceivable but probable, that the Inkstand itself, and the dark-coloured Stone on the Wall, which Luther[5] perhaps had never till then noticed, might have a considerable influence in the production of the Fiend, and of the hostile act with which his obstrusive visit was repelled.

(*CC* IV ii 117–19)

Notes

1. This extract is taken from an essay devoted to the elucidation of a theory of Luther's Apparitions'; the essay was reprinted in *The Friend* both in 1812 and in 1818–where in each case STC's long footnote (n 4 below) was incorporated into the text.

2. No such essays appeared in later numbers of *The Friend*; and in 1818 this sentence begins: 'I have long wished to devote an entire work to the subject of Dreams, Visions, Ghosts, Witchcraft, &c. in which I might first give . . .' (*CC* IV i 145). STC did, however, write a good deal on dreams, witchcraft and ghosts, much of it not yet published. See also Beer (1977).

3. Cf Extract 13–B and n 1.

4. *STC's note*: 'A Lady once asked me if I believed in Ghosts and Apparitions, I answered with truth and simplicity: *No, Madam! I have seen far too many myself*. I have indeed a whole memorandum Book filled with records of these Phænomena, many of them interesting as facts and data for Psychology, and affording some valuable materials for a Theory of Perception and its dependence on the memory and Imagination. "In omnem actum Perceptionis imaginatio influit efficienter." WOLFE.[a] But HE[b.] is no more, who would have realized this idea: who had already established the foundations and the law of the Theory; and for whom I had so often found a pleasure and a comfort,

even during the wretched and restless nights of sickness, in watching and instantly recording these experiences of the world within us, of the "gemina natura, quæ fit et facit, et creat et creatur!"[c] He is gone, my Friend! my munificient Co-patron, and not less the Benefactor of my Intellect!'

a. Christian von Wolff, *Psychologia rationalis* 1 i 24. In *CN* 1 1648 STC translates Wolff's phrase as follows: 'the images of Memory flowing in on the impulses of immediate impression'; STC had quoted Wolff's Latin phrase as early as 1801: cf *CN* 1 905.

b. Thomas Wedgwood, STC's friend and benefactor, died in 1805; prior to his death, Wedgwood had been engaged in a study of the laws of perception.

c. *gemina . . . creatur*: 'that dual nature, which is made and makes, both creates and is created' (Joannes Scotus Erigena, *De divisione naturae* 1 13). Cf also Extract 39–B, n 6; *CN* 1 1382; and *CL* 11 954.

5. During his 'friendly imprisonment' in Wartburg Castle, Luther 'is said to have hurled his inkstand at the Devil, the black spot from which yet remains on the stone wall of the room he studied in' (*CC* 1v ii 115).

15. from the *NOTEBOOKS*

(A) March 1810

I wish much to investigate the connection of the Imagination with the Bildungstrieb[1]—Imaginatio = imitatio vel repetitio *Imaginis*—per motum? ergo, et motuum[2]—The Variolæ[3]—generation—Is not there a *link* between physical Imitation & Imagination?[4]

(CN III Entry 3744)

Notes

1. *Bildungstrieb*: 'creative impulse'. The word may, however, have a more limited and technical meaning here, for it was a term used by J. F. Blumenbach (whose lectures STC had attended at Göttingen in 1799) to denote 'a kind of entelechy, an innate principle of development in organic nature, the mysterious but vitally definitive factor in generation, growth, and the preservation of physical types' (Coburn's note).

2. *Imaginatio . . . Imaginis*: 'Imagination = the imitation or repetition of an Image—by movement? therefore, of movements'.

3. *Variolæ*: 'pustules caused by smallpox innoculation'. The meaning of

this cryptic ellipsis would seem to be that the vaccination pustules
'imitate' the pustules of the disease itself; and this reading 'appears to
lead' (Coburn) to sections 22 and 39 of Erasmus Darwin's *Zoonomia*
(1794–6).

4. Miss Coburn, whose annotations on this entry should be read in full,
concludes: 'It is not difficult to believe that Blumenbach's word, and
Darwin's insistence on links between generation, imitation, motion, and
the imagination, led to the questions adumbrated in this entry, and that
Coleridge's later answers to these entered into the famous definition of
the "primary Imagination" at the end of Chap XIII and also into Chap XIV
[cf Extracts 33–F and 33–G]. Typically, by examining words that are
used on several levels— *Bildungstrieb, Imagination, Imitation*—he tries to
understand some links between the processes of art and life.'

(B) *c.* May 1810

Tho' the dependence of all theologic speculation on the practical
Reason[1] & its moral postulates will always preserve the religious faith
of a true philosopher within the modesty of the Gospel; yet it would
not be amiss if our belle esprits[2] had made part of their intellectual
voyages in the groves & enchanted Islands of Plato, Plotin. & even
Proclus[3]—rendering the mind lofty and generous & *abile*[4] by
splendid Imaginations that receive the beauty of form by the
proportions of Science/ Fancy moulded in Science, & thence no
unbecoming Symbols—Counters at least—of moral Truth/ holding
to truth the same ascetic & preparatory relations as the Game of Chess
to War.[5]

(*CN* III Entry 3820)

Notes

1. Perhaps the most important distinction for STC's philosophic system is
that between Reason and Understanding—a polarity grounded in
Kant's distinction between *Vernunft* and *Verstand*: cf Extract 35–A, n 5,
Extract 35–B, n 1 and Extract 41–A, n 3. The functions proper to the
Understanding, the lower of the two faculties, are 'reflection' and
'generalizing the notices received from the senses'. Reason, the higher
faculty, is divided into two types, *speculative* and *practical*: 'Reason is the
Power of Universal and necessary Convictions, the Source and
Substance of Truths above Sense, and having their evidence in
themselves. Its presence is always marked by the *necessity* of the position
affirmed: this necessity being *conditional*, when a truth of Reason is
applied to Facts of Experience, or to the rules and maxims of the
Understanding; but *absolute*, when the subject matter is itself the growth

or offspring of the Reason. Hence arises a distinction in the Reason itself, derived from the different mode of applying it, and from the objects to which it is directed: accordingly as we consider one and the same gift, now as the ground of formal principles, and now as the origin of *ideas*. Contemplated distinctively in reference to *formal* (or abstract) truth, it is the *speculative* reason; but in reference to *actual* (or moral) truth, as the fountain of ideas, and the *light* of the conscience, we name it the *practical* reason' (*AR* 143). Immanuel Kant's major treatise on ethics, *Kritik der praktischen Vernunft* ('Critique of Practical Reason') published in 1788, postulates such first principles as the existence of God, immortality, and the freedom of the will on the ground that morality is inconceivable without them. For a helpful modern analysis of STC's relation to Kant on this point, see Park (1968).

2. *belle esprits*: 'fashionable spirits; wits' – an ironic and slighting reference (presumably) to Dr Priestley and the Unitarians, as well as to the historians William Warburton and Edward Gibbon, all of whom figure in the preceeding Notebook entries where STC has jotted down notes prompted by his reading of a wide range of sceptics and rationalists in preparation for his proposed 'Defence of Christianity'.

3. Plotinus, the main exponent of Alexandrian Neoplatonism in the third century AD. Proclus, an Athenian Neoplatonist of the fifth century AD. Among Neoplatonists, writes STC (*CN* III 3818), 'Metaphysics ceased to be a science of speculation: it had already become an art of life, a discipline, a religion!'

4. *abile* (Italian): 'skilful, adroit, dextrous'.

5. The Chess/War image is 'a recurrent simile in Coleridge's political writings' (Coburn): cf *CC* IV ii 363.

(C) *c.* May 1810

Many might be the equally good definitions of Poetry, as metrical Language—I have given the former the preference as comprizing the essential of all the fine Arts, and applying to Raphael & Handel equally as to Milton/ But of Poetry commonly so called we might justly call it—A mode of composition that calls into action & gratifies the largest number of the human Faculties in Harmony with each other, & in just proportions—at least, it would furnish a scale of merit if not a definition of *genus* [genius?]—

Frame a numeration table of the primary faculties of Man, as Reason, *unified per Ideas*, Mater Legum [Arbitrement, Legibilitatis mater][1] Judgement, the discriminative, Fancy, the aggregative, Imagination, the modifying & *fusive*, the Sense & Sensations—and from these the different Derivatives of the Agreeable from the Senses, the Beautiful, the Sublime/ the Like and the Different—the spontaneous and the receptive—the Free and the Necessary—And whatever calls into consciousness the greatest number of these in due proportion & perfect harmony with each other, is the noblest Poem.—[2]

(CN III from Entry 3827)

Notes

1. A later insertion by STC. *Mater Legum*: 'Mother of Law'; *Legibilitatis mater*: 'mother of amenability' (Coburn).
2. 'The efforts to express here the ideas of maximum pleasure from whole and parts, the rejection of metre as a defining factor, and the view of the need to bring *the human Faculties in Harmony* point towards [*Biographia*] Chaps XIV and XV. Here too appears to be an early struggle with *Reason*, the mother of laws, *Judgement* as discrimination, *Fancy* as *aggregative*, and *Imagination* as *modifying* and *fusive* (esemplastic?); we find here also some indication of what Coleridge meant (Chap XIV) by "the subordination of its [the soul's] faculties to each other, according to their relative worth and dignity" ' (Coburn).

16. from CRABB ROBINSON'S DIARY (15 November 1810)

A very delightful evening at Charles Lamb's; Coleridge, Morgan, Mr Burney, &c., there. Coleridge very eloquent on German metaphysics and poetry, Wordsworth, and Spanish politics.

Of Wordsworth he spoke with great warmth of praise, but objected to some of his poems. Wishing to avoid an undue regard to the high and genteel in society, Wordsworth had unreasonably attached himself to the low, so that he himself erred at last. He should have recollected that verse being the language of passion, and passion dictating energetic expressions, it became him to make his subjects and style accord.[1] One asks why tales so simple were not in prose. With 'malice prepense'[2] he fixes on objects of reflection, which do not naturally excite it. Coleridge censured the disproportion in the machinery of the poem on the Gipsies.[3] Had the whole world been standing idle, more powerful arguments to expose the evil could not have been brought forward. Of Kant he spoke in terms of high admiration. . . . The 'Kritik der Urtheilskraft'[4] he considered the most astonishing of Kant's works. Both Fichte and Schelling[5] he thought would be found at last to have erred where they deviated from Kant; but he considered Fichte a great logician, and Schelling perhaps a still greater man. In both he thought the want of gratitude towards their master a sign of the absence of the highest excellence. Schelling's system resolves itself into fanaticism, not better than that of Jacob Boehme.[6] Coleridge had known Tieck[7] at Rome, but was not aware of his eminence as a poet. He conceded to Goethe[8] universal talent, but felt a want of moral life to be the defect of his poetry. Schiller[9] he spoke more kindly of. He quoted 'Nimmer, das glaubt mir, erscheinen die Götter, nimmer allein.' (He has since translated it.) Of Jean Paul[10] he said that his wit consisted not in pointing out analogies in themselves striking, but in finding unexpected analogies. You admire not the things combined, but the act of combination. He applied this also to Windham.[11] But is not this the character of all wit? That which he contrasted with it as a different kind of wit is in reality not wit, but acuteness. He made an elaborate distinction between fancy and imagination. The excess of fancy is delirium, of imagination mania.[12] Fancy is the arbitrarily bringing together of things that lie remote, and forming them into a unity. The materials lie ready for the fancy, which acts by a sort of juxtaposition.[13] On the other hand, the imagination under excitement generates and produces a form of its own. The 'seas of milk and ships of amber'[14] he quoted as fanciful delirium. He related, as a sort of disease of imagination, what occurred to himself. He had been watching intently the motions of a kite among the mountains of Westmoreland, when on a sudden he saw two kites in an opposite direction. This delusion lasted some time. At last he discovered that the two kites were the fluttering branches of a tree beyond a wall.[15]

(*DRC* I 304–6)

Notes

1. For STC on poetic diction and Wordsworth's choice of subjects, see *Biographia* Chaps xvii–xx. In a letter to R. H. Brabant (Extract 31), STC urges that Wordsworth had 'never acted on [his theory of poetic diction] except in particular Stanzas which are the Blots of his Compositions.'

2. *malice prepense*: 'malice aforethought'.

3. Wordsworth's 'Gipsies' (1807), a poem in which all nature is seen as censuring the torpid life of a group of gipsies: 'Life which the very stars reprove/ As on their silent tasks they move!' (23–4).

4. Immanuel Kant's (1724–1804) *Kritik der Urtheilskraft* ('Critique of

Judgment') was published in 1790. The third and last of the *Critiques*, the *Urtheilskraft* is Kant's contribution to aesthetic theory; it contains his views on the critical functions of the mind and on those qualities inherent in objects which prompt either admiration or dislike.

5. J. G. Fichte (1762–1814) and F. W. J. von Schelling (1775–1854) are post-Kantian idealists. For the influence of Kant, Fichte and Schelling on STC, see for example Orsini (1969); on Schelling, see below Extract 33–E, nn 8 and 24. Cf also Crabb Robinson's Diary for 3 May 1812: 'From Fichte and Schelling [STC said] he has not gained any one great idea. To Kant his obligations are infinite, not so much from what Kant has taught him in the form of doctrine as from the discipline Kant has taught him to go through. Coleridge is indignant at the low estimation in which the Post-Kantians affect to treat their master. At the same time Coleridge himself adds Kant's writings are not metaphysics, only a propaedeutic' (*HCR* 1 70).

6. For Boehme, see Extract 41–B, n 3. Almost two years later, again according to Crabb Robinson (Diary, 13 August 1812), STC made a similar statement: 'Coleridge spoke of Schelling in terms of greater praise than I ever heard him use before, but without giving up any part of Kantianism to him. Yet he says Schelling alone understands Kant. . . . Schelling, he says, appears greatest in his last work on *Freiheit*. His is, however, altogether the philosophy of Jacob Boehmen. But I suspect Coleridge himself is now floating between Kant and Schelling with a greater uncertainty than he is himself aware of' (*HCR* 1 107–8). Some of STC's critics, intent on pillorying him for plagiarism, would do well to bear Crabb Robinson's closing remark in mind.

7. STC met J. L. Tieck (1773–1853), the German poet, novelist and critic, in Rome in the spring of 1806. Tieck visited England in 1817, and through the offices of Crabb Robinson, a 'dies Attico-germanica' was arranged with Coleridge at Highgate: cf *CL* IV 742–3, 750–1; *HCR* 1 207–9.

8. STC never held Goethe's (1749–1832) works in very high regard. 'The least agreeable part of Coleridge's talk', Crabb Robinson records of an evening at Highgate in 1824, 'was about German literature. He called Herder a coxcomb, and set Goethe far below Schiller, allowing no other merit than that of exquisite taste, repeating his favourite reproach that Goethe wrote from an idea that a certain thing was to be done in a certain style, not from the fullness of sentiment on a certain subject. He treats Goethe with more plausibility as utterly unprincipled' (10 June 1824; *HCR* 1 308). Cf also *TT* for 16 February 1833.

9. J. C. F. von Schiller (1759–1805) was perhaps STC's favourite German author (cf n 8 above). In 1800 he translated Schiller's historical tragedy *Wallenstein* (1799) into English verse. Schiller's lyric 'Dithyrambe' ('Nimmer, das glaubt mir', &c) appears as 'The Visit of the Gods' (with

the subtitle 'Imitated from Schiller') in *Sibylline Leaves* (1817): cf *CPW* I
310–11. STC's rendering of the opening lines, for which Crabb
Robinson gives the German, is as follows:

> Never, believe me,
> Appear the Immortals,
> Never alone . . .

10. Johann Paul Friedrich Richter (1763–1825), usually called simply 'Jean
    Paul' (the pseudonym he used as a signature in his early books), was a
    German novelist and romance writer. Jean Paul became popular with
    Englishmen like De Quincey and Carlyle both for his Sterne-like sense
    of humour and for his popularisation of the new gospel of idealism
    grounded on Fichte's philosophy. On 13 March 1811 Crabb Robinson
    recorded in his Diary that STC had 'read passages from Jean Paul in
    illustration of his absurd accumulation of images, and his unpicturesque
    and incongruous collection of features in one picture' (*HCR* I 26). For
    Jean Paul, see also Extract 22, n 3.
11. William Windham (1750–1810), Edmund Burke's follower, was a
    Member of Parliament well known for his abilities as speaker and
    debater.
12. Cf Extracts 33–C and 51–E.
13. The description of Fancy here, and its conjunction with *wit*, recalls
    Samuel Johnson's anatomy of 'metaphysical wit' in his *Life of Cowley*
    (1779): 'But wit, abstracted from its effects upon the hearer, may be
    more rigorously and philosophically considered as a kind of *discordia
    concors* [harmonious discord]; a combination of dissimilar images, or
    discovery of occult resemblances in things apparently unlike. Of wit,
    thus defined, [the Metaphysical poets] have more than enough. The
    most heterogeneous ideas are yoked by violence together; nature and art
    are ransacked for illustrations, comparisons, and allusions. . . .' Cf
    Extracts 13–G, 33–C and n 14, and 51–E.
14. Thomas Otway, *Venice Preserv'd* (1682) v i 369. STC often cited this
    line as an instance of Fancy: e.g., Extract 33–C.
15. Cf Extract 11.

17. from the *NOTEBOOKS*

(A) *c.* April 1811
The image-forming or rather re-forming power, the imagination in
its passive sense, which I would rather call Fancy = Phantasy,

a φαίνειν,[1] this, the Fetisch & Talisman of all modern Philosophers (the Germans excepted)[2] may not inaptly be compared to the Gorgon Head,[3] which *looked* death into every thing—and this not by accident, but from the nature of the faculty itself, the province of which is to give consciousness to the Subject by presenting to it its conceptions *objectively* but the Soul differences itself from any other Soul for the purposes of symbolical knowledge by *form* or body only—but all form as body, i.e. as shape, & not as forma efformans,[4] is dead—Life may be *inferred*, even as intelligence is from black marks on white paper—but the black marks themselves *are truly 'the dead letter'*.[5] Here then is the error—not in the faculty itself, without which there would be no *fixation*, consequently, no distinct perception or conception, but in the gross idolatry of those who abuse it, & make that the goal & end which should be only a means of arriving at it. Is it any excuse to him who treats a living being as inanimate Body, that we cannot arrive at the knowledge of the living Being but thro' the Body which is its Symbol[6] & outward & visible Sign?—

From the above deduce the worth & dignity of poetic Imagination, of the fusing power, that fixing unfixes & while it melts & bedims the Image, still leaves in the Soul its living meaning—[7]

(CN III Entry 4066)

Notes

1. φαίνειν : 'to make appear'. 'The image-forming power, or re-forming power, a mode of memory, it is here emphasized, [is] the passive aspect of imaginative activity, preferably called *Fancy = Phantasy.* . . . It is the mind's mere mechanical reception of the "fixities and definites" of the phenomenal world of body and shape, as contrasted with the active, creative *forma efformans* of the imagination, which by organic processes deals in "living meaning", i.e. art' (Coburn).
2. While rejecting the empirical, associationalist psychologies of the eighteenth century, STC of course does not dismiss German metaphysics, from which he drew support for 'his dynamic organicism as expressed in his attempts to describe what he meant by imagination and the symbol' (Coburn).
3. The Gorgon's head turned to stone all things that met its gaze directly: cf Hesiod, *Theogony* 270ff and Ovid, *Metamorphoses* iv 792ff (Perseus and Medusa myth).
4. '*Forma efformans* appears to be Coleridge's coinage (by analogy with *natura naturans* and very like Schiller's *lebendige Gestalt*) . . . lit. the "forming", i.e. form-forming "form", as opposed to the

"formed form", active form as against passive shape. . . . A footnote in the 1818 *Friend* enlarges on the meaning: "The word Nature has been used in two senses, viz. actively and passively; energetic (= forma formans), and material (= forma formata). In the first . . . it signifies the inward principle of whatever is requisite for the reality of the thing, as *existent* . . ." ' (Coburn).

5. A slighting reference to John Locke. In his *Essay Concerning Human Understanding* (1690), Locke likens the human mind to a blank sheet of paper on which the external world, through the agency of the five senses, makes impressions; in Locke's system, the mind is a passive receiver of external stimuli, and knowledge is the result of relating or associating the 'ideas' left in the mind by sensation. Cf Introduction, p. 1 , and Extract 4, 42–A, n 7.

6. For STC's later elaborated view of *symbol*, see Extract 35–A and n 9.

7. This entire Notebook entry, opposing *Fancy* which operates only with 'fixities and definites' to *Imagination* which works with 'vital' symbols, represents one of STC's early attempts to formulate the famous distinction so briefly stated in *Biographia* Chap xiii (Extract 33–F). An even earlier attempt appears in *CN* III 4058 (March–April 1811): 'In other words, Definites, be they Sounds or Images, that must be thought of either as being or as capable of being, *out* of us. Nay, is not this faulty?—for an Imagination quoad [insofar as it is] Imagination cannot be thought of as capable of being out of us? Answer. No. For while we imagine, we never do think thus. We always think of it as an *it*, & intimately mix the Thing & the Symbol.'

(B) October–November 1811[1]
We are certain indeed, that the Venus & Adonis, and the Rape of Lucrece were his two earliest Poems— [. . .]
The Venus & Adonis—

1. The perfect sweetness of the Versification so adapted to the subject, and the powers of varying it without passing into a loftier & more majestic rhythm than the subject required & the propriety of preserving the sense of melody predominant required—/.— The delight in richness & sweetness of sound, even to a faulty excess, [if evidently original not mechanical,][2] I cannot but regard as an highly favorable promise in the first complete composition of a young Poet—./ The Man, that hath not music in his Soul—can never be a true Poet—Imagery even from nature, much more from Books, whether Poem, Travels & Voyages, works of natural History—affecting Incidents—and interesting domestic feelings—may be acquired as an art, by incessant effort, by a young man of Talents &

good Education, who has mistaken an intense desire of poetic reputation for a natural Genius for the *Means*—but the sense of musical delight with the power of producing it, and the Gift of true Imagination asking either in itself to reduce multitude into Unity of Effect, or by means of Passion to modify a series of Thoughts by some one predominant Thought or Feeling, these are faculties which may be cultivated & improved but can never be acquired—In these it is that Poeta nascitur, non fit.—[3]

2.—a second sure promise of Genius is the choice of Subjects very remote from private Interests, Feelings, & circumstances of the Poet himself— [. . .] His Venus and Adonis seem at once the characters themselves, and the whole representation of those Characters by the most consummate Actors. You seem to be *told* nothing; but to see & hear every thing. Hence it is from the perpetual activity required on the part of the Reader's Attention, the rapid flow, quick change, [and the playful nature][4] of the Thoughts & Images, and the utter aloofness of the Poet's own *feelings* from those of which he is at once the Painter & Analyst, that, tho' the very subject renders it less pleasing at all times, & in a still greater degree less fit for public recitation, yet never Poem was less dangerous in a moral account/ Instead of doing, as Ariosto[5] & still more offensively, Wieland[6] have done—degrading and disforming the passion of Love into the Struggles of an animal Impulse, Shakespere has here precluded all sympathy with the Desire by dissipating the readers attention into the thousand outward images, & now beautiful, now fanciful circumstances which form its Drapery[7] and Scenery, or by diverting it in those frequent witty or profound reflections, which the active mind of the Poet has deduced or connected with the imagery & incidents. The reader's Mind & Fancy are forced into too much action to sympathize with the merely *Passive* of our Nature—As little can the mind thus roused & awakened doze and be brooded on by indistinct Passions, as the low lazy Mist can creep upon the surface while a strong Gale is driving the Lake on in waves and billows before it—/

3.—I have said before that Images tho' taken immediately from Nature & most accurately represented in words, do yet not characterize the poet.—In order to do this, they must either be blended with or merged in, other images, the offering of the Poet's Imagination, by the Passion, by the specific modification of pleasurable Feelings which the contemplation of the Image had awakened in the Poet himself—

Full many a glorious morning have I seen
Flatter the Mountain Tops with Sovereign Eye—[8]

or by blending it with some deeper emotion, arising out of and
consonant with the state or circumstances of the Person describing
it—an effect which how true it is to Nature, Shakespere himself has
finely enforced in the instance of Love (113 Sonnet)[9]—and of which
we shall hereafter [have] so many occasions to point out in his Lear
&c, or at least with the poetic feeling itself, so that the pleasure of the
Reader as well as the vividness of the Description is in part derived
from the force and fervour of the Describer. The very nature of the
Venus & Adonis treated as Sh[akespeare] has treated it, and as alone a
Sh[akespeare] could condescend to treat it confines the merit of the
Descriptions to this latter excellence, the lowest indeed of a great
Poet, but yet an excellence, characteristic & indispensible.
   —615th page—first red Card—Horse.[10]
619th—2nd red Card—the Hare.
   —The V[enus] and Ad[onis] = the Faery Queen and
Bottom—[11]
Yet quote—

> With this he breaketh from the sweet Embrace
> Of those fair arms that held him to her heart,
> And homeward thro' the dark lawns runs apace:
> Look how a bright Star shooteth from the Sky,
> So glides he in the Night from Venus' Eye—[12]

The Rape of Lucrece—

The Venus & Adonis, we have seen, did not allow the display of any
of the deeper passions—but the story of Lucretia seems to demand
it—and yet pathos or any thing truly dramatic we do not find—The
same minute & faithful Imagery in the same vivid Colors inspirited
by the Same impetuous Vigor & activity of Thought & true
associative & assimilative faculties—with a larger display of profound
reflection & a perfect Dominion, often Domination over, the whole
World of Language—/ What then shall we say?—Even this, that
Shakespear, no mere child of Nature, no Automaton of Genius,
possessed by the Muse not possessing, first studied, deeply meditated,
understood minutely—the knowledge become habitual gradually
wedded itself with his habitual feelings, & at length gave him that

wonderful Power by which he stands alone, with no equal or second in his own class, any where—seated him [on] one of the two Golden Thrones of the English Parnassus, with Milton on the other/—the one darting himself forth, & passing into all the forms of human character & passion, the other attracting all forms & things to himself, into the unity of his own grand Ideal—/ Sh[akespeare] became all things, yet for ever remaining himself—/ while all things & forms became Milton.

(*CN* III from Entry 4115)

Notes

1. This Notebook entry comprises STC's notes for his lecture on Shakespeare's narrative poems; the lecture itself was delivered at Scot's Corporation Hall on 28 November 1811. The material in this entry eventually became *Biographia* Chap xv (Extract 33—H). For STC's earlier remarks on the *Venus and Adonis* in the lectures of 1808, see Extracts 13—L to 13—N.
2. A later insertion by STC.
3. *Poeta nascitur, non fit*: 'a poet is born, not made'.
    A man named J. Tomalin, who may have been Robert Southey's agent but about whom nothing is known for certain, made shorthand notes of STC's 1811—12 lectures; three of these reports have survived, including that for Lecture IV (our present concern) on Shakespeare's narrative poems. It is both helpful and instructive to compare Tomalin's account of the lecture with STC's own outline. Tomalin's report at this point reads: 'That gift of true Imagination, that capability of reducing a multitude into unity of effect, or by strong passion to modify series of thoughts into one predominant thought or feeling—those were faculties which might be cultivated and improved, but could not be acquired. Only such a man as possessed them deserved the title of *poeta* who *nascitur non fit*—he was that child of Nature, and not the creature of his own efforts' (*SC* II 63).
4. A later insertion by STC.
5. Ludovico Ariosto (1474—1533), author of *Orlando Furioso*.
6. Christoph Martin Wieland (1733—1813), author of *Oberon*, a verse romance published in 1780 and later translated into English by STC's friend, William Sotheby.
7. Cf the last sentence of Extract 33—G.
8. Shakespeare, Sonnet 33, 1—2 (*variatim*).
9. Shakespeare, Sonnet 113:

> Since I left you, mine eye is in my mind;
> And that which governs me to go about

Doth part his function and is partly blind,
Seems seeing, but effectually is out;
For it no form delivers to the heart
Of bird, of flower, or shape, which it doth latch:
Of his quick objects hath the mind no part,
Nor his own vision holds what it doth catch;
For if it see the rudest or gentlest sight,
The most sweet favour or deformed'st creature,
The mountain or the sea, the day or night,
The crow or dove, it shapes them to your feature:
    Incapable of more, replete with you,
    My most true mind thus makes mine eye untrue.

10. Tomalin's report reads: 'Coleridge here read the description of the horse of Adonis from the line—"Imperiously he leaps, he neighs, he bounds" [line 265] to the line—"Fanning the hairs which heave like feather'd wings" [306]. The lecturer also read the description of the hare [679–708]. In these quotations the auditors would perceive that there was accuracy of description blended with the fervour of the poet's mind, thereby communicating pleasure to the reader. In the description where Adonis flies from Venus prior to the hunt in which he lost his life, there seemed to be all that could be expected from imagination. It was a complete picture [in]formed with all the passions of the person viewing it' (SC II 65–6). The description of Adonis's horse is probably that which, in the 1808 lecture, STC had deemed 'less fitted for public recitation' than the description of the hunted hare: cf Extract 13–M. Nevertheless, STC did manage to preserve decorum in the 1811 lecture, for (as Tomalin's line-references show) he omitted Shakespeare's lively accounts of the breeding jennet and the final consummation of equine passion.

    red Card: STC had either written out the passages he wished to read on red cards, or he had used such cards as markers in his copy of Shakespeare.

11. A parallel was here to be drawn between Venus–Adonis and Titania–Bottom in *A Midsummer Night's Dream*; doubtless the analogy would have been a humorous one. Lamentably Tomalin is silent at this point.

12. *Venus and Adonis* 811–13, 815–16 (*variatim*).

18. from CRABB ROBINSON'S DIARY (24 November 1811)

Rose late; breakfasted with Serjeant Rough and then walked with him to see Coleridge at Hammersmith. We found him not quite well, but very eloquent. He soon mounted his hobby, and I was not a little surprised to find him very much of a Schellingianer, [1] of which I had no idea. At least, his mode of comparing the fine arts and of antithetically considering all their elements appeared to me very similar. [2] He observed of poetry that it united passion with order, [3] and he very beautifully illustrated the nature of the human mind, which requires and seeks to gratify contrary propensities (as sloth and the horror of vacancy) [4] at the same time, and from this he deduced many of our likings and dislikings. He spoke of Calderon, [5] defining him to be a Shakespeare but without his philosophy [6]—having all his imagination and fancy. His usual distinction between these last-mentioned qualities he repeated on this occasion, assigning great fancy but no imagination to Southey, and much imagination but a sterile fancy to Wordsworth. [7] Our visit was short. . . .

(HCR 1 52)

Notes

1. I.e., a disciple of Schelling: cf Extract 16, nn 5 and 6.
2. The reference is to Schelling's *Ueber das Verhältniss der bildenen Künste zu der Natur* (1807): cf Extract 40−C, n 1. There is some doubt, however, as to whether or not STC had read Schelling's oration as early as 1811: cf *CN* III 4066 n.
3. Cf *Biographia* Chap xiv (Extract 33−G): 'a more than usual state of emotion, with more than usual order. . . .'
4. Cf Extract 40−B and n 9.
5. Pedro Calderón de la Barca (1600−81), Spanish dramatist who composed some 120 plays as well as numerous short religious *autos* (dramatic presentations of the Eucharist). 'Coleridge's reading of Calderón', writes Miss Coburn, 'is a *terra incognita*, his claim to knowledge (at this date [1810]) of Spanish unconfirmed. . . . By June 1814 he was "perfecting himself in the Spanish", reading the minor works of Cervantes . . .' (*CN* III 3924 n).
6. Shakespeare's *judgement*, as STC frequently asserted, *was equal to his genius*: cf 33−H, n 21. In the 1818 *Friend* he devotes an entire essay to Shakespeare's method (*CC* IV i 450−7) and then later remarks that 'From Shakespeare to Plato, from the philosophic poet to the poetic philosopher, the transition is easy . . .' (ibid. 472).

7. Cf *Biographia* Chap xxii: 'Last, and pre-eminently, I challenge for this poet [Wordsworth] the gift of IMAGINATION in the highest and strictest sense of the word. In the play of *Fancy*, Wordsworth, to my feelings, is not always graceful, and sometimes *recondite.* . . . Indeed his fancy seldom displays itself, as mere and unmodified fancy' (*BL* II 124). For Southey, see Introduction, pp. 12–13.

19. from a LECTURE ON *ROMEO AND JULIET* (9 December 1811)[1]

[*Collier Report.*][2]

. . . I can understand and allow for an effort of the mind, when it would describe what it cannot satisfy itself with the description of, to reconcile opposites and qualify contradictions, leaving a middle state of mind more strictly appropriate to the imagination than any other, when it is, as it were, hovering between images. As soon as it is fixed on one image, it becomes understanding; but while it is unfixed and wavering between them, attaching itself permanently to none, it is imagination.[3] Such is the fine description of Death in Milton:—

> 'The other shape,
> If shape it might be call'd, that shape had none
> Distinguishable in member, joint, or limb,
> Or substance might be call'd, that shadow seem'd,
> For each seem'd either: black it stood as night;
> Fierce as ten furies, terrible as hell,
> And shook a dreadful dart: what seem'd his head
> The likeness of a kindly crown had on.'
>
> *Paradise Lost* Book II.[4]

The grandest efforts of poetry are where the imagination is called forth, not to produce a distinct form, but a strong working of the mind, still offering what is still repelled, and again creating what is again rejected; the result being what the poet wishes to impress, namely, the substitution of a sublime feeling of the unimaginable for a mere image.[5] I have sometimes thought that the passage just read might be quoted as exhibiting the narrow limit of painting, as compared with the boundless power of poetry: painting cannot go beyond a certain point; poetry rejects all control, all confinement. Yet we know that sundry painters have attempted pictures of the meeting between Satan and Death at the gates of Hell; and how was Death represented? Not as Milton has described him, but by the most defined thing that can be imagined—a skeleton, the dryest and hardest image that it is possible to discover; which, instead of keeping the mind in a state of activity, reduces it to the merest passivity,—an image, compared with which a square, a triangle, or any other mathematical figure, is a luxuriant fancy.

(*SC* II 103–4)

Notes

1. This lecture was the seventh (and perhaps the best) in a series of seventeen on Shakespeare and Milton delivered at Scot's Corporation Hall between 18 November 1811 and 27 January 1812. Of this lecture Crabb Robinson wrote in his Diary: 'Accompanied Mrs R[ough] to Coleridge's 7th and incomparably best lecture. C. declaimed with great eloquence on *Love* without wandering from his subject, *Romeo and Juliet*. He was spirited; for the greater part intelligible, tho' profound; and he was methodical . . .' (*SC* II 171; *HCR* I 54).

2. John Payne Collier (1789–1883) took shorthand notes of STC's 1811–12 lectures, some of which he rediscovered much later among his papers and published in 1856 as *Seven Lectures on Shakespeare and Milton. By the late S. T. Coleridge.* R. A. Foakes has recovered Collier's original shorthand transcript of STC's lectures and published them: see *Coleridge on Shakespeare* (London: Routledge & Kegan Paul, 1971).

3. 'The Imagination, then, starts with sensible images of the concrete world, and is able, even from images that contradict each other, to form a *synthesis*—not a fixed image, as the original ones were, but something which is possible only because the Imagination is constantly working and hovering. The Imagination is indeed "that synthetic and magical power" ' (*BL* II 12): Keppel-Jones (1967) 62.

4. Lines 666–73.

5. Raysor (*SC* II 104 n) here cites Kant's *Critique of Judgement*: 'The beautiful in nature is a question of the form of the object, and this consists in limitation, whereas the sublime is to be found in an object even devoid of form, so far as it immediately involves, or else by its presence provokes, a representation of *limitlessness*, yet with a super-added thought of its totality'.

20. from a LECTURE ON *ROMEO AND JULIET* (12 December 1811)[1]

[*Collier Report.*][2]

It is impossible to pay a higher compliment to poetry, than to consider the effects it produces in common with religion, yet distinct (as far as distinction can be, where there is no division) in those qualities which religion exercises and diffuses over all mankind, as far as they are subject to its influence.

I have often thought that religion (speaking of it only as it accords with poetry, without reference to its more serious impressions) is the poetry of mankind, both having for their objects:—

1. To generalise our notions; to prevent men from confining their attention solely, or chiefly, to their own narrow sphere of action, and to their own individual circumstances. By placing them in certain awful relations it merges the individual man in the whole species, and makes it impossible for any one man to think of his future lot, or indeed of his present condition, without at the same time comprising in his view his fellow-creatures.

2. That both poetry and religion throw the object of deepest interest to a distance from us, and thereby not only aid our imagination, but in a most important manner subserve the interest of our virtues; for that man is indeed a slave, who is a slave to his own senses, and whose mind and imagination cannot carry him beyond the distance which his hand can touch, or even his eye can reach.[3]

3. The grandest point of resemblance between them is, that both have for their object (I hardly know whether the English language supplies an appropriate word) the perfecting, and the pointing out to us the indefinite improvement of our nature, and fixing our attention upon that. They bid us, while we are sitting in the dark at our little fire, look at the mountain-tops,[4] struggling with darkness, and announcing that light which shall be common to all, in which individual interests shall resolve into one common good, and every man shall find in his fellow man more than a brother.

Such being the case, we need not wonder that it has pleased Providence, that the divine truths of religion should have been revealed to us in the form of poetry;[5] and that at all times poets, not the slaves of any particular sectarian opinions, should have joined to support all those delicate sentiments of the heart (often when they were most opposed to the reigning philosophy of the day) which may be called the feeding streams of religion.

I have heard it said that an undevout astronomer is mad. In the strict sense of the word, every being capable of understanding must be mad, who remains, as it were, fixed in the ground on which he treads—who, gifted with the divine faculties of indefinite hope and fear, born with them, yet settles his faith upon that, in which neither hope nor fear has any proper field for display. Much more truly, however, might it be said that, an undevout poet is mad: in the strict sense of the word, an undevout poet is an impossibility. I have heard of verse-makers (poets they are not, and never can be) who introduced into their works such questions as these:—Whether the world was made of atoms?—Whether there is a universe?—Whether there is a governing mind that supports it?[6] As I have said, verse-makers are not poets: the poet is one who carries the simplicity of childhood into the powers of manhood;[7] who, with a soul unsubdued by habit, unshackled by custom, contemplates all things with the freshness and wonder of a child; and, connecting with it the inquisitive powers of riper years, adds, as far as he can find knowledge, admiration; and, where knowledge no longer permits admiration, gladly sinks back again into the childlike feeling of devout wonder.[8]

The poet is not only the man made to solve the riddle of the universe, but he is also the man who feels where it is not solved. What is old and worn-out, not in itself, but from the dimness of the intellectual eye, produced by worldly passions and pursuits, he makes new:[9] he pours upon it the dew that glistens, and blows round it the breeze that cooled us in our infancy. I hope, therefore, that if in this single lecture I make some demand on the attention of my hearers to a most important subject, upon which depends all sense of the worthiness or unworthiness of our nature, I shall obtain their pardon.

(*SC* II 111–12)

Notes

1. Cf Extract 19, n 1. The eighth lecture was not well received, largely owing to the lecturer's tendency to digress from his subject; Crabb Robinson recorded in his Diary the following assessment: 'C. unhappily relapsed into his desultory habit and delivered, I think, his *worst* lecture. He began with identifying religion and love, delivered a rhapsody on brotherly and sisterly love, which seduced him into a dissertation on incest. I at last lost all power of attending to him any longer . . .' (*SC* II 172; *HCR* I 55).

2. The reports of this lecture published in the *Morning Chronicle* and *The Courier* (13 and 14 December 1811) are similar to the summary quoted from Collier: 'Mr Coleridge commenced his eighth lecture by pointing out the great similarity in the effects produced by poetry and religion, the latter of which he had ever deemed the poetry of all mankind, in which the divinest truths were revealed. He had heard it said that "an undevout astronomer is mad"; much more truly might it be stated that an undevout poet is insane; in fact, it was an impossibility. After impressing upon his audience what a poet was, viz., that he combined all the feelings of the child with the powers of the man, he proceeded to trace the passion of love from its earliest origin . . .' (*SC* II 161–2).

3. Raysor (*SC* II 111 n) points to 'Schiller's essay on "The Moral Utility of Aesthetic Manners" for an interesting parallel, which is not close enough to suggest an influence.'

4. For a similar image, see Extract 1 and n 4, and Extract 33–E.

5. Cf Extract 9. In order to counter the strictures of Plato (and Cornelius Agrippa), Renaissance apologists had frequent recourse to the observation that many parts of Scripture are in verse, thereby demonstrating poetry's divine pedigree. Ben Jonson, for instance, in *Timber, or Discoveries made upon Men and Matters* (1640) denominates poetry 'the Queene of Arts, which had her Originall from heaven, received thence from the '*Ebrewes*.'

6. The reference is to the early Greek poet-philosophers Democritus and Leucippus who propounded an atomic theory; apart from scattered fragments, their works are no longer extant. STC would also have had in mind their followers Epicurus and (especially) Lucretius, whose long didactic poem *De Rerum Natura* expounds a physical theory of atomism 'with a view to abolishing superstitious fears of the intervention of the gods in the world and of the punishment of the soul in an after-life. This he accomplishes by demonstrating that the world is governed by the mechanical laws of nature ("Foedera naturai") and that the soul is mortal and perishes with the body' (*OCD* 623). Doubtless STC intended also to include such contemporary 'infidel' poet-philosophers as Erasmus Darwin and, at the same time, to indicate *how far* from poetic truth were the 'mechanical' systems of philosophers like Locke and Hartley.

7. Cf Wordsworth's line (which STC was fond of quoting) in 'The Rainbow': 'The Child is father of the Man'. Cf also Extract 33–C.

8. Raysor (*SC* II 112 n) suggests that STC is here echoing Schiller's essay 'Naive and Sentimental Poetry'; he adds, however, that the 'development of the idea is . . . entirely Coleridge's own'.

9. A common Coleridgean idea: cf Extract 33–C and n 6, and Extract 33–G.

21. from a LETTER TO AN UNKNOWN CORRESPONDENT (December 1811)

It will not be by Dates, that Posterity will judge of the originality of a Poem; but by the original spirit itself. This is to be found neither in a Tale however interesting, which is but the Canvass, no nor yet in the Fancy or the Imagery—which are but Forms & Colors—it is a subtle Spirit, all in each part, reconciling & unifying all—. Passion and Imagination are it's *most* appropriate names; but even these say little—for it must be not merely Passion but poetic Passion, poetic Imagination.— [MS breaks off here]

(*CL* III 361)

22. from the *NOTEBOOKS* (May 1812)

The Heimweh[1] of the Mountain-born—Lie on our Nurse's bosom (the Earth) and hear tales of our great Father not yet seen/—but the effect of the Sky—how purely intellectual—

The Rainbow of our Morning in the West before us—of our Evening in the East behind us—The eye reaches to Heaven, the Hands but the Fruit of the Soul—Why this?—the Eye & Ear first emancipating themselves from the Thier-dienst[2] & became Organs, Glasses that shelter & admit Light, into the inner World of our Nature—but even as the Images of our sensuous Memory prove a correspondent outward World—so does the inward ideal World in us prove a correspondent World, in which ideal & real are one & the same/[3]

—The unsensualized Mind[4] like the Sojourner in Greenland in the sixteen days before the ascent of the Sun above the Horizon—It is refracted and *appears* before it really *is* there/

(*CN* III Entry 4153)

Notes

1. *Heimweh*: 'home-sickness'. Cf *CN* III 4088: 'We are born in the mountains, in the Alps—and when we hire ourselves out to the Princes of the Lower Lands, sooner or later we feel an incurable Home-

sickness—& every Tune that recalls our native Heights, brings on a relapse of the Sickness.—I seem to myself like a Butterfly who having foolishly torn or bedaubed his wings, is obliged to crawl like a Caterpillar with all the restless Instincts of the Butterfly.'

2. *Thierdienst*: 'animal need, brute servitude' (Coburn).

3. Cf the discussion of the 'philosophic imagination' in *Biographia* Chap xii: Extract 33—E. The imagery in this Notebook entry is influenced by Jean Paul Richter's *Geist oder Chrestomathie* (1801) I 29—33. (For Richter, see Extract 16, n 10.) Miss Coburn quotes (and translates) the relevant section from Jean Paul at length (*CN* III 4088 n); her translation reads in part: 'This inner universe, more splendid and marvellous than the external one, requires a different heaven from the one above us and a loftier world than is warmed by any sun.—The triple chord of Virtue, Truth, and Beauty, drawn from the music of the spheres, summons us from this dull earth and announces for us the nearness of a melodious world. . . . But once our necessary *animal needs* [Thierdienst] are met, the howling circle of wild beasts within us fed, the animal combat over, then the *inner* man demands his nectar and ambrosia. . . . Strangers born in the *mountains* are consumed in the *lowlands* by an incurable homesickness. We are made for a higher place, and that is why we are gnawed at by an eternal longing. In the morning of our lives, we see the joys that satisfy the timid wishes our hearts *aspire to*, far off, shimmering towards us from *later* years; once we have reached *these* years, we turn round at this deceptive place and see our happiness blossoming *behind* us in our strong and lusty youth, and enjoy now, instead of our hopes, *the memories of our hopes*. So in this too, joy resembles the rainbow in this respect, that it shines before us in the *West* in the morning, and arches over the *East* in the evening.—Our *eye* can travel as far as *light*, but our arm is short, and can reach only the fruit of our earth. 'And what are we to conclude from this?' Not that we are unhappy, but that we are immortal, and that the *second* world *within* us demands and demonstrates a second world *outside* us.'

For the idea that the human soul, imprisoned in the body, has (through love) some power of recollecting the world of ideal and immutable Forms from which it has come, see Plato, *Phaedo* 72e—76 (quoted in part in Extract 40—C, n 20) and *Phaedrus* 247c—252c. Cf also STC's 'Dejection: An Ode' 17—20, 59—93; and Wordsworth's 'Ode: Intimations of Immortality' sections i, v—vi, viii—ix.

4. Cf lines 80—8 of Extract 2.

23. from *OMNIANA* (1812)[1]

If I have life and health, and leisure, I purpose to compile from the works, memoirs, transactions, &c., of the different philosophical societies in Europe, from magazines, and the rich store of medical and psychological publications furnished by the English, French, and German press, all the essays and cases, that relate to the human faculties under unusual circumstances (for pathology is the crucible of physiology); excluding such only as are not intelligible without the symbols or terminology of science. These I would arrange under the different senses and powers: as the eye, the ear, the touch, &c.; the imitative power, voluntary and automatic; the imagination, or shaping and modifying power; the fancy, or the aggregative and associative power; the understanding, or the regulative, substantiating, and realizing power; the speculative reason,—*vis theoretica et scientifica*,[2] or the power by which we produce, or aim to produce, unity, necessity, and universality in all our knowledge by means of principles *a priori*; the will, or practical reason; the faculty of choice (*Germanicè, Willkühr*),[3] and (distinct both from the moral will, and the choice) the sensation of volition, which I have found reason to include under the head of single and double touch.[4] Thence I propose to make a new arrangement of madness. . . .[5]

(*TT* 361−2)

Notes

1. *Omniana* was a miscellany compiled by Robert Southey; STC contributed several pieces to this *omnium gatherum*.
2. *vis theoretica et scientifica*: 'the speculative and scientific power'. In *Aids to Reflection* (1825), STC says that 'by *reason*' he means 'exclusively the speculative or scientific power so called, the νοῦς or *mens* of the ancients' (*AR* 135). For STC's distinction between *speculative* and *practical* Reason, see Extract 15−B, n 1; for his distinction between Reason and Understanding, see Extract 35−A and n 5, Extract 35−B and n 1, and Extract 41−A and n 3.
3. *Germanicè, Willkühr*: 'In German, *free choice*'. (*Die Willkühr* is a compound formed from *Wille* 'will, intent, purpose' and *Kür* 'choice'.)
4. For the meaning of 'single and double touch', see Beer (1977) 81−8, 256−7.
5. Although the work on abnormal psychology and madness was never written, these and similar phenomena (cf Extract 14) were of continuing interest to STC: cf Beer (1977). This passage from *Omniana*, however, is

important in connection with STC's concern with 'desynonymization' and his desire to discriminate among the powers of the soul on the basis of 'their relative worth and dignity': cf Extract 15—C. In writing (12 August 1812) to Richard Saumarez, STC included the prospectus for his lectures of 1812—13 at the Surrey Institution, containing the following outline of his purpose in the first lecture: 'That to use each word in a sense peculiarly it's own, is an indispensable Condition of all just thinking, and at once the surest, easiest, and even most entertaining Discipline of the mind.—On the words, Beautiful, Sublime, Majestic, Grand, Picturesque, Fancy, Imagination, Taste' (*CL* III 418). STC's most sustained and elaborate attempts at *desynonymization* occur in the quinquepartite Appendix of *The Statesman's Manual* (1816), which STC himself described on the back fly-leaf of Gillman's copy as being 'an attempt to fix the true meaning of the Terms, Reason, Understanding, Sense, Imagination, Conscience & Ideas, with reflections on the theoretical & practical Consequences of their perversion from the Revolution (1688) to the present day, 1816.' For *The Statesman's Manual*, see Extracts 35—A and 35—B; also, STC quotes part of this passage from *Omniana* in *Biographia* Chap xii: cf end of Extract 33—E.

24. from the *NOTEBOOKS* (February–June 1813)

His Imagination, if it must be so called, is at all events of the pettiest kind—it is an Imagunculation.[1]—How excellently the German Einbildungskraft[2] expresses this prime & loftiest Faculty, the power of co-adunation,[3] the faculty that forms the many into one, *in eins Bildung*.[4]

Eisenoplasy, or esenoplastic Power,[5])({* Fantasy, or the Mirrorment, either catoptric or metoptric[6]—repeating simply, or by transposition—& again, involuntary (as in dreams) or by an act of the will.—[7]

*)({ = in opposition to, or as contradistinguished from—

(*CN* III Entry 4176)

Notes

1. *Imagunculation*: 'little imagination'. (STC's coinage; not in *OED*.) To whom is STC here referring? Miss Coburn cautiously suggests ('speculation is dangerous') that it may have been Robert Southey, and

she points to a disagreement between the two men in February 1812 and, as well, to STC's statement (recorded in Crabb Robinson's Diary, 13 March 1811) that Southey 'wanted modifying power—he was a jewel-setter; whatever he read he instantly applied to the formation or adorning of a story' (*HCR* 1 26). I am less hesitant than Miss Coburn in believing that Southey is the subject of this Notebook entry; the critical sentiment here expressed, albeit more tart than usual, is perfectly consonant with STC's earlier assessments of Southey's literary talents. As early as 1796–7, STC was concerned about Southey's lack of 'opulence of Imagination', and he did not hesitate to make his views known in letters of those years to Thelwall and Cottle: cf Introduction, p. 13; also Extract 18. While we shall probably never know for certain precisely to whom STC was referring in the Notebook entry, Robert Southey, I think, must be thought the leading candidate.

2. *Einbildungskraft*: 'Coleridge may have "misapprehended" the etymology of the German *Einbilden, Einbildungskraft* (from *ein* = in, not *eins* = one) and *das Bild*, "image"; or he may have been punning. Schelling could hardly be misapprehending the word *In-Eins-Bildung* when he used it in *Jahrbücher der Medicin als Wissenschaft* (Tübingen 1806–8) 1 ii 22, meaning, "formation into one"; in this instance it was not applied to imagination' (*CN* III 4176 n). Cf also Shawcross, *BL* 1 249.

3. *co-adunation*: 'the joining together into one'. The word is used frequently by STC: e.g., Extract 13–J; and as early as 1802 he had described Imagination as 'the *modifying* and *co-adunating* Faculty' (Extract 9). Coburn cites another interesting instance in the 1818 *Friend*: 'For Thought, Imagination (and we may add, Passion), are, in their very essence, the first, connective, the latter co-adunative' (*CC* IV i 456).

4. *in eins Bildung*: 'formation into one'. Cf n 2 above.

5. *Eisenoplasy, or esenoplastic Power*: 'the power of shaping or making into one'. *Esenoplastic* and *Esemplastic* are synonyms; of the latter STC writes: '"Esemplastic. The word is not in Johnson, nor have I met with it elsewhere." Neither have I. I constructed it myself from the Greek words, εἰς ἕν πλάττειν, to shape into one; because, having to convey a new sense, I thought that a new term would both aid the recollection of my meaning, and prevent its being confounded with the usual import of the word, imagination' (*BL* 1 107). The sub-title of *Biographia* Chap XIII is 'On the imagination, or esemplastic power'.

6. *catoptric*: 'of mirror, reflector, or reflexion'—i.e., *repeating simply*. (Cf *CL* II 698).

   metoptric: 'of the same objects differently arranged'—i.e., *repeating . . . by transposition*. (Not in *OED*.)

7. Miss Coburn's comment (*CN* III 4176 n) on this important Notebook entry is very helpful: 'the making-into-one of the imagination is here illuminated by the contrast with fantasy, described as a direct mirror-

ment by repetition or by transcription. As in [*Biographia*] Chap XIII he says of "Fancy", *Fantasy* here deals with "fixities and definites" and "is blended with, and modified by that empirical phenomenon of the will, which we express by the word CHOICE". Or it may be involuntary, as in dreams. The imagination, on the other hand, builds-into-one both the materials it works on and the person who does the work, calling "the whole soul of man into activity". Hence his own belittling of *Kubla Khan*, a dream poem, though perhaps it is his best evidence for that possibility of the co-presence of the esemplastic power and the fancy for which he contended at the close of [*Biographia*] Chap XII.' It is not clear, in fact, how far STC 'belittled' 'Kubla Khan'; his prefatory note does not necessarily represent his private view of the matter: cf Extract 34 and nn 1 and 3.

25. from a LETTER TO CHARLES MATHEWS (30 May 1814)

A great Actor, comic or tragic, is not to be a mere *Copy*, a *fac simile*, but an *imitation*, of Nature. Now an *Imitation* differs from a Copy in this, that it of necessity implies & demands *difference*—whereas a Copy aims at *identity*.[1] What a marble peach on a mantlepiece, that you take up deluded, & put down with pettish disgust, is compared with a fruit-piece of Vanhuysen's,[2] even such is a mere *Copy* of nature compared with a true histrionic *Imitation*. A good actor is Pygmalion's Statue,[3] a work of exquisite *art, animated* & gifted with *motion*; but still *art*, still a species of *Poetry*.

(*CL* III 501)

Notes

1. The distinction between *imitation* and *copy* is another instance of Coleridgean 'desynonymization'. Cf also the following:
   (*a*) 'To defend the *Opera* = all the objections against *equally* applicable to Tragedy & Comedy without music, & all proceed on the false principle, that Theatrical representations are *Copies* of nature whereas they are imitations' (October 1804; *CN* II 2211).
   (*b*) 'Hard to express that sense of the analogy or likeness of a Thing which enables a Symbol to represent it, so that we think of the Thing itself—& yet knowing that the Thing is not present to us.—Surely, on this universal fact of words & images depends by more or less mediations

the *imitation* instead of *copy* which is illustrated in very nature *shakespearianized/*—that Proteus Essence that could assume the very form, but yet known & felt not to be the Thing by that difference of the Substance which made every atom of the Form another thing/ —that likeness not identity—and exact web, every line of direction miraculously the same, but the one worsted, the other silk' (November 1804; *CN* II 2274). For STC's use of the word *symbol*, see Extract 35—A and nn 5, 9 and 11.

(*c*) 'The second [cause of pleasure excited by Wordsworth's poetry] is the apparent naturalness of the *representation*, as raised and qualified by an imperceptible infusion of the author's own knowledge and talent, which infusion does, indeed, constitute it an *imitation* as distinguished from a mere *copy*' (Chap xvii; *BL* II 30).

(*d*) '. . . the composition of a poem is among the *imitative* arts; and . . . imitation, as opposed to copying, consists either in the interfusion of the SAME throughout the radically DIFFERENT, or of the different throughout a base radically the same' (Chap xviii; *BL* II 56).

For other examples see *MC* 49, 207; *SC* II 258; *BL* II 185—8; *TT* 3 July 1833; Extract 40—C and n 6.

2. Jan van Huysum (1682—1749), Dutch still-life painter.

3. Pygmalion—having renounced women—fell in love with an ivory statue of a maiden; he prayed to Aphrodite that he might be given a wife as beautiful as the statue and, in answer to his prayer, Aphrodite gave life to the statue itself; Pygmalion then married the lady (Galatea) so created: Ovid, *Metamorphoses* x 243ff. Given the histrionic context of this passage, STC may also be alluding to the restoration of Hermione in Shakespeare's *The Winter's Tale* V iii.

26. from 'ON THE PRINCIPLES OF GENIAL CRITICISM' (1814)[1]

AGREEABLE.[2]—We use this word in two senses; in the first for whatever agrees with our nature, for that which is congruous with the primary constitution of our senses. Thus green is naturally agreeable to the eye. In this sense the word expresses, at least involves, a pre-established harmony between the organs and their appointed objects. In the second sense, we convey by the word *agreeable*, that the thing has by force of habit (thence called a second nature) been made to agree with us; or that it has become agreeable to us by its recalling to our minds some one or more things that were dear and pleasing to us; or lastly, on account of some after pleasure or advantage, of which it has been the constant cause or occasion. Thus by force of custom men *make* the taste of tobacco, which was at first hateful to the palate, agreeable to them. [. . .]

The BEAUTIFUL,[3] contemplated in its essentials, that is, in *kind* and not in *degree*, is that in which the *many*, still seen as many, becomes one. Take a familiar instance, one of a thousand. The frost on a window-pane has by accident crystallized into a striking resemblance of a tree or a sea-weed. With what pleasure we trace the parts, and their relations to each other, and to the whole! Here is the stalk or trunk, and here the branches or sprays—sometimes even the buds or flowers. Nor will our pleasure be less, should the caprice of the crystallization represent some object disagreeable to us, provided only we can see or fancy the component parts each in relation to each, and all forming a whole. A lady would see an admirably painted tiger with pleasure, and at once pronounce it beautiful,—nay, an owl, a frog, or a toad, who would have shrieked or shuddered at the sight of the things themselves. So far is the Beautiful from depending wholly on association, that it is frequently produced by the mere removal of associations. Many a sincere convert to the beauty of various insects, as of the dragon-fly, the fangless snake, &c., has Natural History made, by exploding the terror or aversion that had been connected with them.

The most general definition of beauty, therefore, is—that I may fulfil my threat of plaguing my readers with hard words—Multëity in Unity.[4] Now it will be always found, that whatever is the definition of the *kind*, independent of degree, becomes likewise the definition of the highest degree of that kind. An old coach-wheel lies in the coachmaker's yard, disfigured with tar and dirt (I purposely take the most trivial instances)—if I turn away my attention from these, and regard the *figure* abstractly, 'still,' I might say to my companion, 'there is beauty in that wheel, and you yourself would not only admit, but would feel it, had you never seen a wheel before. See how the rays proceed from the centre to the circumferences, and how many different images are distinctly comprehended at one glance, as forming one whole, and each part in some harmonious relation to each and to all.' But imagine the polished golden wheel of the chariot of the Sun, as the poets have described it: then the figure, and the real thing so figured, exactly coincide. There is nothing heterogeneous, nothing to abstract from: by its perfect smoothness and circularity in width, each part is (if I may borrow a metaphor from a sister sense) as perfect a melody, as the whole is a complete harmony. This, we should say, is beautiful throughout. Of all 'the many,' which I actually see, each and all are really reconciled into unity: while the effulgence from the whole coincides with, and seems to represent, the effluence of delight from my own mind in the intuition of it.

It seems evident then, first, that beauty is harmony, and subsists only in composition, and secondly, that the first species of the Agreeable can alone be a component part of the beautiful, that namely which is naturally consonant with our senses by the pre-established harmony between nature and the human mind; and thirdly, that even of this species, those objects only can be admitted (according to rule the first) which belong to the eye and ear, because they alone are susceptible of distinction of parts. Should an Englishman gazing on a mass of cloud rich with the rays of the rising sun exclaim, even without distinction of, or reference to its form, or its relation to other objects, how beautiful! I should have no quarrel with him. First, because by the law of association there is in all visual beholdings at least an indistinct subsumption of form and relation: and, secondly, because even in the coincidence between the sight and the object there is an approximation to the reduction of the many into one. But who, that heard a Frenchman call the flavor of a leg of mutton a beautiful taste, would not immediately recognize him for a Frenchman, even though there should be neither grimace or characteristic nasal twang?[5] The result, then, of the whole is that the shapely (i.e. *formosus*) joined with the naturally agreeable, constitutes what, speaking accurately, we mean by the word beautiful (i.e. *pulcher*).

[.   .   .   .   ]

The Beautiful arises from the perceived harmony of an object, whether sight or sound, with the inborn and constitutive rules of the judgement and imagination: and it is always intuitive. As light to the eye, even such is beauty to the mind, which cannot but have complacency[6] in whatever is perceived as pre-configured to its living faculties. Hence the Greeks called a beautiful object καλόν quasi καλοῦν, i.e. *calling on*[7] the soul, which receives instantly, and welcomes it as something connatural.

(*BL* II 231−4, 243)

Notes

1. STC's essays on 'Genial Criticism' first appeared in *Felix Farley's Bristol Journal* in August–September 1814; all of the passages here quoted are from 'Essay III'.

2. STC's use of the terms *agreeable* and *beautiful* is discussed in Fogle (1962) 34–48. Cf also Vol. 3 of the 1818 *Friend*: *CC* IV i 501–2. An early Notebook entry (December 1803) also shows STC discriminating between these terms: '*The Good* for all who have reason/ & so perhaps the Beautiful—*the Agreeable* depends on each man's internal nature/ on the Subject, not the Object/ Now what is it, if there be any thing, which belongs to the very nature of a rational Being, & which, it is matter of Fact, that all men have, who have Reason?—In short, REASON—N.B.' (*CN* I 1719).

3. For STC's later examination of the *Idea* of the Beautiful, see his letter of 12 August 1829 to J. H. Green: *CL* VI 811–13.

4. *Multëity*: 'the quality or condition of being many (i.e. more than one); manifoldness' (*OED*, which cites STC's use here). Earlier in 'Essay III' STC had explicated the term in this way: 'in order to express "*the many*," as simply contra-distinguished from "*the one*," I have hazarded the smile of the reader, by introducing to his acquaintance, from the forgotten terminology of the old schoolmen, the phrase, *multëity*, because I felt that I could not substitute *multitude*, without more or less connecting it with the notion of "a *great* many." Thus the Philosopher [i.e. Plotinus] of the later Platonic, or Alexandrine school, named the triangle the first-born of beauty, it being the first and simplest symbol of *multëity in unity*' (*BL* II 230). Multëity is one of a family of terms that STC coined on the analogy of such scholastic terms as haecceitas ('this-ness'), &c. Cf omnëity ('all-ness') in Extract 35–B.

5. Although initially an admirer of the French, STC came to believe that a 'Frenchified' taste for aphoristic truth in lieu of sound principles and methodology was responsible in large part for a decline in government and in social behaviour. Derogatory references to the French are scattered through his published and private writings—for example, in a letter of 1809 to his brother George STC deplored 'the asthmatic sententiolae of the French School' (*CL* III 237), and in the 1818 *Friend* he likewise voiced his 'aversion to the epigrammatic unconnected periods of the fashionable *Anglo-gallican taste*' (*CC* IV i 20). Cf also *CL* IV 667. For helpful comments on STC's view of the French, see Jackson (1969) 21–35.

6. '*The sense of beauty subsists in simultaneous intuition of the relation of parts, each to each, and of all to a whole: exciting an immediate and absolute complacency, without intervention, therefore, of any interest, sensual or intellectual.* The BEAUTIFUL is thus at once distinguished both from the

AGREEABLE, which is beneath it, and from the GOOD, which is above it:
for both these have an interest necessarily attached to them: both act on
the WILL, and excite a desire for the actual existence of the image or idea
contemplated: while the sense of beauty rests gratified in the mere
contemplation or intuition, regardless whether it be a fictitious Apollo,
or a real Antinous' (*BL* II 239).

7. καλόν *quasi* καλοῦν : '*beautiful*, as it were, *a calling on*'. As Shawcross
notes, STC's 'etymology is ingenious, but without foundation' (*BL* II
314, n 18).

27. from a LETTER TO JOHN KENYON (3 November 1814)

Jer. Taylor's[1] Discursive Intellect dazzle-darkened his Intuitions—:
the principle of becoming all Things to all men if by *any* means he
might save *any*, with him as with Burke,[2] thickened the protecting
Epidermis of the Tact-nerve of Truth into something too like a
Callus. But take him all in all, such a miraculous Combination of
Erudition broad, deep, and omnigenous,[3] of Logic subtle as well as
acute, and as robust as agile; of psychological Insight, so fine yet so
secure!—of public Prudence & practical *Sageness* that one ray of
creative Faith would have lit up and transfigured into Wisdom; and of
genuine Imagination, with it's streaming Face unifying all at one
moment like that of the setting Sun when thro' one interspace of blue
Sky no larger than itself it emerges from the Cloud to sink behind the
Mountain—but a face seen only at starts, when some Breeze from the
higher Air scatters for a moment the cloud of Butterfly Fancies,
which flutter around him like a moving Garment of ten thousand
Colors—(Now how shall I get out of this sentence?—The Tail is too
big to be taken up into the Coiler's Mouth—) well, as I was saying, I
believe, such a complex Man hardly shall we meet again—.

(*CL* III 541–2)

Notes

1. Jeremy Taylor (1613–67), a highly respected Anglican preacher and
prose stylist (whom the eighteenth-century dubbed 'the Shakespeare of
divines'), was the author of *The Rule and Exercise of Holy Living* (1650),
The Rule and Exercise of Holy Dying (1651), two volumes of sermons
(1651, 1653) and a book of prayers (1655). 'Lamb's copy of Jeremy

Taylor's *Polemicall Discourses* (London, 1674) is the most copiously annotated book—by Coleridge—that we have record of' (George Whalley). STC contrasts Taylor with Milton in Extract 38.
2. Edmund Burke (1729–97), enlightened politician and statesman best known today for his *Reflections on the Revolution in France* (1790).
3. *omnigenous*: 'of all kinds'.

28. from a LETTER TO JOSEPH COTTLE (7 March 1815)

I received by means of Mr Wade's Son your 'Messiah'[1] a few days ago: or by Mr Hood, I do not remember which. I have read about one half; and tho' I myself see your plan, yet I find it difficult to explain it to the Public, so as to make it consistent with the received conception of a Poem, call it epic, heroic, divine or what you like. The common end of all *narrative*, nay, of *all*, Poems is to convert a *series* into a *Whole*:[2] to make those events, which in real or imagined History move on in a *strait* Line, assume to our Understandings a *circular* motion—the snake with it's Tail in it's Mouth.[3] Hence indeed the almost flattering and yet appropriate Term, Poesy—i.e. poiësis = *making*.[4] Doubtless, to *his* eye, which alone comprehends all Past and all Future in one eternal Present, what to our short sight appears strait is but a part of the great Cycle—just as the calm Sea to us *appears* level, tho' it be indeed only a part of a *globe*. Now what the Globe is in Geography, *miniaturing* in order to *manifest* the Truth, such is a Poem to that Image of God, which we were created into, and which still seeks that Unity, or Revelation of the *One* in and by the *Many*, which reminds it, that tho' in order to be an individual Being it must go forth *from* God, yet as the receding from *him* is to *proceed* towards Nothingness and Privation, it must still at every step turn back toward him in order to *be* at all—Now a straight Line, continuously retracted forms of necessity a circular orbit. Now God's Will and Word CANNOT be frustrated. His aweful *Fiat*[5] was with ineffable awefulness applied to Man, when all things and all living Things, Man himself (as a mere animal) included, were called forth by the Universal—*Let there be*—and then the Breath of the Eternal super-added to make an *immortal* Spirit[6]—immortality being, as the author of the 'Wisdom of Solomon' profoundly expresses it, the only possible Reflex or Image of Eternity.[7] The Immortal Finite is the contracted Shadow of the Eternal Infinite.—Therefore *nothingness* or *Death*, to which we move as we recede from God & the Word, *cannot* be nothing; but that tremendous Medium between Nothing and true Being, which Scripture & inmost Reason present as most, most horrible! I have said this to shew you the connection between things in themselves comparatively trifling, and things the most important, by their derivation from common sources.—

(*CL* IV 545—6)

Notes

1. Joseph Cottle (1770—1853) was the Bristol bookseller who published STC's first two volumes of poetry and, as well, the first edition of *Lyrical Ballads* (1798). In 1799 Cottle, who fancied himself a poet, retired from business to devote his whole energy to the Muse. His works include *John the Baptist* (1801), *Alfred* (1801), *Fall of Cambria* (1809) and *Messiah* (1815). Cottle's literary pretensions are humorously lampooned by Byron in *English Bards and Scotch Reviewers* (1809) 384—91:

   > Another epic! who inflicts again
   > More books of blank upon the sons of men?
   > Boeotian Cottle, rich Bristowa's boast,
   > Imports old stories from the Cambrian coast,
   > And sends his goods to market—all alive!
   > Lines forty thousand, cantos twenty-five?
   > Fresh fish from Helicon! who'll buy, who'll buy?
   > The precious bargain's cheap—in faith, not I.

   On 1 June 1814 STC had written in high spirits to J. J. Morgan: 'By the bye, Jo. Cottle, who is *fizzling* & desperately disposed, spite of all poetic Decency, to *let* a third Epic, called Messiah (O such an Epic!!!) he gave me 10 pounds for reading thro', and correcting seven books out of TWENTY FOUR! & never galley-slave earned a penny so painfully and laboriously' (*CL* III 502).

2. The striking feature of STC's organicism, as noted above (Extract 13—A, n 2), is that he stresses both the parts *and* the whole, both the unity itself *and* the things unified. It is important to recognise that STC's organicism is not limited to literary criticism alone:
   (*a*) 'I have been, and am, most anxious to write a small, but full, plain, and popular work of the *doctrines* really contained in the Old and New Testament, shewing the bounds of each; and how, as living members of one organic body, each at once supports and limits the other, and how all are modified by it, and subordinated to *the whole*. I shall at every

important part point out the origination of some erroneous or heretical sect from *exclusive* attention to that one part, forgetting that there can be no absolutely predominant, self-existing, and separable *Part* in the living Body, of which Christ is the Head!—and having thus explained to the humblest capacity the cause and origin of all known sects, either from the neglect, or the ignorance, or the misinterpretation of Scripture by unpermitted partiality to particular parts, which, separated from the rest, and no longer modified by each and all of the living whole, cease to be themselves, as the eye plucked out ceased to be an eye' (Letter to T. A. Methuen, 2 August 1815; *CL* IV 582).

(*b*) 'But by the eternal Identity of Allness and Oneness, the whole Universe becomes an infinity of Concentric Circles—i.e. every thing has it's own system, besides it's relations to the Universe' (Letter to James Gillman, 10 November 1816; *CL* IV 689). The letter as a whole is devoted to exploring this point (and its ramifications) in great detail.

(*c*) The different mode in which the imagination is acted on/ Pantheon [i.e. the splendid building in Rome erected in 27 B.C. by M. Vipsanius Agrippa], the whole perceived in *perceived* harmony with the parts that compose it—where the Parts preserve their distinct individuality, this is Beauty simply—where they melt undistinguished into the Whole, it is Majestic Beauty—in Chr[istian cathedrals] the parts are in themselves sharply distinct, and this distinction counterbalanced only by their multitude & variety—while the Whole, and that there is a Whole produced, is altogether a Feeling, in which all the thousand several impressions lose themselves as in a universal Solvent' (Notes for a lecture on Dante, 11 March 1819; *CN* III 4498). The contrast between Graeco-Roman and Christian religious architecture is more fully stated in the eighth of STC's philosophical lectures: cf *PL* 256–7 and also Extract 29, n 1.

3. The same image appears in a marginal comment, probably written in January 1807, in which STC explains his motive in omitting from later editions the closing lines of the 1798 version of 'Frost at Midnight': 'The six last lines I omit because they destroy the rondo, and return upon itself of the Poem. Poems of this kind of length ought to be coiled with its' tail round its' head' (B. Ifor Evans, 'Coleridge's Copy of "Fears in Solitude"' *TLS* 18 April 1935 255). The six lines in question, omitted in all editions after 1798, are available in *CPW* I 243 n.

4. The belief that the poet is a *maker* (Greek ποιητής, poiëtes) and that, in his role as maker, he mirrors *in parvo* the divine act of the universal Creator is a staple of Renaissance poetics both on the Continent and in England. An example will make this point more clear and will, at the same time, serve to elucidate STC's meaning here. Like Sidney and Webbe before him and Jonson and Milton after him, George Puttenham firmly asserts in his *Arte of English Poesie* (1589) that the poet's is a high and

consecrated office: 'A Poet is as much to say as a maker. And our English name well conformes with the Greeke word, for of ποιεῖν, to make, they call a maker *Poeta*. Such as (by way of resemblance and reuerently) we may say of God; who without any trauell [travail] to his diuine imagination, made all the world of nought, nor also by any paterne or mould, as the Platonicks with their Idees do phantastically suppose. Euen so the very Poet makes and contriues out of his owne braine both the verse and matter of his poeme. . . . The premises considered, it giueth to the name and profession no smal dignitie and preheminence, aboue all other artificers, Scientificke or Mechanicall.' Cf also Extract 13–D, n 2, and Extract 40–B, n 7.

5. *Fiat*: 'Let there be'. Cf Genesis 1: 3 (Vulgate): *fiat lux*, 'let there be light'; also Genesis 1: 26 – 'And God said, Let us make man in our image, after our likeness . . .' (*AV*)

6. Genesis 2: 7 – 'And the Lord God formed man of the dust of the ground, and breathed into his nostrils the breath of life; and man became a living soul.' (*AV*)

7. Wisdom of Solomon 2: 23 – 'For God created man to be immortal, and made him to be an image of his own eternity' (*AV*). STC quotes the second half of this verse in a letter (11 April 1832) to H. B. Owen: cf *CL* VI 900. That STC (at least in his middle years) held the Wisdom of Solomon in high regard is apparent from a footnote in *A Lay Sermon* (1817): 'It were perhaps to be wished, that this work [i.e., Ecclesiasticus], and the wisdom of Solomon had alone received the honor of being accompaniments to the inspired writings, and that these should, with a short precautionary preface and a few notes have been printed in *all* our Bibles. The remaining books [of the Apocrypha] might without any loss have been left for the learned or for as many as were prompted by curiosity to purchase them, in a separate volume' (*CC* VI 129–30).

29. from a LETTER TO SAMUEL ROGERS (25 May 1815)

. . . the unhappy attempt at picture petrifactions by Bernini,[1] in whom a great genius was bewildered and lost by excess of fancy over imagination, the aggregative over the unifying faculty.

(*CL* IV 569)

Note

1. Gianlorenzo Bernini (1598–1680), Italian Baroque sculptor. Cf the following statement from STC's lecture on the Gothic Mind (27

January 1818): 'The contemplation of the works of antique [i.e., Graeco-Roman] art excites a feeling of elevated beauty, and exalted notions of the human self; but the Gothic architecture impresses the beholder with a sense of self-annihilation; he becomes, as it were, a part of the work contemplated. An endless complexity and variety are united into one whole, the plan of which is not distinct from the execution. A Gothic cathedral is the petrifaction of our religion. The only work of truly modern sculpture is the Moses of Michel Angelo' (*MC* 7). Cf also Extract 28, n 2.

30. from 'TO WILLIAM WORDSWORTH' (30 May 1815)[1]

Theme hard as high!

Of smiles spontaneous, and mysterious fears
(The first-born they of Reason and twin-birth),
Of tides obedient to external force,
And currents self-determined, as might seem,   15
Or by some inner Power; of moments awful,
Now in thy inner life, and now abroad,
When power streamed from thee, and thy soul received
The light reflected, as a light bestowed—
Of fancies fair, and milder hours of youth,   20
Hyblean murmurs of poetic thought
Industrious in its joy, in vales and glens
Native or outland, lakes and famous hills!
Or on the lonely high-road, when the stars
Were rising; or by secret mountain-streams,   25
The guides and the companions of thy way!

Of more than Fancy, of the Social Sense
Distending wide, and man beloved as man,
Where France in all her towns lay vibrating
Like some becalméd bark beneath the burst   30
Of Heaven's immediate thunder, when no cloud
Is visible, or shadow on the main.
For thou wert there, thine own brows garlanded,
Amid the tremor of a realm aglow,
Amid a mighty nation jubilant,   35
When from the general heart of human kind

Hope sprang forth like a full-born Deity!
—Of that dear Hope afflicted and struck down,
So summoned homeward, thenceforth calm and sure
From the dread watch-tower of man's absolute self,   40
With light unwaning on her eyes, to look
Far on—herself a glory to behold,
The Angel of the vision! Then (last strain)
Of Duty, chosen Laws controlling choice,
Action and joy!—An Orphic song indeed,   45
A song divine of high and passionate thoughts
To their own music chaunted!

                                        (*CPW* I 404–6)

Note

1. The subtitle of this poem is 'Composed on the Night after his Recitation of a Poem on the Growth of an Individual Mind'—i.e., Wordsworth's *The Prelude*. STC's poem, in its first form, was composed in January 1807 (cf *CPW* I 579–82); however, the lines reproduced above from the letter of 1815 vary widely from the comparable passage in the earlier version. There are, as one might expect, numerous echoes of *The Prelude* in STC's lines.

31. from a LETTER TO R. H. BRABANT (29 July 1815)[1]

I have given a full account (raisonné) of the Controversy concerning Wordsworth's Poems & Theory,[2] in which my name has been so constantly included—I have no doubt, that Wordsworth will be displeased[3]—but I have done my Duty to myself and to the Public, in (as I believe) compleatly subverting the Theory & in proving that the Poet himself has never acted on it except in particular Stanzas which are the Blots of his Compositions.[4]—One long passage[5]—a disquisition on the powers of association, with the History of the Opinions on this subject from Aristotle to Hartley, and on the generic difference between the faculties of Fancy and Imagination—I did not indeed altogether insert, but I certainly extended and elaborated, with a view to your perusal—as laying the foundation Stones of the

Constructive or Dynamic Philosophy in opposition to the merely mechanic—.[6]

(*CL* IV 579)

Notes

1. The subject of this letter is *Biographia Literaria*, which STC was then composing. Although the work was completed by mid-September 1815, it was not finally published until July 1817, over twenty months after it had been sent to the publisher, Rest Fenner.

2. STC is probably referring both to Wordsworth's theory of poetic diction in the various prefaces and appendices to *Lyrical Ballads*, and also to Wordsworth's Fancy—Imagination distinction in the Preface to *Poems* (1815); the latter is reprinted in the Appendix below. For STC's earlier view of Wordsworth's poetic theory, see Introduction, pp. 17–20 and Extract 5. The fully reasoned account of the discrepancies between Wordsworth's poetic theory and practice, mentioned in the letter to Brabant, is found in *Biographia* Chaps iv, xiv, xvii–xx, and xxii: cf Extract 33. For a fine assessment of the genesis and structure of *Biographia*, see Whalley (1953).

3. Cf Crabb Robinson's Diary for 4 December 1817: 'Coleridge's book [*Biographia*] has given him [Wordsworth] no pleasure, and he finds just fault with Coleridge for professing to write about himself and writing merely about Southey and Wordsworth. With the criticism on the poetry too he is not satisfied. The praise is extravagant and the censure inconsiderate. I recollected hearing Hazlitt say that Wordsworth would not forgive a single censure mingled with however great a mass of eulogy' (*HCR* I 213).

4. 'In short, were there excluded from Mr Wordsworth's poetic compositions all, that a literal adherence to the theory of his preface *would* exclude, two-thirds at least of the marked beauties of his poetry must be erased. For a far greater number of lines would be sacrificed than in any other recent poet . . .' (Chap xx; *BL* II 84).

5. Presumably Chaps iv–viii, although he may also have Chap xiii in mind.

6. The basis of of the 'Dynamic Philosophy' is laid in Chap xii: cf Extract 33–E. The 'merely mechanic' system is, of course, the empirical philosophy of Locke, Hume, Hartley *et al*.

32. from a LETTER TO LORD BYRON (15 October 1815)

. . . your Censure,[1] however extensive it should be, would be welcomed by me with unfeigned pleasure, as a mark of your kindness. The first Volume is entitled, Biographical Sketches of my own literary Life and Opinions, on Politics, Religion, Philosophy and the Theory of Poetry, my object to reduce Criticism to a system, by the deduction of Canons from Principles involved in our faculties.[2] The Chapters on the Γένεσις[3] and Functions of the Imagination, it's *contra*-distinction from the Fancy (as to which I unexpectedly find my convictions widely different from those of Mr Wordsworth, as explained in the new Preface to his Collection of his poems[4]) and the conditional Necessity of the Fine Arts.—The second Volume I entitle, SIBYLLINE LEAVES: as a collection of all the Poems, that are my own property, which I wish to have preserved.—

(*CL* VI 1037)

Notes

1. This letter inviting Byron's candid opinion accompanied presentation copies of *Biographia Literaria* and *Sibyline Leaves*.
2. 'The ultimate end of criticism is much more to establish the principles of writing, than to furnish *rules* how to pass judgement on what has been written by others; if indeed it were possible that the two could be separated' (Chap xviii; *BL* II 63). For STC on *methodology*, see his 'Essays on the Principles of Method' in the 1818 *Friend* (*CC* IV i 448–524); and for a helpful modern commentary and assessment of methodology in STC's critical thought, see Jackson (1969) 21–74.
3. Γένεσις: 'genesis: origin, source; mode of formation'.
4. The first collected edition of Wordsworth's poetry, together with a revised Preface explaining the principles of grouping the poems and, as well, a long disquisition on the distinction between Fancy and Imagination, was published in March 1815. Cf Appendix, below.

33. from *BIOGRAPHIA LITERARIA* (1815; published 1817)

(A) from Chapter i

I learnt from him,[1] that Poetry, even that of the loftiest and, seemingly, that of the wildest odes, had a logic of its own, as severe as that of science; and more difficult, because more subtle, more complex, and dependent on more, and more fugitive causes.[2] In the truly great poets, he would say, there is a reason assignable, not only for every word, but for the position of every word;[3] and I well remember that, availing himself of the synonimes to the Homer of Didymus,[4] he made us attempt to show, with regard to each, *why* it would not have answered the same purpose; and *wherein* consisted the peculiar fitness of the word in the original text.

In our own English compositions, (at least for the last three years of our school education,) he showed no mercy to phrase, metaphor, or image, unsupported by a sound sense, or where the same sense might have been conveyed with equal force and dignity in plainer words. Lute, harp, and lyre, muse, muses, and inspirations, Pegasus, Parnassus, and Hippocrene were all an abomination to him. In fancy I can almost hear him now, exclaiming '*Harp? Harp? Lyre? Pen and ink, boy, you mean! Muse, boy, Muse? Your Nurse's daughter, you mean! Pierian spring? Oh aye! the cloister-pump, I suppose!*' Nay, certain introductions, similes, and examples, were placed by name on a list of interdiction.

(BL 1 4–5)

Notes

1. *STC's note*: 'The Rev. James Bowyer, many years Head Master of the Grammar School, Christ's Hospital.' James Boyer (1736–1814); note that STC misspells Boyer's name here, although he spells it correctly (e.g.) in *CN* 1 1649 and 1726. In Extract 9 a similar remark is ascribed, not to Boyer, but to Edward Young. There is a manuscript biography of Boyer, perhaps by his son, in the Bristol Library.

2. Later, in the 'Treatise on Method' (1818), STC wrote that 'Those who tread the enchanted ground of POETRY, oftentimes do not even suspect that there is such a thing as *Method* to guide their steps', and then later in the same work: 'Let it not after this be said that Poetry—and under the word Poetry we will now take leave to include all the Works of the higher Imagination, whether operating by measured sound, or by the harmonies of form and colour, or by words, the more immediate and universal representatives of Thought—is not strictly Methodical; nay, does not owe its whole charm, and all its beauty, and all its power, to the Philosophical Principles of Method' (*S. T. Coleridge's Treatise on Method as Published in the Encyclopaedia Metropolitana*, ed. A. D. Snyder, London: Constable, 1934, 25, 35–6).

3. Cf also *BL* 1 14–15: 'Our genuine admiration of a great poet is a

continuous *under-current* of feeling; it is everywhere present, but seldom anywhere as a separate excitement. I was wont boldly to affirm, that it would be scarcely more difficult to push a stone out from the pyramids with the bare hand, than to alter a word, or the position of a word, in Milton or Shakespeare, (in their most important works at least,) without making the author say something else, or something worse, than he does say.'

4. Didymus of Alexandria (*c.* 65 BC–AD 10) wrote a commentary on the poems of Homer embodying the opinions of a number of earlier commentators.

(B) from Chapter ii

I have often thought, that it would be neither uninstructive nor unamusing to analyze, and bring forward into distinct consciousness, that complex feeling, with which readers in general take part against the author, in favor of the critic; and the readiness with which they apply to *all* poets the old sarcasm of Horace upon the scribblers of his time: 'Genus irritabile vatum.'[1] A debility and dimness of the imaginative power, and a consequent necessity of reliance on the immediate impressions of the senses, do, we well know, render the mind liable to superstition and fanaticism. Having a deficient portion of internal and proper warmth, minds of this class seek in the crowd *circum fana*[2] for a warmth in common, which they do not possess singly. [. . .] But where the ideas are vivid, and there exists an endless power of combining and modifying them, the feelings and affections blend more easily and intimately with these ideal creations than with the objects of the senses; the mind is affected by thoughts, rather than by things;[3] and only then feels the requisite interest even for the most important events and accidents, when by means of meditation they have passed into *thoughts*. The sanity of the mind is between supersitition with fanaticism on the one hand, and enthusiasm with indifference and a diseased slowness to action on the other. For the conceptions of the mind may be so vivid and adequate, as to preclude that impulse to the realizing of them, which is strongest and most restless in those, who possess more than mere *talent*, (or the faculty of appropriating and applying the knowledge of others,) yet still want something of the creative, and self-sufficing power of absolute *Genius.*[4] For this reason therefore, they are men of *commanding* genius. While the former rest content between thought and reality, as it were in an intermundium[5] of which their own living spirit supplies the *substance*, and their imagination the ever-varying *form*; the latter must impress their preconceptions on the world without, in order to present them back to their own view with the satisfying degree of clearness, distinctness, and individuality.

(*BL* I 19—20)

Notes

1. *Genus irritabile vatum*: 'the peevish race of poets' (Horace, *Epistles* II ii 102).

2. *circum fana*: 'round about the temples'. 'Coleridge is likely to have the semantic link with "fanaticism" in mind, also' (John Beer).

3. Writing as early as February 1801 to Humphry Davy, STC noted: 'I have been *thinking* vigorously during my Illness—so that I cannot say, that my long long wakeful nights have been all lost to me. The subject of my meditations has been the Relations of Thoughts to Things, in the language of Hume, of Ideas to Impressions . . .' (*CL* II 671–2). Cf also the letter to Thomas Clarkson of 13 October 1806: *CL* II 1193–9. There is also an important statement in *Biographia* Chap v: 'These conjectures, however, concerning the mode in which our perceptions originated, could not alter the natural difference of *things* and *thoughts*. In the former, the cause appeared wholly external, while in the latter, sometimes our will interfered as the producing or determining cause, and sometimes our nature seemed to act by a mechanism of its own, without any conscious effort of the will, or even against it. Our inward experiences were thus arranged in three separate classes, the passive sense, or what the school-men call the merely receptive quality of mind; the voluntary; and the spontaneous, which holds the middle place between both' (*BL* I 66). The relationship of a *thought* to a *thing* was a subject of abiding interest to STC; it is, indeed, a subject integral to his whole philosophy and is intimately connected with other polarities—e.g., Subject and Object, 'I Am' and 'It Is', Reason and Understanding, and (of course) Imagination and Fancy. Two helpful reconstructions of this aspect of STC's thought are McFarland (1969) and Barfield (1972).

4. 'Talent, lying in the understanding, is often inherited; genius, being the action of reason and imagination, rarely or never' (*TT* 21 May 1830). In Lecture v (18 January 1819) of his series on the history of philosophy, STC writes: 'To have a genius is to live in the universal, to know no self but that which is reflected not only from the faces of all around us, our fellow creatures, but reflected from the flowers, the trees, the beasts, yea from the very surface of the [*waters and the*] sands of the desert. A man of genius finds a reflex to himself, were it only in the mystery of being' (*PL* 179). Cf also McKenzie (1939) 64–8 for a discussion of STC's theory of *genius*.

5. *intermundium*: 'a space between two worlds'.

(C) from Chapter iv

I was in my twenty-fourth year,[1] when I had the happiness of knowing Mr Wordsworth personally, and while memory lasts, I shall hardly forget the sudden effect produced on my mind, by his recitation of a manuscript poem, which still remains unpublished. . . .[2] It was not however the freedom from false taste, whether as to common defects, or to those more properly his own, which made so unusual an impression on my feelings immediately, and subsequently on my judgement. It was the union of deep feeling with profound thought;[3] the fine balance of truth in observing, with the imaginative faculty of modifying the objects observed; and above all the original gift of spreading the tone, the *atmosphere*, and with it the depth and height of the ideal world around forms, incidents, and situations, of which, for the common view, custom had bedimmed all the lustre, had dried up the sparkle and the dew drops. 'To find no contradiction in the union of old and new; to contemplate the ANCIENT of days and all his works with feelings as fresh, as if all had then sprang forth at the first creative fiat; characterizes the mind that feels the riddle of the world, and may help to unravel it. To carry on the feelings of childhood into the powers of manhood;[4] to combine the child's sense of wonder and novelty with appearances, which every day for perhaps forty years had rendered familiar;

> "With sun and moon and stars throughout the year,
>   And man and woman;"[5]

this is the character and privilege of genius, and one of the marks which distinguish genius from talents. And therefore is it the prime merit of genius and its most unequivocal mode of manifestation, so to represent familiar objects as to awaken in the minds of others a kindred feeling concerning them and that freshness of sensation which is the constant accompaniment of mental, no less than of bodily, convalescence.[6] Who has not a thousand times seen snow fall on water? Who has not watched it with a new feeling, from the time that he has read Burns' comparison of sensual pleasure

> "To snow that falls upon a river
> A moment white—then gone for ever!"[7]

In poems, equally as in philosophic disquisitions, genius produces the strongest impressions of novelty, while it rescues the most admitted truths from the impotence caused by the very circumstance of their universal admission. Truths of all others the most awful and mysterious, yet being at the same time of universal interest, are too often considered as *so* true, that they lose all the life and efficiency of truth, and lie bed-ridden in the dormitory of the soul, side by side with the most despised and exploded errors.'[8] THE FRIEND, p. 76, No. 5.[9]

This excellence, which in all Mr Wordsworth's writings is more or less predominant, and which constitutes the character of his mind, I no sooner felt, then I sought to understand. Repeated meditations led me first to suspect, (and a more intimate analysis of the human faculties, their appropriate marks, functions, and effects matured my conjecture into full conviction,) that fancy and imagination were two distinct and widely different faculties, instead of being, according to the general belief,[10] either two names with one meaning, or, at furthest, the lower and higher degree of one and the same power. It is not, I own, easy to conceive a more opposite[11] translation of the Greek *Phantasia* than the Latin Imaginatio;[12] but it is equally true that in all societies there exists an instinct of growth, a certain collective, unconscious good sense working progressively to desynonymize those words originally of the same meaning, which the conflux of dialects had supplied to the more homogeneous languages, as the Greek and German:[13] and which the same cause, joined with accidents of translation from original works of different countries, occasion in mixt languages like our own. The first and most important point to be proved is, that two conceptions perfectly distinct are confused under one and the same word, and (this done) to appropriate that word exclusively to one meaning, and the synonyme (should there be one) to the other. But if (as will be often the case in the arts and sciences) no synonyme exists, we must either invent or borrow a word. In the present instance the appropriation has already begun, and been legitimated in the derivative adjective: Milton had a highly *imaginative*, Cowley a very *fanciful* mind.[14] If therefore I should succeed in establishing the actual existences of two faculties generally different, the nomenclature would be at once determined. To the faculty by which I had characterized Milton, we should confine the term *imagination*; while the other would be con- tradistinguished as *fancy*. Now were it once fully ascertained, that this division is no less grounded in nature, than that of delirium from mania,[15] or Otway's

'Lutes, lobsters, seas of milk, and ships of amber,'[16]

from Shakespear's

'What! have his daughters brought him to this pass?'[17]

or from the preceding apostrophe to the elements;[18] the theory of the fine arts, and of poetry in particular, could not, I thought, but derive some additional and important light. It would in its immediate effects furnish a torch of guidance to the philosophical critic; and ultimately to the poet himself. In energetic minds, truth soon changes by domestication into power; and from directing in the discrimination and appraisal of the product, becomes influencive in the production. To admire on principle, is the only way to imitate without loss of originality.

It has been already hinted, that metaphysics and psychology have long been my hobby-horse. But to have a hobby-horse, and to be vain of it, are so commonly found together, that they pass almost for the same. I trust therefore, that there will be more good humour than contempt, in the smile with which the reader chastises my self-complacency, if I confess myself uncertain, whether the satisfaction from the perception of a truth new to myself may not have been rendered more poignant by the conceit, that it would be equally so to the public. There was a time, certainly, in which I took some little credit to myself, in the belief that I had been the first of my countrymen,[19] who had pointed out the diverse meaning of which the two terms were capable, and analyzed the faculties to which they should be appropriated. Mr W. Taylor's recent volume[20] of synonymes I have not yet seen; but his specification of the terms in question has been clearly shown to be both insufficient and erroneous by Mr Wordsworth in the Preface added to the late collection of his 'Lyrical Ballads and other poems.'[21] The explanation which Mr Wordsworth has himself given will be found to differ from mine, chiefly perhaps, as our objects are different. It could scarcely indeed happen otherwise, from the advantage I have enjoyed of frequent conversation with him on a subject to which a poem of his own first directed my attention, and my conclusions concerning which, he had made more lucid to myself by many happy instances drawn from the operation of natural objects on the mind. But it was Mr

Wordsworth's purpose to consider the influences of fancy and imagination as they are manifested in poetry, and from the different effects to conclude their diversity in kind;[22] while it is my object to investigate the seminal principle, and then from the kind to deduce the degree. My friend has drawn a masterly sketch of the branches with their *poetic* fruitage. I wish to add the trunk, and even the roots as far as they lift themselves above ground, and are visible to the naked eye of our common consciousness.

(*BL* 1 58–64)

Notes

1. I.e., September 1795. For a fine assessment of the intellectual interrelationship between STC and Wordsworth, see Prickett (1970).
2. Wordsworth's 'Guilt and Sorrow', composed between 1791 and 1794, was not published until 1842; part of the poem did, however, appear in *Lyrical Ballads* under the title 'The Female Vagrant'. Cf *The Salisbury Plain Poems of William Wordsworth*, ed. S. Gill (Hassocks, Sussex: Harvester Press, Ithaca, N.Y.: Cornell University Press, 1975).
3. Cf Introduction, p. 12, and Extract 12.
4. Cf Extract 20.
5. Lines 5–6 (*variatim*) of Milton's 'Sonnet XXII' ('Cyriack, this three years' day these eyes . . .').
6. Cf the early statement in a letter to Josiah Wedgwood (1 November 1800): 'Often when in a deep Study I have walked to the window & remained there *looking without seeing*, all at once the Lake of Keswick & the fantastic Mountains of Borrodale at the head of it have entered into my mind with a suddenness, as if I had been snatched out of Cheapside & placed for the first time on the spot where I stood.—And that is a delightful Feeling—these Fits & Trances of *Novelty* received from a long known Object' (*CL* 1 644). Cf also Extract 20. There are also similar statements in Shelley's *Defence of Poetry* (1821): 'Poetry lifts the veil from the hidden beauty of the world, and makes familiar objects be as if they were not familiar; it reproduces all that it represents . . .'; Poetry 'makes us the inhabitants of a world to which the familiar world is chaos. It reproduces the common universe of which we are portions and percipients, and it purges from our inward sight the film of familiarity which obscures from us the wonder of our being. It compels us to feel that which we perceive, and to imagine that which we know. It creates anew the universe, after it has been annihilated in our minds by the recurrence of impressions blunted by reiteration.'

7. Variant of Robert Burns's 'Tam O'Shanter' 61–2:

> Or like the snow-fall in the river,
> One moment white—then melts for ever.

8. Cf the opening aphorism in *Aids to Reflection* (1825): 'In philosophy equally as in poetry, it is the highest and most useful prerogative of genius to produce the strongest impressions of novelty, while it rescues admitted truths from the neglect caused by the very circumstance of their universal admission. Extremes meet. Truths, of all others the most awful and interesting, are too often considered as *so* true, that they lose all the power of truth, and lie bed-ridden in the dormitory of the soul, side by side with the most despised and exploded errors' (*AR* 1). The earliest statement of this belief occurs in a notebook entry of April 1805: *CN* II 2535.

9. Actually pp. 76–7 (*variatim*) of the fifth number (14 September 1809) of *The Friend*: *CC* IV ii 73–4.

10. Cf Introduction, pp. 1–2.

11. Although 'opposite' is the correct reading, the sense suggests that STC originally wrote 'apposite'.

12. *Phantasia*: 'a making visible, displaying'. *Imaginatio*: 'a mental image'—e.g., *libidinum imaginationes in somno*, 'mental images of desires in sleep'.

13. Cf *CN* III 4247: 'Homogeneous Languages favorable to Metaphysics—exemplified in the Greek and in the German. And why?—the Words, as percipere, i.e. capere per sensus [to perceive, that is, to apprehend through the senses]; concipere, i.e. capere aliquid *cum* alio vel aliis [to conceive, that is, to apprehend *with* another or through others]—Einbildung, i.e. formatio in unum [Imagination, that is, formation into a whole]—bedingt, bedingung [conditioned, stipulated], i.e. what presupposes some thing as the condition of its existence, i.e. *be-thinged*—all are like a series of historical medals—the stamps remain—while in derivative Languages they are mere *Coins*, current for so much, by a *credit*, without any distinct knowledge or reference. It was given One—& *it goes* in our Market.—Hence Indistinctness—& as the human mind still craves for distinctness, thence the turning to & resting wholly in *imagible* things/ but as there must likewise be a sense of indefiniteness (or all activity would cease) this is wasted on what is called common sense—i.e. the Shells, or the Wampum, or the Minted Coin, or the Bank, or Country, or Town Notes, which happen at *the moment* to be current & in credit, tho' the month after a Bankruptcy shews the hollowness of the Foundation.' Miss Coburn (*CN* III 4247 n) writes: 'In its (merely) apparent disjointedness this whole entry with its elided arguments based on the sense of various levels of language and

imagination, and its rejection of "common sense", is moving swiftly towards the dynamic idea of imagination, as e.g. in [*Biographia*] Chap VII: *BL* I 86.' With the Notebook entry above which dates probably from April 1812, compare Extracts 13–K, 33–D, 35–A and 40–C.

14. Abraham Cowley (1618–67), a contemporary of Milton, was a militant Royalist during the Civil Wars. He wrote a number of prose works; his major poems are 'The Mistress' (1647), and his 'imitations' of the Pindaric Ode form and the biblical epic 'Davideis', both of the latter being included in *Miscellanies* (1656).

As early as October 1800 STC had included Cowley among those poets 'who have written delightful Poems with good sense, & the common feelings of *all* good & sensible men; but without the passion, or the peculiar feelings, & stronger excitements of the poetic character—Deserted Village, but especially Cowley's Cromwell—' (*CN* I 829; cf also *BL* II 97). The references are to Oliver Goldsmith's 'The Deserted Village' (1770) and Cowley's 'Vision concerning his late pretended Highness Cromwell the wicked' (1661), a prose piece with verses interspersed.

There are two comments of 1815 which express much the same view of Cowley and at the same time explicitly contrast him with Milton. First, in a letter to Wordsworth (30 May 1815), STC writes: 'After the opinions, I had given publicly, for the preference of the Lycidas (moral no less than poetical) to Cowley's Monody, I could not have printed it* consistently—. It is for the Biographer, not the Poet, to give the *accidents* of *individual* Life. Whatever is not representative, generic, may be indeed most poetically exprest, but is not Poetry' (*CL* IV 572). [**it*: STC's poem 'To William Wordsworth' (Extract 30) written in January 1807 after he had heard Wordsworth recite *The Prelude*. Wordsworth, concerned that STC might publish the poem (in fact he did, in 1817, under the title 'To a Gentleman'), wrote on 22 May 1815 to ask him to refrain from so doing. STC replied, in the letter quoted above, that it would be inconsistent with his own poetic principles to publish it, for his poem on Wordsworth—*like* Cowley's 'On the Death of Mr William Hervey', but *unlike* Milton's 'Lycidas'—was versified biography and dealt with a particular experience *per se* rather than with that particular event as an illustration of generic experience. And Poetry, as he states in *Biographia* Chap xvii, 'is essentially *ideal*, it avoids and excludes all *accident*' (BL II 33; cf ibid. 106–7).] Secondly, in *Biographia* Chap i, having just discussed Milton, STC describes the characteristic fault of Cowley and his school as that of expressing 'the most fantastic out-of-the-way thoughts, but in the most pure and genuine mother English'; they characteristically 'sacrificed the passion and passionate flow of poetry, to the subtleties of intellect, and to the starts of wit'—in short, they 'sacrificed the heart to the head' (*BL* I 15; cf also ibid. II 66–7,

209). Cf also Dr Johnson's strictures on Cowley and the 'wit' of the Metaphysical School in his *Life of Cowley* (quoted in part in Extract 16, n 13).

To return to the extract from *Biographia* Chap iv: Not all readers are prepared to treat STC's ascription of *fancy* to Cowley and *imagination* to Milton with the seriousness that I believe it merits. T. S. Eliot (1933), for example, argues that 'The distinction is too simple. The last sentence, "Milton has a highly imaginative, Cowley a very fanciful mind", should be enough to arouse suspicion. It represents a course of argument which is specious. You assert a distinction, you select two authors who illustrate it to your satisfaction, and you ignore the negative instances or difficult cases. If Coleridge had written, "Spenser had a highly imaginative, Donne a very fanciful mind", the assumed superiority of imagination to fancy might not appear quite so immediately convincing. Not only Cowley, but all the metaphysical poets, had very fanciful minds, and if you removed the fancy and left only imagination, as Coleridge appears to use these terms, you would have no metaphysical poetry. The distinction is admittedly a distinction of value; the term "fancy" is really made derogatory, just applicable to clever verse that you do not like' (58; cf also ibid. 29). It may of course seem to readers familiar with Eliot's own essays that he employs a not dissimilar method of argument in his effort to establish the reputation of the Metaphysical poets—at Milton's expense. For a brief reply to Eliot, see Richards (1934, 3rd ed. 1962) 73—4, n 1.

15. Cf Extracts 16 and 51—E.

16. Thomas Otway, *Venice Preserv'd* (1682) v i 369: 'Lutes, laurels, seas of milk and ships of amber'. The word *lobsters* has probably crept into the quotation here from Butler's *Hudibras*, another favourite example of Fancy: cf Extracts 13—C and 51—E. Like Chatterton, Otway was a vogue figure of the gifted poet killed by an indifferent world; he died destitute at 33.

17. *King Lear* III iv 63.

18. Ibid. III ii 1ff.

19. Cf Bate and Bullitt (1945) and Wasserman (1949). Notice, however, that STC here uses the past tense ('There *was* a time . . .'), and remember his observation in Extract 13—F, 'I fear not him for a Critic who can confound a Fellow-thinker with a Compiler.'

20. W. Taylor, *British Synonymes Discriminated* (London, 1813).

21. Cf Appendix.

22. Wordsworth's declared intention in the 1815 Preface was to justify the classification of his poems: 'Certain poems are placed according to the powers of mind, in the Author's conception, predominant in the production of them; *predominant*, which implies the exertion of other faculties in less degree. Where there is more imagination than fancy in a

poem, it is placed under the head of imagination, and *vice versa.*'

(D) from Chapter vii

Let us consider what we do when we leap. We first resist the gravitating power by an act purely voluntary, and then by another act, voluntary in part, we yield to it in order to light on the spot, which we had previously proposed to ourselves.[1] Now let a man watch his mind while he is composing; or, to take a still more common case, while he is trying to recollect a name;[2] and he will find the process completely analogous. Most of my readers will have observed a small water-insect on the surface of rivulets, which throws a cinque-spotted shadow fringed with prismatic colours on the sunny bottom of the brook; and will have noticed, how the little animal *wins* its way up against the stream, by alternate pulses of active and passive motion, now resisting the current, and now yielding to it in order to gather strength and a momentary *fulcrum* for a further propulsion.[3] This is no unapt emblem of the mind's self-experience in the act of thinking. There are evidently two powers at work, which relatively to each other are active and passive; and this is not possible without an intermediate faculty, which is at once both active and passive. (In philosophical language, we must denominate this intermediate faculty in all its degrees and determinations, the IMAGINATION. But, in common language, and especially on the subject of poetry, we appropriate the name to a superior degree of the faculty, joined to a superior voluntary controul over it.)

(*BL* I 85–6)

Notes

1. Cf *CN* III 3708 (10 March 1810): 'I had been talking of the association of Ideas, and endeavoring to convince an Idolator of Hume & Hartley, that this was strictly speaking a law only of the memory & imagination, of the *Stuff out* of which we make our conceptions & perceptions, not of the thinking faculty, by which we make them—that it was as the force of gravitation to leaping to any given point—without gravitation this would be impossible, and yet equally impossible to leap except by a *power* counteracting first, and then using the *force* of gravitation. . . .'

2. Cf Extract 39–B.

3. Cf Alexander Pope, 'First Epistle of the First Book of Horace Imitated' (1738) 33–4:

   > Back to my native Moderation slide,
   > And win my way by yielding to the tyde.

(E) from Chapter xii

The first range of hills,[1] that encircles the scanty vale of human life, is the horizon for the majority of its inhabitants. On *its* ridges the common sun is born and departs. From *them* the stars rise, and touching *them* they vanish. By the many, even this range, the natural limit and bulwark of the vale, is but imperfectly known. Its higher ascents are too often hidden by mists and clouds from uncultivated swamps, which few have courage or curiosity to penetrate. To the multitude below these vapors appear, now as the dark haunts of terrific agents, on which none may intrude with impunity; and now all *a-glow*, with colors not their own, they are gazed at as the splendid palaces of happiness and power. But in all ages there have been a few, who measuring and sounding the rivers of the vale at the feet of their furthest inaccessible falls have learned, that the sources must be far higher and far inward; a few, who even in the level streams have detected elements, which neither the vale itself or the surrounding mountains contained or could supply. How and whence to these thoughts, these strong probabilities, the ascertaining vision, the intuitive knowledge may finally supervene, can be learnt only by the fact.[2] I might oppose to the question the words with which Plotinus supposes NATURE to answer a similar difficulty. 'Should any one interrogate her, how she works, if graciously she vouchsafe to listen and speak, she will reply, it behoves thee not to disquiet me with interrogatories, but to understand in silence even as I am silent, and work without words.'[3]

Likewise in the fifth book of the fifth *Ennead*, speaking of the highest and intuitive knowledge as distinguished from the discursive, or in the language of Wordsworth,

'The vision and the faculty divine;'[4]

he says: 'it is not lawful to enquire from whence it sprang, as if it were a thing subject to place and motion, for it neither approached hither, nor again departs from hence to some other place; but it either appears to us or it does not appear. So that we ought not to pursue it with a view of detecting its secret source, but to watch in quiet till it suddenly shines upon us; preparing ourselves for the blessed spectacle as the eye waits patiently for the rising sun.'[5] They and they only can acquire the philosophic imagination, the sacred power of self-intuition, who within themselves can interpret and understand the symbol, that the wings of the air-sylph are forming within the skin of the caterpillar; those only, who feel in their own spirits the same instinct, which impels the chrysalis of the horned fly to leave room in its involucrum for antennæ yet to come. They know and feel, that the *potential* works *in* them, even as the *actual* works on them![6] In short, all the organs of sense are framed for a corresponding world of sense; and we have it. All the organs of spirit are framed for a correspondent world of spirit: though the latter organs are not developed in all alike. But they exist in all, and their first appearance discloses itself in the *moral* being.[7]

[.   .   .   .   .   .   ]

THESIS VI.[8]

This principle,[9] and so characterized, manifests itself in the SUM or I AM ; which I shall hereafter indiscriminately express by the words spirit, self, and self-consciousness. In this, and in this alone, object and subject,[10] being and knowing are identical, each involving, and supposing the other. In other words, it is a subject which becomes a subject by the act of constructing itself objectively to itself; but which never is an object except for itself, and only so far as by the very same act it becomes a subject. It may be described therefore as a perpetual self-duplication of one and the same power into object and subject, which presuppose each other, and can only exist as antitheses.

SCHOLIUM. If a man be asked how he *knows* that he is? he can only answer, sum quia sum.[11] But if (the absoluteness of this certainty having been admitted) he be again asked, how he, the individual person, came to be, then in relation to the ground of his *existence*, not to the ground of his *knowledge* of that existence, he might reply, sum quia Deus est, or still more philosophically, sum quia in Deo sum.[12]

But if we elevate our conception to the absolute self, the great eternal I AM, then the principle of being, and of knowledge, of idea, and of reality; the ground of existence, and the ground of the knowledge of existence, are absolutely identical, Sum quia sum;[13] I am, because I affirm myself to be; I affirm myself to be, because I am.

THESIS VII.

If then I know myself only through myself, it is contradictory to require any other predicate of self, but that of self-consciousness. Only in the self-consciousness of a spirit is there the required identity of object and of representation; for herein consists the essence of a spirit, that it is self-representative. If therefore this be the one only immediate truth, in the certainty of which the reality of our collective knowledge is grounded, it must follow that the spirit in all the objects which it views, views only itself. If this could be proved, the immediate reality of all intuitive knowledge would be assured. It has been shown, that a spirit is that, which is its own object, yet not originally an object, but an absolute subject for which all, itself included, may become an object. It must therefore be an ACT; for every object is, as an *object*, dead, fixed, incapable in itself of any action, and necessarily finite. Again the spirit (originally the identity of object and subject) must in some sense dissolve this identity, in order to be conscious of it: fit alter et idem.[14] But this implies an act, and it follows therefore that intelligence or self-consciousness is impossible, except by and in a will. The self-conscious spirit therefore is a will; and freedom must be assumed as a *ground* of philosophy, and can never be deduced from it.

THESIS VIII.
Whatever in its origin is objective, is likewise as such necessarily finite. Therefore, since the spirit is not originally an object, and as the subject exists in antithesis to an object, the spirit cannot originally be finite. But neither can it be a subject without becoming an object, and, as it is originally the identity of both, it can be conceived neither as infinite nor finite exclusively, but as the most original union of both. In the existence, in the reconciling, and the recurrence of this contradiction consists the process and mystery of production and life.

THESIS IX.
This principium commune essendi et cognoscendi,[15] as subsisting in a WILL, or primary ACT of self-duplication, is the mediate or indirect principle of every science; but it is the immediate and direct principle of the ultimate science alone, i.e. of transcendental philosophy alone. For it must be remembered, that all these Theses refer solely to one of the two Polar Sciences, namely, to that which commences with, and rigidly confines itself within, the subjective, leaving the objective (as far as it is exclusively objective) to natural philosophy, which is its opposite pole. In its very idea therefore as a systematic knowledge of our collective KNOWING, (scientia scientiæ)[16] it involves the necessity of some one highest principle of knowing, as at once the source and accompanying form in all particular acts of intellect and perception. This, it has been shown, can be found only in the act and evolution of self-consciousness. We are not investigating an absolute principium

essendi; for then, I admit, many valid objections might be started against our theory; but an absolute principium cognoscendi. The result of both the sciences, or their equatorial point, would be the principle of a total and undivided philosophy, as, for prudential reasons, I have chosen to anticipate in the Scholium to Thesis VI. and the note subjoined. In other words, philosophy would pass into religion, and religion become inclusive of philosophy. We begin with the I KNOW MYSELF, in order to end with the absolute I AM. We proceed from the SELF, in order to lose and find all self in GOD.

THESIS X.

The transcendental philosopher does not inquire, what ultimate ground of our knowledge there may lie out of our knowing, but what is the last in our knowing itself, beyond which we cannot pass. The principle of our knowing is sought within the sphere of our knowing. It must be something therefore, which can itself be known. It is asserted only, that the act of self-consciousness is for us the source and principle of all our possible knowledge.[17] Whether abstracted from us there exists any thing higher and beyond this primary self-knowing, which is for us the form of all our knowing, must be decided by the result. [...] ... we must arrive at the same principle from which as transcendental philosophers we set out; that is, in a self-consciousness in which the principium essendi does not stand to the principium cognoscendi in the relation of cause to effect, but both the one and the other are co-inherent and identical. Thus the true system of natural philosophy places the sole reality of things in an ABSOLUTE, which is at once causa sui et effectus, πατηρ αὐτοπάτωρ, υἱὸς ἑαυτοῦ[18]—in the absolute identity of subject and object, which it calls nature, and which in its highest power is nothing else than self-conscious will or intelligence. In this sense the position of Malbranche,[19] that we see all things in God, is a strict philosophical truth; and equally true is the assertion of Hobbs, of Hartley, and of their masters in ancient Greece,[20] that all real knowledge supposes a prior sensation.[21] For sensation itself is but vision nascent, not the cause of intelligence, but intelligence itself revealed as an earlier power in the process of self-construction.

$$Μάκαρ, ἵλαθί μοι$$
$$Πάτερ, ἵλαθί μοι$$
$$Εἰ παρὰ κόσμον,$$
$$Εἰ παρὰ μοῖραν$$

Τῶν σῶν ἔθιγον![22]

Bearing then this in mind, that intelligence is a self-developement, not a quality supervening to a substance, we may abstract from all *degree*, and for the purpose of philosophic construction reduce it to *kind*, under the idea of an indestructible power with two opposite and counteracting forces, which by a metaphor borrowed from astronomy, we may call the centrifugal and centripetal forces. The intelligence in the one tends to *objectize* itself, and in the other to *know* itself in the object. It will be hereafter my business to construct by a series of intuitions the progressive schemes, that must follow from such a power with such forces, till I arrive at the fulness of the *human* intelligence.[23] For my present purpose, I *assume* such a power as my principle, in order to deduce from it a faculty, the generation, agency, and application of which form the contents of the ensuing chapter.[24]

[. . . . . .]

I shall now proceed to the nature and genesis of the imagination; but I must first take leave to notice, that after a more accurate perusal of Mr Wordsworth's remarks on the imagination, in his preface[25] to the new edition of his poems, I find that my conclusions are not so consentient with his as, I confess, I had taken for granted.[26] In an article contributed by me to Mr Southey's Omniana, on the soul and its organs of sense, are the following sentences.[27] 'These (the human faculties) I would arrange under the different senses and powers: as the eye, the ear, the touch, &c.; the imitative power, voluntary and automatic; the imagination, or shaping and modifying power; the fancy, or the aggregative and associative power; the understanding, or the regulative, substantiating and realizing power; the speculative reason, vis theoretica et scientifica, or the power by which we produce or aim to produce unity, necessity, and universality in all our knowledge by means of principles a priori;[28] the will, or practical reason; the faculty of choice (*Germanice*, Willkür) and (distinct both from the moral will and the choice,) the *sensation* of volition, which I have found reason to include under the head of single and double touch.' To this, as far as it relates to the subject in question, namely the words (*the aggregative and associative power*) Mr Wordsworth's 'only objection is that the definition is too general. To aggregate and to associate, to evoke and to combine, belong as well to the imagination as to the fancy.'[29] I reply, that if, by the power of evoking and combining, Mr Wordsworth means the same as, and no more than, I meant by the aggregative and associative, I continue to deny, that it belongs at all to the imagination; and I am disposed to conjecture, that he has mistaken the co-presence of fancy with imagination for the operation of the latter singly.[30] A man may work with two different tools at the same moment; each has its share in the work, but the work effected by each is distinct and different. But it will probably appear in the next Chapter, that deeming it necessary to go back much further than Mr Wordsworth's subject required or permitted, I have attached a meaning to both fancy and imagination, which he had not in view, at least while he was writing that preface. He will judge. Would to Heaven, I might meet with many such readers.[31] I will conclude with the words of Bishop Jeremy Taylor: he to whom all things are one, who draweth all things to one, and seeth all things in one, may enjoy true peace and rest of spirit. (*J. Taylor's* VIA PACIS).[32]

(*BL* I 164—7, 183—8, 193—4)

Notes

1. For a similar image, see Extracts 1 and 20. The extended metaphor here functions (in Appleyard's words) as an appeal 'to experience to confirm the difference between the spontaneous and the philosophic consciousness. The capacity for the higher kind of knowledge is not to be acquired by labour and searching . . .' (191).

2. Appleyard (1965) writes: 'What more precisely is the specific power which these descriptions attempt to suggest? The key word seems to be intuition, that is, intellectual intuition, the capacity to know truths without a medium' (191).

3. *Enneads* III viii 4. Plotinus (*c.* AD. 203—62) was the chief exponent of Alexandrian Neoplatonism.

4. *The Excursion* (1814) I 79.

5. *Enneads* V v 8.

6. Cf *CN* III 4088 (May–July 1811): 'And what is Faith?—it is to the Spirit of Man the same Instinct, which impels the chrysalis of the horned fly to build its involucrum as long again as itself to make room for the Antennæ, which are to come, tho' they never yet have been—O the *Potential* works *in* us even as the Present mood works *on* us!—'

7. Cf Extract 22.

8. Sara Coleridge (STC's daughter) points out in the notes to her critical edition of *Biographia* (London, 1847) that these Theses depend heavily on Friedrich von Schelling's *System des Transcendentalen Idealismus* (1800). Orsini (1969) shows how STC 'proceeds to condense a dozen pages or so of the *System* into a series of Theses. . . . These theses are an abstract of Schelling with some explanatory interpolations . . .

reaffirming [STC's] theistic positions' (206). The relevant passages from Schelling's *System* are available (in German, with an English translation) in *CN* III 4265 n; cf also ibid. 4186. STC annotated several of Schelling's works; for a list, see *PL* 464–5, n 36.

The nature and extent of STC's borrowings from Schelling (and other writers) has been the subject of a long and acrimonious scholarly debate. Thomas De Quincey, in an article contributed to *Tait's Edinburgh Magazine* (September 1834), was the first to draw attention to STC's 'barefaced plagiarism' from Schelling's *System*; and J. F. Ferrier's patronising 'Plagiarisms of S. T. Coleridge'–a paper sated with sanctimonious ejaculations of outraged 'fair play'–appeared in *Blackwood's Edinburgh Magazine* in 1840. Since then, the charge of plagiarism has been revived again and again, most recently by Fruman (1971). The injustice of the charge was argued in the early years by STC's daughter and by his friend J. H. Green, and has been reasserted in more recent times by critics like Sir Herbert Read and M. H. Abrams. The most able and systematic defence, however, is provided by McFarland (1969) who, aided by immense erudition, argues that STC's 'borrowings, though skirting and sometimes crossing the boundary of propriety, were not the thefts of a poverty-stricken mind, but the mosaic materials of a neurotic technique of composition. We see this mosaic organization, in fact, not only in a work like the *Biographia Literaria*, but as the central reality of the composition of such poems as *The Ancient Mariner*. Lowes's *Road to Xanadu* would not have been possible, there would have been no phrasings and snippets lifted from travel books, had not Coleridge's method of composition been to work with larger elements—phrases and connected image patterns—than is conventional' (32). McFarland demonstrates (convincingly, to my mind) the substantial truth in STC's claim that 'In Schelling's "NATUR-PHILOSOPHIE", and the "SYSTEM DES TRANSCENDENTALEN IDEALISMUS", I first found a genial coincidence with much that I had toiled out for myself, and a powerful assistance in what I had yet to do' (*BL* I 102). Cf also Extract 16 and n 6.

Schelling (1775–1854) was the 'founder of the philosophy of identity which holds that subject and object coincide in the Absolute, a state to be realized in intellectual intuition. Deeply involved in romanticism, Schelling's philosophy of nature culminates in a transcendental idealism where nature and spirit are linked in a series of developments by unfolding powers or potencies, together forming one great organism in which nature is dynamic visible spirit and spirit invisible nature' (*DP* 279).

9. In Theses III–v STC (with Schelling's aid) has argued that philosophic investigation must be based on a truth that is 'self-grounded, unconditional and known by its own light' (III); 'that there can be but one such

principle' (IV); and that this principle cannot be either an object independent of a subject or a subject independent of an object– and therefore, 'it must be found in that which is neither subject nor object exclusively, but which is the identity of both' (V). This 'principle' is then defined as the SUM or I AM (VI). A few pages earlier STC had anticipated this very argument: 'All knowledge rests on the coincidence of an object with a subject. . . . For we can *know* that only which is true: and the truth is universally placed in the coincidence of the thought with the thing, of the representation with the object represented' (*BL* I 174). Appleyard (1965) comments: 'All that is objective Coleridge calls nature, in its passive and material sense, the phenomena by which its active existence is made known to us. All that is subjective he calls the self or intelligence. In all acts of knowledge there is a reciprocal and instantaneous concurrence of conscious intelligence and unconscious nature' (192).

10. Cf also *CN* III 4244. The identification of subject and object was a topic of interest to STC as early as 1801, as is clear from a Notebook entry (February–March 1801) beginning with lines 48–9 of Wordsworth's 'Tintern Abbey':

> '—and the deep power of Joy
> We see into the *Life* of Things—

i.e.—By deep feeling we make our *Ideas dim*—& this is what we mean by our Life—ourselves. I think of the Wall—it is before me, a distinct Image—here. I necessarily think of the *Idea* & the Thinking I as two distinct & opposite Things. Now let me think of *myself*—of the thinking Being—the Idea becomes dim whatever it be—so dim that I know not what it is—but the Feeling is deep & steady—and this I call *I*—identifying the Percipient & the Perceived—' (*CN* I 921). Orsini (1969) examines this 1801 Notebook entry in detail and traces it to a probable source in Fichte's *Versuch einer neuen Darstellung der Wissenschaftslehre* (1797), where 'Fichte repeatedly invites the reader to think of some common object, such as a wall, and then to think of himself. The passage that perhaps comes nearest to Coleridge is: "When you thought of your table or your wall (*deine Wand*), you, my intelligent reader, *you* who are conscious to yourself of the activity of your thought, you were yourself *the thinker* in your thinking; but *the thing-thought-of* (*das Gedachte*) was for you not yourself, but something different from yourself. In short . . . the thinker and the thing-thought-of must be two. But when you think *yourself*, you are not only the thinker, but also at the same time the thought-of (*das Gedachte*); thinker and thought-of must therefore be one"' (182– 3).

11. *sum quia sum*: 'I am because I am' (am ='exist').

12. *sum quia Deus est*: 'I am because God is'; *sum quia in Deo sum*: 'I am because I am in God'.

13. *STC's note*: 'It is most worthy of notice, that in the first revelation of himself, not confined to individuals; indeed in the very first revelation of his absolute being, Jehovah at the same time revealed the fundamental truth of all philosophy, which must either commence with the absolute, or have no fixed commencement; that is, cease to be philosophy. I cannot but express my regret, that in the equivocal use of the word *that*, for *in that*, or *because*, our admirable version [i.e. *AV*] has rendered the passage [Exodus 3:14] susceptible of degraded interpretation in the mind of common readers or hearers, as if it were a mere reproof to an impertinent question, I am what I am, which might be equally affirmed of himself by any existent being.'

14. *fit alter et idem*: 'become other and the same'. '"Alter et Idem" is a recurrent phrase in STC's marginalia on Bohme, for evolving the relation between the Father and the Son in Trinitarian doctrine' (George Whalley).

15. *principium commune essendi et cognoscendi*: 'general principle of being and knowing'.

16. *scientia scientiæ*: 'science of knowledge', i.e. epistemology.

17. To the transcendental philosopher, 'self-consciousness is not a kind of *being*, but a kind of *knowing*'[STC].

18. *causa sui et effectus*, &c.: 'his own cause and effect, father self-engendered, and son of himself'.

19. Cf Nicolas Malebranche, *De la Recherche de la Vérité* (1674–5) III vi.

20. Cf Thomas Hobbes, *De homine* (1658); David Hartley, *Observations on Man* (1749); Aristotle, *Parva Naturalia* and *De Anima*. STC discusses these figures in detail in *Biographia* Chaps v–vii.

21. STC has in mind the peripatetic aphorism *nihil in intellectu quod non prius in sensu* ('There is nothing in the mind that is not first in the senses'): cf Extract 35–B and n 5.

22. Μάκαρ, etc.: 'Blessed One, be gracious to me; Father, be gracious to me, if against decency, if contrary to what is meet and right, I have touched your divinity' (Synesius of Cyrene, *Hymns* iii 113–17).

23. Jackson (1969) examines these ten Theses and concludes: 'Coleridge has now completed his attempt to establish an initial Idea, the initiative of the critical system he wishes to expound. I do not think that one can praise his organization of material, and yet, for all his irresolution, for all his circling and weaving around the point he is trying to make, his meaning is fairly clear. He is belittling thought based on the observation of phenomena (the relation of Theory, the method of natural science) and advocating thought based on scrutiny of the mind itself (the relation of Law). If we are to attain the sort of absolute knowledge which Coleridge believes is essential, we must begin with the Self and not with

Nature. Coleridge declares his ultimate ambition to be "to construct by a series of intuitions the progressive schemes . .: till I arrive at the fulness of the *human* intelligence." For the present, however, he is only concerned with arriving at an explanation of the poetic faculty of imagination; he assumes the fuller exposition of the position "I Am" into "the fulness of the *human* intelligence" as his principle, "in order to deduce from it a faculty, the generation, agency, and application of which form the contents of the ensuing chapter". . . . we are being asked to accept the results and implications of an argument which he promises to expound later. He is not giving up the attempt to arrive at a description of the creative act of poetry derived from first principles' (70—1).

24. Chap xiii, the 'ensuing chapter', is entitled 'On the Imagination, or esemplastic power'. The ten Theses in Chap xii were originally to have been applied in Chap xiii to 'the deduction of the Imagination, and with it the principles of production and of genial criticism in the fine arts' (*BL* 1 180). The promised chapter on the Imagination, however, was never written; the only portion of the promise to be fulfilled (formally, at least) is the famous Fancy—Imagination distinction reproduced in Extract 33—F.

Only a month before his death STC is reported to have asserted that 'The metaphysical disquisition [Chaps xii and xiii] at the end of the first volume of the *Biographia Literaria* is unformed and immature; it contains the fragments of the truth, but it is not fully thought out. It is wonderful to myself to think how infinitely more profound my views now are, and yet how much clearer they are withal. The circle is completing; the idea is coming round to, and to be, the common sense' (*TT* 28 June 1834). The significance of this statement is fully explored by McFarland (1969) who points out that STC's 'invocation of Schelling as the reconciler of "objective" [= "it is"] and "subjective" [= "I am"] philosophies is . . . a wistful imposition of philosophical need upon logical fact, and such an imposition must necessarily be of brief duration'—for 'it was only as the *soi-disant* reconciler of "it is" and "I am" thought (and to a less urgent degree as offering the aesthetic justification of artistic activity) that Schelling seriously engaged Coleridge's attention' (158—9).

25. For Wordsworth's remarks on Imagination in his 1815 Preface, see Appendix.

26. Cf Extracts 5, 31 and 32.

27. Cf Extract 23 and nn.

28. *STC's note*: 'This phrase, *a priori*, is in common, most grossly misunderstood, and an absurdity burdened on it, which it does not deserve. By knowledge, *a priori*, we do not mean, that we can know anything previously to experience, which would be a contradiction ir

terms; but that having once known it by occasion of experience (that is, something acting upon us from without) we then know, that it must have pre-existed, or the experience itself would have been impossible. By experience only I know, that I have eyes; but then my reason convinces me, that I must have had eyes in order to [have had] the experience.'

29. Wordsworth's Preface to *Poems* (1815): cf Appendix.

30. Cf *Table Talk* (20 August 1833): 'Genius must have talent as its complement and implement, just as in like manner imagination must have fancy. In short, the higher intellectual powers can only act through a corresponding energy of the lower.'

31. STC's mature attitude to Wordsworth was not, however, characterised by blind idolatry; see for example *CN* III 4243 (probably dating from 1815), which reads in part: 'I would almost wager my life, that if Αξ[ιολογος] published το ποιημα περι του πνευματος του σεαυτου, he would cancel all the passages relating to στς. φιλοσοφια as instances of mutual interpenetration of 2 = 1— φιλοσοφια = η σοφια της φιλοτητος : the Love of Wisdom = the Wisdom of Love.' By translation and transliteration, Miss Coburn renders this passage as follows: '*if* "Ax." *published* "the poem about his own mind", *he would cancel all the passages relating to* "STC's philosophy" *as instances of mutual interpenetration of 2 = 1—* "philosophy = the wisdom of love": *the Love of Wisdom = the Wisdom of Love.*' The Greek word ἀξίολογος ('axiologos'), STC's code-word for Wordsworth, literally means 'remarkable' and is a compound from ἄξιος ('worthy') and λόγος ('word').

32. 'Sunday' i 8 in Taylor's *Golden Grove* (1655), a manual of daily prayers.

(F) from Chapter xiii[1]

The IMAGINATION then, I consider either as primary, or secondary. The primary IMAGINATION I hold to be the living Power and prime Agent of all human Perception, and as a repetition in the finite mind of the eternal act of creation in the infinite I AM.[2] The secondary Imagination I consider as an echo of the former, co-existing with the conscious will, yet still as identical with the primary in the *kind* of its agency, and differing only in *degree*, and in the *mode* of its operation. It dissolves, diffuses, dissipates, in order to re-create; or where this process is rendered impossible, yet still at all events it struggles to idealize and to unify. It is essentially *vital*, even as all objects (*as* objects) are essentially fixed and dead.[3]

FANCY, on the contrary, has no other counters to play with, but fixities and definites. The Fancy is indeed no other than a mode of Memory emancipated from the order of time and space; while it is blended with, and modified by that empirical phenomenon of the will, which we express by the word CHOICE. But equally with the ordinary memory the Fancy must receive all its materials ready made from the law of association.[4]

(BL I 202)

Notes

1. The sources, critical utility, and meaning of the Fancy—Imagination distinction here outlined have been almost endlessly discussed by critics. On STC's *sources*, see for example Shawcross, *BL* I xi—lxxxix; Muirhead (1930) 198—211; Carver (1940); Thorpe (1944); Bate and Bullitt (1945); Kennedy (1947); Brett (1949); Wasserman (1949); McFarland (1969) 306—10 and (1972). On the *critical utility* of the distinction, see for example: *contra* = Abercrombie (1925) 58; Lucas (1936) 157—80; Leavis (1940); and *pro* = Richards (1934); James (1937) 44—74; Willey (1946). On the *meaning* of the terms, see for example Bate (1950); Brooke (1960); Appleyard (1965) 188—208; Jackson (1969) 109—21; Barfield (1972) 61—91.

2. See Introduction, pp. 3, 21—3; also Extract 1, n 2. This statement in *Biographia* is an important affirmation of the poietic nature of perception—i.e. seeing as making. By describing the power of perception as 'primary Imagination', STC at one stroke establishes that perception (on which the poetic Imagination depends) is, like the poetic Imagination, poietic; it repeats at the finite level the eternally generative activity of God.

   In her edition (1847) of *Biographia*, Sara Coleridge notes: 'The last clause "and as a repetition" etc. I find stroked out in a copy of the B.L.' Some later commentators—Bate (1950) and Appleyard (1965)—basing their cases on an ambiguous version of Sara's note in Shawcross's edition of *Biographia*, have argued or suggested that STC considered removing the whole sentence about Primary Imagination; Hume (1969) reviews the evidence and concludes that Sara's note makes it clear that 'Coleridge wished to preserve the first half of his sentence: "The primary Imagination I hold to be the living Power and prime Agent of all human Perception" '. In the final analysis, none of these arguments is convincing: first, the second half of the sentence is perfectly consonant with STC's habitual description of the poietic power of perception in theological terms (e.g. Extracts 4, 9, and 12); second, Sara found the clause stroked out *in a single copy* of the *Biographia*; third, there is no evidence that the deletion was made by STC himself and no annotation accompanied the deletion (as was STC's habit).

3. Cf Extract 9 and also Thesis VII in Extract 33—E.

4. STC discusses the law of association (with special reference to Hartley's

Observations on Man of 1749) in *Biographia* Chaps v–viii. In Chap v he traces the law to its origin in Aristotelian psychology: 'The *general law* of association . . . according to Aristotle is this. Ideas by having been together acquire a power of recalling each other; or every partial representation awakes the total representation of which it had been a part. . . . In association then consists the whole mechanism of the reproduction of impressions, in the Aristotelian Psychology. It is the universal law of the *passive* fancy and *mechanical* memory; that which supplies to all other faculties their objects, to all thought the elements of its materials' (*BL* 1 72–3). On Hartley and associationism, see for example H. N. Fairchild, 'Hartley, Pistorius, and Coleridge' *PMLA* 62 (1947) 1010–21; R. Haven, 'Coleridge, Hartley, and the Mystics' *JHI* 20 (1959) 477–94; Appleyard (1965) 22–38. Cf also Introduction, pp. 22–3.

(G) from Chapter xiv

During the first year that Mr Wordsworth and I were neighbours, [1] our conversations turned frequently on the two cardinal points of poetry, the power of exciting the sympathy of the reader by a faithful adherence to the truth of nature, and the power of giving the interest of novelty by the modifying colors of imagination. The sudden charm, which accidents of light and shade, which moon-light or sun-set diffused over a known and familiar landscape, appeared to represent the practicability of combining both. These are the poetry of nature. [2] The thought suggested itself (to which of us I do not recollect) that a series of poems might be composed of two sorts. In the one, the incidents and agents were to be, in part at least, supernatural; and the excellence aimed at was to consist in the interesting of the affections by the dramatic truth of such emotions, as would naturally accompany such situations, supposing them real. And real in *this* sense they have been to every human being who, from whatever source of delusion, has at any time believed himself under supernatural agency. For the second class, subjects were to be chosen from ordinary life; the characters and incidents were to be such, as will be found in every village and its vicinity, where there is a meditative and feeling mind to seek after them, or to notice them, when they present themselves.

In this idea originated the plan of the 'Lyrical Ballads'; [3] in which it was agreed, that my endeavours should be directed to persons and characters supernatural, or at least romantic; yet so as to transfer from our inward nature a human interest and a semblance of truth sufficient to procure for these shadows of imagination that willing suspension of disbelief for the moment, which constitutes poetic faith.[4] Mr Wordsworth, on the other hand, was to propose to himself as his object, to give the charm of novelty to things of every day, and to excite a feeling analogous to the supernatural, by awakening the mind's attention from the lethargy of custom, and directing it to the loveliness and the wonders of the world before us; an inexhaustible treasure, but for which, in consequence of the film of familiarity and selfish solicitude we have eyes, yet see not, ears that hear not, and hearts that neither feel nor understand.[5]

With this view I wrote 'The Ancient Mariner,' and was preparing among other poems, 'The Dark Ladie,' and the 'Christabel,' in which I should have more nearly realized my ideal, than I had done in my first attempt. But Mr Wordsworth's industry had proved so much more successful, and the number of his poems so much greater, that my compositions, instead of forming a balance, appeared rather an interpolation of heterogeneous matter.[6]

[. . . . .]

A poem is that species of composition, which is opposed to works of science, by proposing for its *immediate* object pleasure, not truth; and from all other species (having *this* object in common with it) it is discriminated by proposing to itself such delight from the *whole*, as is compatible with a distinct gratification from each component *part*.[7]

[. . . . .]

My own conclusions on the nature of poetry, in the strictest use of the word, have been in part anticipated in the preceding[8] disquisition on the fancy and imagination. What is poetry? is so nearly the same question with, what is a poet? that the answer to the one is involved in the solution of the other. For it is a distinction resulting from the poetic genius itself, which sustains and modifies the images, thoughts, and emotions of the poet's own mind.

The poet, described in *ideal* perfection, brings the whole soul of man into activity, with the subordination of its faculties to each other, according to their relative worth and dignity.[9] He diffuses a tone and spirit of unity, that blends, and (as it were) *fuses*, each into each, by that synthetic and magical power, to which we have exclusively appropriated the name of imagination. This power, first put in action by the will and understanding, and retained under their irremissive, though gentle and unnoticed, controul (*laxis effertur habenis*)[10] reveals itself in the balance or reconciliation of opposite or discordant qualities:[11] of sameness, with difference; of the general, with the concrete; the idea, with the image; the individual, with the representative; the sense of novelty and freshness, with old and familiar objects; a more than usual state of emotion, with more than usual order; judgement ever awake and steady self-possession, with enthusiasm and feeling profound or vehement; and while it blends and harmonizes the natural and the artificial, still subordinates art to nature; the manner to the matter; and our admiration of the poet to our sympathy with the poetry.[12] 'Doubtless,' as Sir John Davies observes of the soul[13] (and his words may with slight alteration be applied, and even more appropriately, to the poetic IMAGINATION)

> 'Doubtless this could not be, but that she turns
>   Bodies to spirit by sublimation strange,
> As fire converts to fire the things it burns,
>   As we our food into our nature change.
>
> From their gross matter she abstracts their forms,
>   And draws a kind of quintessence from things;
> Which to her proper nature she transforms,
>   To bear them light on her celestial wings.
>
> Thus does she, when from individual states
>   She doth abstract the universal kinds;
> Which then re-clothed in divers names and fates
>   Steal access through our senses to our minds.'

Finally, GOOD SENSE is the BODY of poetic genius, FANCY its DRAPERY,[14] MOTION its LIFE, and IMAGINATION the SOUL that is everywhere, and in each; and forms all into one graceful and intelligent whole.

(BL II 5–6, 10, 12–13)

Notes

1. STC moved to Nether Stowey on 31 December 1796. Wordsworth paid him a visit in March 1797, which STC returned by spending some three weeks with the Wordsworths at Racedown in June. By the middle of July 1797 the Wordsworths had moved to Alfoxden, a mere three miles from Stowey. During the year that followed—the *annus mirabilis*—the two poets spent a great deal of time together roaming the Quantocks, discussing poetic theory, composing the *Lyrical Ballads* and other poems.

In the months between July 1797 and September 1798, STC wrote much of his best verse: the Conversation Poems, 'Kubla Khan', 'The Ancient Mariner', and Part I of 'Christabel'. The manuscript of *Lyrical Ballads* was (apart from 'Tintern Abbey') ready for the printer by late May 1798 but did not in fact appear until the following September, only a fortnight before STC and the Wordsworths, the *annus mirabilis* behind them, set sail from Yarmouth for Germany.

2. The phrase 'poetry of nature' does not refer to *nature-poetry* but to *nature behaving like a poet.*

3. Wordsworth gives a rather different account of the origin of the volume in the 'Fenwick note' to 'We Are Seven'; there, he maintains that the original plan was that the two poets should collaborate on 'The Ancient Mariner' in order to defray the expenses of a walking-tour to Linton; the plan was soon altered, however, 'and we began to talk of a volume which was to consist, as Mr Coleridge has told the world, of poems chiefly on natural subjects taken from common life but looked at, as much as might be, through an imaginative medium.' See Mark L. Reed, 'Wordsworth, Coleridge, and the "Plan" of the *Lyrical Ballads*' *UTQ* 34 (1964–5) 238–53. For STC's account of the genesis of 'The Ancient Mariner', see his Preface to 'The Wanderings of Cain' (1828): *CPW* 1 285–7.

4. As Wellek (1955) has pointed out, STC's famous dictum about the 'willing suspension of disbelief' had been anticipated (in rather more turgid formulations) by the German critic Moses Mendelssohn (1729–86) both in *Rhapsodie über die Empfindungen* (1761) – 'A certain capability is needed to surrender to illusion and to resign the consciousness of the present in its favour' – and again in *Morgenstunden* (1785): 'If we carry with us the intention to let ourselves be deceived in an agreeable manner, sensuous knowledge will do its usual job; from the signs of passion, from the signs of free actions we shall draw inferences as to intention and motivation and shall thus become interested in nonexistent persons. We take a real part in unreal actions and feelings because, for the sake of being pleased, we abstract intentionally from their unreality' (1 149).

Numerous possible 'sources' (e.g., Lord Kames, Herder, Schiller, Erasmus Darwin) have been suggested for this idea: for a short bibliography, see *SC* (1960) 1 178 n; the closest parallel cited by Raysor in *SC* is Schlegel's statement: 'the theatrical as well as every other poetical illusion, is a waking dream, to which we voluntarily surrender ourselves.' STC may have articulated a theory of dramatic illusion as early as 1808, if Raysor is correct in assigning to that year a note containing the following sentence: 'These and all other stage presentations are to produce a sort of temporary half-faith, which the spectator encourages in himself and supports by a voluntary contribution on his own part, because he knows that it is at all times in his power to see the thing as it really is' (*SC* i 178). For other formulations of this idea, see *BL* ii 107, 189; *SC* i 113–18 and ii 257–8; and STC's letter of 13 May 1816 to Daniel Stuart (*CL* iv 641–2).

5. Cf Isaiah 6: 9–10–a text frequently cited in the New Testament (e.g., Matthew 13: 14–15 and Acts 28: 26–7). Cf also Extract 20, and Extract 33–C and n 6.

6. Of the twenty-three poems in *Lyrical Ballads* (1798), only four are by STC: 'The Ancient Mariner', 'The Foster-Mother's Tale', 'The Nightingale' and 'The Dungeon'. STC's 'Lewti', which had been published in *The Morning Post* (13 April 1798) under the pseudonym Nicias Erythraeus, was to have been included in the volume; however, perhaps because it had already been published and might, therefore, have compromised the anonymity of *Lyrical Ballads*, it was excluded at the last moment and replaced by 'The Nightingale'. Of the two other poems which STC says he was preparing for the volume, thus much may be briefly noted: 'Christabel', in which he would have 'more nearly realized' his ideal than in 'The Ancient Mariner', was begun in 1797 or 1798 but was not published (and even then as a fragment) until 1816; 'The Ballad of the Dark Ladié' (begun in 1798 and published as a fragment in 1834) appeared in an incomplete form in *The Morning Post* (21 December 1799) and then under the title 'Love' in the second edition (1800) of *Lyrical Ballads*. On the abrupt exclusion of *Christabel* from *Lyrical Ballads* (1800), see STC's letter to Josiah Wedgwood (1 November 1800): 'But immediately on my arrival in this country I undertook to finish a poem which I had begun, entitled Christabel, for a second volume of the Lyrical Ballads. . . . my poem grew so long & in Wordsworth's opinion so impressive, that he rejected it from his volume as disproportionate both in size & merit, & as discordant in it's character' (*CL* i 643; cf also ibid. 631–2).

7. There are a number of drafts (dating as early as 1809) of this famous definition of poetry: cf *CN* iii 3615, 3827, 4111, 4112; *SC* i 148 and ii 41, 50–1, 68. On the relationship of *parts* to the *whole*, see Extract 13–A, n 2, and Extract 28 and n 2.

8. I.e. in Chap xiii: Extract 33–F.

9. Cf Extracts 15–C, 23, and 33–E.

10. *laxis effertur habenis*: 'it is brought out with loose reins' (variant of Virgil, *Georgics* ii 364: *laxis . . . immissus habenis*).

11. On the reconciliation of opposites, see 'Kubla Khan' 31–6 (Extract 3), and also Extracts 21 and 40–C.

12. The preceding sentences are examined in detail by Fogle (1962) 59–62.

13. The stanzas here quoted are from Section iv of Davies's 'Nosce Teipsum' (1599), a long philosophic poem on the nature of man and the immortality of the soul. STC's 'slight alteration' occurs in the final

stanza quoted above where, in the original poem, the last two lines are:

> Which bodyless and immaterial are,
> And can be only lodged within our minds.

14. Cf point 2 in Extract 17–B.

(H) Chapter xv[1]
The specific symptoms of poetic power elucidated in a critical analysis of Shakespeare's Venus and Adonis, and Lucrece.
In the application of these principles[2] to purposes of practical criticism as employed in the appraisal of works more or less imperfect, I have endeavoured to discover what the qualities in a poem are, which may be deemed promises and specific symptoms of poetic power, as distinguished from general talent determined to poetic composition by accidental motives, by an act of the will, rather than by the inspiration of a genial and productive nature. In this investigation, I could not, I thought, do better, than keep before me the earliest work of the greatest genius, that perhaps human nature has yet produced, our *myriad-minded*[3] Shakespeare. I mean the 'Venus and Adonis,' and the 'Lucrece'; works which give at once strong promises of the strength, and yet obvious proofs of the immaturity, of his genius. From these I abstracted the following marks, as characteristics of original poetic genius in general.[4]

1. In the 'Venus and Adonis,' the first and most obvious excellence is the perfect sweetness of the versification; its adaptation to the subject; and the power displayed in varying the march of the words without passing into a loftier and more majestic rhythm than was demanded by the thoughts, or permitted by the propriety of preserving a sense of melody predominant. The delight in richness and sweetness of sound, even to a faulty excess, if it be evidently original, and not the result of an easily imitable mechanism, I regard as a highly favourable promise in the compositions of a young man. 'The man that hath not music in his soul'[5] can indeed never be a genuine poet. Imagery (even taken from nature, much more when transplanted from books, as travels, voyages, and works of natural history); affecting incidents; just thoughts; interesting personal or domestic feelings; and with these the art of their combination or intertexture in the form of a poem; may all by incessant effort be acquired as a trade, by a man of talents and much reading, who, as I once before observed,[6] has mistaken an intense desire of poetic

reputation for a natural poetic genius; the love of the arbitrary end for a possession of the peculiar means. But the sense of musical delight, with the power of producing it, is a gift of imagination; and this together with the power of reducing multitude into unity of effect, and modifying a series of thoughts by some one predominant thought or feeling, may be cultivated and improved, but can never be learned. It is in these that 'poeta nascitur non fit.'[7]

2. A second promise of genius is the choice of subjects very remote from the private interests and circumstances of the writer himself. At least I have found, that where the subject is taken immediately from the author's personal sensations and experiences, the excellence of a particular poem is but an equivocal mark, and often a fallacious pledge, of genuine poetic power. We may perhaps remember the tale of the statuary, who had acquired considerable reputation for the legs of his goddesses, though the rest of the statue accorded but indifferently with ideal beauty; till his wife, elated by her husband's praises, modestly acknowledged that she herself had been his constant model. In the 'Venus and Adonis' this proof of poetic power exists even to excess. It is throughout as if a superior spirit more intuitive, more intimately conscious, even than the characters themselves, not only of every outward look and act, but of the flux and reflux of the mind in all its subtlest thoughts and feelings, were placing the whole before our view; himself meanwhile unparticipating in the passions, and actuated only by that pleasureable excitement, which had resulted from the energetic fervor of his own spirit in so vividly exhibiting, what it had so accurately and profoundly contemplated.[8] I think, I should have conjectured from these poems, that even then the great instinct, which impelled the poet to the drama, was secretly working in him, prompting him by a series and never broken chain of imagery, always vivid and, because unbroken, often minute; by the highest effort of the picturesque in words, of which words are capable, higher perhaps than was ever realized by any other poet, even Dante not excepted; to provide a substitute for that visual language, that constant intervention and running comment by tone, look and gesture, which in his dramatic works he was entitled to expect from the players. His 'Venus and Adonis' seem at once the characters themselves, and the whole representation of those characters by the most consummate actors. You seem to be told nothing, but to see and hear everything. Hence it is, that from the perpetual activity of attention required on the part of the reader; from the rapid flow, the quick change, and the playful nature of the thoughts and

images; and above all from the alienation, and, if I may hazard such an expression, the utter *aloofness* of the poet's own feelings, from those of which he is at once the painter and the analyst; that though the very subject cannot but detract from the pleasure of a delicate mind, yet never was poem less dangerous on a moral account. Instead of doing as Ariosto, and as, still more offensively, Wieland[9] has done, instead of degrading and deforming passion into appetite, the trials of love into the struggles of concupiscence; Shakespeare has here represented the animal impulse itself, so as to preclude all sympathy with it, by dissipating the reader's notice among the thousand outward images, and now beautiful, now fanciful circumstances, which form its dresses and its scenery; or by diverting our attention from the main subject by those frequent witty or profound reflections, which the poet's ever active mind has deduced from, or connected with, the imagery and the incidents. The reader is forced into too much action to sympathize with the merely passive of our nature. As little can a mind thus roused and awakened be brooded on by mean and indistinct emotion, as the low, lazy mist can creep upon the surface of a lake, while a strong gale is driving it onward in waves and billows.

3. It has been before observed that images, however beautiful, though faithfully copied from nature, and as accurately represented in words, do not of themselves characterize the poet.[10] They become proofs of original genius only as far as they are modified by a predominant passion; or by associated thoughts or images awakened by that passion; or when they have the effect of reducing multitude to unity, or succession to an instant; or lastly, when a human and intellectual life is transferred to them from the poet's own spirit,

'Which shoots its being through earth, sea, and air.'[11]

In the two following lines for instance, there is nothing objectionable, nothing which would preclude them from forming, in their proper place, part of a descriptive poem:[12]

'Behold yon row of pines, that shorn and bow'd
Bend from the sea-blast, seen at twilight eve.'

But with a small alteration of rhythm, the same words would be equally in their place in a book of topography, or in a descriptive tour. The same image will rise into semblance of poetry if thus conveyed:

'Yon row of bleak and visionary pines,
By twilight glimpse discerned, mark! how they flee
From the fierce sea-blast, all their tresses wild
Streaming before them.'

I have given this as an illustration, by no means as an instance, of
that particular excellence which I had in view, and in which
Shakespeare even in his earliest, as in his latest, works surpasses all
other poets. It is by this, that he still gives a dignity and a passion to the
objects which he presents. Unaided by any previous excitement, they
burst upon us at once in life and in power.

'Full many a glorious morning have I seen
Flatter the mountain tops with sovereign eye.'
                              Shakespeare, Sonnet 33rd.[13]

'Not mine own fears, nor the prophetic soul
Of the wide world dreaming on things to come—

  * * * * * * * * *
  * * * * * * * * * *[14]

The mortal moon hath her eclipse endur'd,
And the sad augurs mock their own presage;
Incertainties now crown themselves assur'd,
And Peace proclaims olives of endless age.
Now with the drops of this most balmy time
My Love looks fresh, and DEATH to me subscribes!
Since spite of him, I'll live in this poor rhyme,
While he insults o'er dull and speechless tribes.
And thou in this shalt find thy monument,
When tyrants' crests, and tombs of brass are spent.
                                        Sonnet 107.

As of higher worth, so doubtless still more characteristic of poetic
genius does the imagery become, when it moulds and colors itself to
the circumstances, passion, or character, present and foremost in the
mind. For unrivalled instances of this excellence, the reader's own
memory will refer him to the LEAR, OTHELLO, in short to which not of
the '*great, ever living, dead man's*' dramatic works? 'Inopem me copia
fecit.'[15] How true it is to nature, he has himself finely expressed in the
instance of love in Sonnet 98.

'From you have I been absent in the spring,
When proud pied April drest in all its trim
Hath put a spirit of youth in every thing,
That heavy Saturn laugh'd and leap'd with him.
Yet nor the lays of birds, nor the sweet smell
Of different flowers in odour and in hue,
Could make me any summer's story tell,
Or from their proud lap pluck them, where they grew:
Nor did I wonder at the lilies white,
Nor praise the deep vermilion in the rose;
They were, tho' sweet, but figures of delight,
Drawn after you, you pattern of all those.
Yet seem'd it winter still, and, you away,
As with your shadow I with these did play!'

Scarcely less sure, or if a less valuable, not less indispensable mark

Γονίμου μὲν ποιητοῦ ——————
—————— ὅστις ῥῆμα γενναῖον λάκοι,[16]

will the imagery supply, when, with more than the power of the painter, the poet gives us the liveliest image of succession with the feeling of simultaneousness!

'With this, he breaketh from the sweet embrace
Of those fair arms, that held him to her heart,
And homeward through the dark lawns runs apace:
Look! how a bright star shooteth from the sky,
So glides he in the night from Venus' eye.'[17]

4. The last character I shall mention, which would prove indeed but little, except as taken conjointly with the former; yet without which the former could scarce exist in a high degree, and (even if this were possible) would give promises only of transitory flashes and a meteoric power; is DEPTH, and ENERGY of THOUGHT. No man was ever yet a great poet, without being at the same time a profound philospher.[18] For poetry is the blossom and fragrancy of all human knowledge, human thoughts, human passions, emotions, language. In Shakespeare's *poems* the creative power and the intellectual energy wrestle as in a war embrace.[19] Each in its excess of strength seems to threaten the extinction of the other. At length in the DRAMA they were reconciled, and fought each with its shield before the breast of

the other. Or like two rapid streams, that, at their first meeting within narrow and rocky banks, mutually strive to repel each other and intermix reluctantly and in tumult; but soon finding a wider channel and more yielding shores blend, and dilate, and flow on in one current and with one voice. The 'Venus and Adonis' did not perhaps allow the display of the deeper passions. But the story of Lucretia [20] seems to favor and even demand their intensest workings. And yet we find in *Shakespeare's* management of the tale neither pathos, nor any other *dramatic* quality. There is the same minute and faithful imagery as in the former poem, in the same vivid colors, inspirited by the same impetuous vigor of thought, and diverging and contracting with the same activity of the assimilative and of the modifying faculties; and with a yet larger display, a yet wider range of knowledge and reflection; and lastly, with the same perfect dominion, often *domination*, over the whole world of language. What then shall we say? even this; that Shakespeare, no mere child of nature; [21] no automaton of genius; no passive vehicle of inspiration possessed by the spirit, not possessing it; first studied patiently, meditated deeply, understood minutely, till knowledge, become habitual and intuitive, wedded itself to his habitual feelings, and at length gave birth to that stupendous power, by which he stands alone, with no equal or second in his own class; to that power which seated him on one of the two glory-smitten summits of the poetic mountain, with Milton as his compeer, not rival. While the former darts himself forth, and passes into all the forms of human character and passion, the one Proteus of the fire and the flood; the other attracts all forms and things to himself, into the unity of his own IDEAL. All things and modes of action shape themselves anew in the being of MILTON; while SHAKESPEARE becomes all things, yet forever remaining himself. [22] O what great men hast thou not produced, England! my country! truly indeed—

> 'Must *we* be free or die, who speak the tongue,
> Which SHAKESPEARE spake; the faith and morals hold,
> Which MILTON held. In every thing we are sprung
> Of earth's first blood, have titles manifold!'
>
> WORDSWORTH [23]

(*BL* II 13—20)

Notes

1. This short but important chapter is here reproduced in full. STC had lectured on Shakespeare's narrative poems both in 1808 and 1811: cf Extracts 13–L to 13–N and Extract 17–B. It is clear that STC's notes for his 1811 lecture–Extract 17–B–were used as the basis for this chapter.

2. I.e., the philosophic principles concerning the poet and poetry at the end of Chap xiv: Extract 33–G.

3. *STC's note:* "Ἀνὴρ μυριόνους, a phrase which I have borrowed from a Greek monk, who applies it to a Patriarch of Constantinople. I might have said, that I have *reclaimed*, rather than borrowed it: for it seems to belong to Shakespeare, "de jure singulari, et ex privilegio naturæ'" Ἀνὴρ μυριόνους: 'myriad-minded man'. *De jure singulari*, etc.: 'by solitary right and natural prerogative'.

   STC discovered the phrase 'myriad-minded' in late 1801, as is clear from *CN* I 1070: 'Ὁ μυριόνους —hyperbole from Naucratius's Panegyric of Theorodorus Studites—Shakespeare?' Miss Coburn traced the reference to William Cave's *Scriptorum Ecclesiasticorum Historia Literaria* (1688–9) where the phrase is quoted in the section on Naucratius and applied to Theodorus Studites, abbot (not patriarch) of the Studium monastery at Constantinople. The relevant passages from Cave are quoted in *CN* I 1070 n.

4. On *genius*, see Extract 33–B and n 4.

5. Shakespeare, *Merchant of Venice* v i 83 (*variatim*).

6. *Biographia* Chap ii: *BL* I 25. Cf also Extract 5, n 3.

7. *poeta nascitur non fit*: ' a poet is born, not made'.

8. Cf Wordsworth's statements in his Preface to *Lyrical Ballads* (1802): 'For all good poetry is the spontaneous overflow of powerful feelings: but though this be true, Poems to which any value can be attached, were never produced on any variety of subjects but by a man, who being possessed of more than usual organic sensibility, had also thought long and deeply. . . . I have said that Poetry is the spontaneous overflow of powerful feelings: it takes its origin from emotion recollected in tranquillity: the emotion is contemplated till by a species of reaction the tranquillity gradually disappears, and an emotion, kindred to that which was before the subject of contemplation, is gradually produced, and does itself actually exist in the mind. In this mood successful composition generally begins, and in a mood similar to this it is carried on. . . .'

9. For Ariosto and Wieland, see Extract 17–B, nn 5 and 6. Cf also STC's remarks on Gessner's 'Der erste Schiffer' in Extracts 7 and 8.

10. For the distinction between *imitation* and *copy*, see Extract 25 and n 1.

11. STC, 'France: An Ode' (1798) 103.

12. These two lines, like the four which follow, are STC's own.

13. Lines 1–2: cf also Extract 17–B.

14. Lines 3–4: 'Can yet the lease of my true love control/ Supposed as forfeit to a confined doom.' As Shawcross (*BL* I 269) notes, STC 'omits them, as disturbing the imaginative sequence.'

15. *Inopem me copia fecit*: 'Plenty has made me poor' (Ovid, *Metamorphoses* iii 466).

16. Γονίμου μὲν ποιητοῦ, etc.: 'of a geniune poet, who can utter a noble speech'. (Adapted from Aristophanes, *Frogs* 96–7.)

17. *Venus and Adonis* 811–13 and 815–16 (*variatim*).

18. A cherished maxim of STC's: cf Extracts 4, 9 and 12.

19. Cf *CN* III 4113 (October–November 1811): 'that two-fold Being of Shakspere, the Poet & the Philosopher, availing himself of it to convey profound Truths in the most lively Images, and yet the whole faithful to the character supposed to utter the lines & a further development of that character.'

20. *The Rape of Lucrece* (1594). The story is that of Lucrece (or Lucretia) whose beauty inflames the passion of Sextus Tarquinius, which he uses threats and violence to satisfy. Lucrece subsequently takes her own life; however, the violation of chaste Lucrece leads to the expulsion of the Tarquins from Rome and the establishment of a republic.

21. Judged by the orthodox creed of neoclassical dramatic criticism, Shakespeare (in Ben Jonson's phrase) 'wanted art'; however, since even the most rigid and rule-bound neoclassical critic could not deny Shakespeare's power and success, it was commonly asserted that he was a natural genius, a 'child of nature' in whom natural and uncultivated genius had triumphed over bad taste and a lack of conscious art. In opposition to this view, STC (following the 'liberal' eighteenth-century school of criticism represented by Lord Kames and Samuel Johnson) always stresses that Shakespeare's art is *conscious and cultivated*, that he is not to be patronised as an unthinking and untutored genius. Although numerous examples of STC's position might be given, two instances from his 1818 lectures must suffice here: 'No man was ever a great poet without being a great philosopher. In [Shakespeare's] earliest poems the poet and philosopher are perpetually struggling with each other till they found a field where they were blended, and flowed in sweetest harmony and strength' (*SC* II 251); 'Shakespear, the only one who has made passion the vehicle of general truth, as in his comedy he has made even folly itself the vehicle of philosophy' (ibid. 252).

22. STC was fond of distinguishing between the centripetal imagination of Milton and the centrifugal imagination of Shakespeare: cf Extracts 7, 13–B n 1, 13–M, 13–N, 17–B and 51–E. Cf also *Table Talk* (12 May 1830): 'There is a subjectivity of the poet, as of Milton, who is himself before himself in everything he writes; and there is a subjectivity of the *persona*, or dramatic character, as in all Shakespeare's great creations,

Hamlet, Lear, &c.'
23. Lines 11—14 of Wordsworth's sonnet 'It is not to be thought of'.

(I) from Chapter xviii

Could a rule be given from *without*, poetry would cease to be poetry, and sink into a mechanical art. It would be μόρφωσις, not ποίησις.[1] The *rules* of the IMAGINATION are themselves the very powers of growth and production. The *words*, to which they are reducible, present only the outlines and external appearance of the fruit. A deceptive counterfeit of the superficial form and colors may be elaborated; but the marble peach feels cold and heavy, and *children* only put it to their mouths.[2]

(*BL* II 65)

Notes

1. μόρφωσις, *not* ποίησις: 'a process of shaping (*or* fashioning), not making'. Cf Extract 28, n 4.
2. *Table Talk* (6 July 1833): 'It is a poor compliment to pay to a painter to tell him that his figure stands out of the canvas, or that you start at the likeness of the portrait. Take almost any daub, cut it out of the canvas, and place the figure looking into or out of a window, and any one may take it for life. Or take one of Mrs Salmon's wax queens or generals, and you will very sensibly feel the difference between a copy, as they are, and an imitation, of the human form, as a good portrait ought to be. Look at that flower vase of Van Huysun, and at these wax or stone peaches and apricots! The last are likest to their original, but what pleasure do they give? None, except to children.' Cf also Extract 25 and n 1.

(J) from Chapter xxii

Such descriptions[1] too often occasion in the mind of a reader, who is determined to understand his author, a feeling of labor, not very dissimilar to that, with which he would construct a diagram, line by line, for a long geometrical proposition. It seems to be like taking the pieces of a dissected map out of its box. We first look at one part, and then at another, then join and dove-tail them; and when the successive acts of attention have been completed, there is a retrogressive effort of mind to behold it as a whole. The poet should paint to the imagination, not to the fancy; and I know no happier case to exemplify the distinction between these two faculties. Master-pieces of the former mode of poetic painting abound in the writings of

Milton, ex. gr.

> 'The fig-tree; not that kind for fruit renown'd,
> But such as at this day, to Indians known,
> In Malabar or Decan spreads her arms
> Branching so broad and long, that in the ground
> The bended twigs take root, *and daughters grow*
> *About the mother tree, a pillar'd shade*
> *High over-arch'd, and* ECHOING WALKS BETWEEN:
> *There oft the Indian Herdsman, shunning heat,*
> *Shelters in cool, and tends his pasturing herds*
> *At loop holes cut through thickest shade.'*

MILTON *P.L.* 9. 1100.[2]

This is *creation* rather than *painting*, or if painting, yet such, and with such co-presence of the whole picture flash'd at once upon the eye, as the sun paints in a camera obscura.[3] But the poet must likewise understand and command what Bacon calls the *vestigia communia*[4] of the senses, the latency of all in each, and more especially as by a magical *penna duplex*,[5] the excitement of vision by sound and the exponents of sound. Thus 'THE ECHOING WALKS BETWEEN,' may be almost said to reverse the fable in tradition of the head of Memnon, in the Egyptian statue.[6] Such may be deservedly entitled *creative words* in the world of imagination.

[. . . . . . .]

Fifth:[7] a meditative pathos, a union of deep and subtle thought with sensibility; a sympathy with man as man; the sympathy indeed of a contemplator, rather than a fellow-sufferer or co-mate, (spectator, haud particeps)[8] but of a contemplator, from whose view no difference of rank conceals the sameness of the nature; no injuries of wind or weather, or toil, or even of ignorance, wholly disguise the human face divine.[9] The superscription and the image of the Creator still remain legible to *him* under the dark lines, with which guilt or calamity had cancelled or cross-barred it. Here the man and the poet lose and find themselves in each other, the one as glorified, the latter as substantiated. In this mild and philosophic pathos, Wordsworth appears to me without a compeer. Such he *is*: so he *writes*. See vol. I. page 134 to 136,[10] or that most affecting composition, the 'Affliction of Margaret————of————,' page 165 to 168, which no mother, and, if I may judge by my own experience, no parent can read without a tear. Or turn to that genuine lyric, in the former edition, entitled 'The Mad Mother,' page 174 to 178, of which I cannot refrain from quoting two of the stanzas, both of them for their pathos, and the former for the fine transition in the two concluding lines of the stanza, so expressive of that deranged state, in which from the increased sensibility the sufferer's attention is abruptly drawn off by every trifle, and in the same instant plucked back again by the one despotic thought, bringing home with it, by the blending, *fusing* power of Imagination and Passion, the alien object to which it had been so abruptly diverted, no longer an alien but an ally and an inmate.[11]

'Suck, little babe, oh suck again!
It cools my blood; it cools my brain:
Thy lips, I feel them, baby! they
Draw from my heart the pain away.
Oh! press me with thy little hand;
It loosens something at my chest:
About that tight and deadly band
I feel thy little fingers prest.
The breeze I see is in the tree!
It comes to cool my babe and me.'

'Thy father cares not for my breast,
'Tis thine, sweet baby, there to rest,
'Tis all thine own!—and, if its hue
Be changed, that was so fair to view,
'Tis fair enough for thee, my dove!
My beauty, little child, is flown,
But thou wilt live with me in love;
And what if my poor cheek be brown?
'Tis well for me, thou canst not see
How pale and wan it else would be.'

Last, and pre-eminently, I challenge for this poet the gift of IMAGINATION in the highest and strictest sense of the word. In the play of *Fancy*, Wordsworth, to my feelings, is not always graceful, and sometimes *recondite*. The *likeness* is occasionally too strange, or demands too peculiar a point of view, or is such as appears the creature of predetermined research, rather than spontaneous presentation. Indeed his fancy seldom displays itself, as mere and unmodified fancy.

But in imaginative power, he stands nearest of all modern writers to Shakespeare and Milton; and yet in a kind perfectly unborrowed and his own.[12] To employ his own words, which are at once an instance and an illustration, he does indeed to all thoughts and to all objects

> '———————————— add the gleam,
> The light that never was, on sea or land,
> The consecration, and the poet's dream.'[13]

I shall select a few examples as most obviously manifesting this faculty;[14] but if I should ever be fortunate enough to render my analysis of imagination, its origin and characters, thoroughly intelligible to the reader, he will scarcely open on a page of this poet's works without recognising, more or less, the presence and the influences of this faculty.

(*BL* II 102–3, 122–4)

Notes

1. I.e., Wordsworth, *The Excursion* III 50–73. The present passage occurs in STC's essay on Wordsworth's poetic defects, and the passage from *The Excursion* is cited in order to illustrate that '*matter-of-factness*' in certain of Wordsworth's poems which manifests itself in 'a laborious minuteness and fidelity in the representation of objects, and their positions, as they appeared to the poet himself.'

2. *Paradise Lost* ix 1101–10. The italics are STC's.

3. *camera obscura* (*lit.* 'dark chamber'): 'a darkened box, into which light is admitted by a lens, forming an image of external objects on the paper or glass placed at the focal point of the lens'.

4. *vestigia communia*: 'common vestiges, general traces'. STC himself provides the translation, 'the latency of all in each'–i.e. the Neoplatonic notion of *multëity in unity* (cf Extract 26, n 4). I have not been able to trace the phrase *vestigia communia* in Bacon; however, compare the following sentence from *Of the Advancement of Learning* (1605), where Bacon is discussing the effect of imagination on the human body: 'But unto all this knowledge *de communi vinculo* [of the common bond], of the concordances between the mind and the body, that part of inquiry is most necessary, which considereth of the *seats* and *domiciles* which the several faculties of the mind do take and occupy in the organs of the body' (II ix 3). It may also be the case, as Professor P. Æ. Hutchings has pointed out to me, that STC's phrase *vestigia communia* may refer to the *sensus communis* (i.e. *common* or *central sense*) of Aristotelian psychology and medieval scholasticism; the *sensus communis* is, hypothetically, an

interior faculty serving as 'a kind of complement to the peripheral organs' of sight, hearing, touch, etc., and 'needed to *combine* external sensations and to compare them and to *discriminate* between them' (*MSP* I 189). See also W. D. Ross, *Aristotle* (London: Methuen, 1923; revised 1930) 139–42.

5. *penna duplex*: 'two-fold wing' or 'double pen'. I suspect that a *penna duplex* may be some sort of mechanical gadget (perhaps a pantograph); however, I have been unable to track it down.

6. A large statue on the Nile near Egyptian Thebes was said to produce a musical sound when struck by the rays of the morning sun. The statue, supposed to be that of Memnon (the Ethiopian chieftain slain by Achilles), in reality represented King Amenophis of the eighteenth dynasty.

The statue of Memnon appears in Mark Akenside's *The Pleasures of Imagination* (1744) I 109–24:

> As Memnon's marble harp, renown'd of old
> By fabling Nilus, to the quivering touch
> Of Titan's ray, with each repulsive string
> Consenting, sounded thro' the warbling air
> Unbidden strains; even so did nature's hand
> To certain species of external things,
> Attune the finer organs of the mind:
> So the glad impulse of congenial pow'rs,
> Or of sweet sound, or fair-proportion'd form,
> The grace of motion, or the bloom of light,
> Thrills thro' imagination's tender frame,
> From nerve to nerve: all naked and alive
> They catch the spreading rays: till now the soul
> At length discloses every tuneful spring,
> To that harmonious movement from without,
> Responsive.

Another treatment of the Memnon story–again both helpful and interesting in connection with STC's use of it–occurs in Erasmus Darwin's *The Economy of Vegetation* (1791) I 183–8:

> So to the sacred Sun in MEMNON'S fane,
> Spontaneous concords quired the matin strain;
> —Touch'd by his orient beam, responsive rings
> The living lyre, and vibrates all it's strings;
> Accordant ailes the tender tones prolong,
> And holy echoes swell the adoring song.

And, in Additional Note VIII, Darwin adds: 'The gigantic statue of Memnon in his temple at Thebes had a lyre in his hands, which many credible writers assure us, sounded when the rising sun shone upon it. Some philosophers have supposed that the sun's light possesses a mechanical impulse, and that the sounds abovementioned might be thence produced. . . . The statue of Memnon was overthrown and sawed in two by Cambyses to discover its internal structure, and is said still to exist. See Savary's Letters on Egypt. The truncated statue is said for many centuries to have saluted the rising sun with chearful tones, and the setting sun with melancholy ones.'

The point of STC's allusion is that, as light prompted sound in the instance of Memnon's statue, so (though in reverse) *sound* in Milton's image prompts *sight*. Milton's image, then, is *synaesthetic*—that is, it excites (independently of association established by experience) the concurrent response of two of the senses by the stimulation of a single sense. Synaesthesia is a technique frequently employed by Keats, as well as by such later poets as Poe, Baudelaire and Sitwell. The concept of synaesthesia is important, both poetically and philosophically, in STC's writings; it is, for example, intimately connected with his theory of the *reconciliation of opposites*—cf Extracts 21 and 33—G—and, more significantly in relation to the passage in *Biographia* Chap xxii, it is connected to his doctrine of the 'One Life': cf especially the eight lines added in 1816—17 to 'The Eolian Harp' (lines 26—33) and containing the line, 'A light in sound, a sound-like power in light'.

7. The following passage is taken from STC's essay on Wordsworth's 'poetic excellences'. The first four excellences adduced are these: *first*, 'an austere purity of language both grammatically and logically; in short a perfect appropriateness of the words to the meaning'; *second*, 'a correspondent weight and sanity of the Thoughts and Sentiments, won—not from books, but—from the poet's own meditative observation'; *third*, 'the sinewy strength and originality of single lines and paragraphs'; *fourth*, 'the perfect truth of nature in his images and descriptions, as taken immediately from nature, and proving a long and genial intimacy with the very spirit which gives the physiognomic expression to all the works of nature.'

8. *spectator, haud particeps*: 'an observer, not a participant at all'.

9. Cf Blake, 'The Divine Image' (1798) 9—12:

> For mercy has a human heart;
> Pity, a human face;
> And love, the human form divine;
> And peace, the human dress.

10. Page references are to Wordsworth's collected *Poems* (1815) in two

volumes. The poem on pp. 134–6 is "'Tis said that some have died for love' (1800); that on pp. 165–8 is 'The Affliction of Margaret ———' (1801?; pub. 1807).

11. 'The Mad Mother' (1798) stanzas 4 and 7. Wordsworth altered the title in 1815, and the poem was thereafter known by its opening line, 'Her Eyes are Wild'. STC cites the last two lines of stanza 4 in Extract 13–C.

12. Cf Extract 12.

13. 'Elegiac Stanzas Suggested by a Picture of Peele Castle, in a Storm' (1805; pub. 1807) 14–16.

14. As instances of Wordsworthian Imagination, STC quotes the following: 'Yew Trees', 13–33; 'Resolution and Independence', 127–31; 'Ode: Intimations of Immortality', 58–76, 133–71; and 'The White Doe of Rylstone', 31–66, 79–90. As further instances, he mentions (but does not quote from) the following seven sonnets: 'Where lies the Land'; 'Even as a dragon's eye'; 'O mountain stream'; 'Earth has not anything to shew more fair'; 'Methought I saw'; 'It is a beauteous evening'; 'Two voices are there'.

34. PREFACE TO 'KUBLA KHAN' (May 1816)[1]

Of the Fragment of Kubla Khan[2]

The following fragment[3] is here published at the request of a poet of great and deserved celebrity,[4] and, as far as the Author's own opinions are concerned, rather as a psychological curiosity, than on the ground of any supposed *poetic* merits.

In the summer of the year 1797,[5] the Author, then in ill health, had retired to a lonely farm-house between Porlock and Linton, on the Exmoor confines of Somerset and Devonshire. In consequence of a slight indisposition, an anodyne[6] had been prescribed, from the effects of which he fell asleep in his chair at the moment that he was reading the following sentence, or words of the same substance, in 'Purchas's Pilgrimage':[7] 'Here the Khan Kubla commanded a palace to be built, and a stately garden thereunto. And thus ten miles of fertile ground were inclosed with a wall.' The Author continued for about three hours in a profound sleep,[8] at least of the external senses, during which time he has the most vivid confidence, that he could not have composed less than from two to three hundred lines; if that indeed can be called composition in which all the images rose up before him as *things*, with a parallel production of the correspondent expressions, without any sensation or consciousness of effort. On awaking he appeared to himself to have a distinct recollection of the whole, and taking his pen, ink, and paper, instantly and eagerly wrote down the lines that are here preserved. At this moment he was unfortunately called out by a person on business from Porlock, and detained by him above an hour, and on his return to his room, found, to his no small surprise and mortification, that though he still retained some vague and dim recollection of the general purport of the vision, yet, with the exception of some eight or ten scattered lines and images, all the rest had passed away like the images on the surface of a stream into which a stone has been cast, but, alas! without the after restoration of the latter!

> Then all the charm
> Is broken—all that phantom-world so fair
> Vanishes, and a thousand circlets spread,
> And each mis-shape's the other. Stay awhile,
> Poor youth! who scarcely dar'st lift up thine eyes—
> The stream will soon renew its smoothness, soon
> The visions will return! And lo, he stays,
> And soon the fragments dim of lovely forms
> Come trembling back, unite, and now once more
> The pool becomes a mirror.[9]

Yet from the still surviving recollections in his mind, the Author has frequently purposed to finish for himself what had been originally, as it were, given to him. Σχμερον αδιον ασω:[10] but the to-morrow is yet to come.

As a contrast to this vision, I have annexed a fragment of a very different character, describing with equal fidelity the dream of pain and disease.[11]

(CPW I 295–7)

Notes

1. In 1934 the Marquis of Crewe loaned a manuscript copy of 'Kubla Khan' to the National Portrait Gallery in London for a centenary exhibition commemorating Coleridge and Lamb. The manuscript, previously unknown to scholars, was in fact an autograph in STC's handwriting. Since its disclosure in 1934, the Crewe Manuscript (as it has come to be known) has very seriously affected critical assessment of

'Kubla Khan' for two reasons: first, it contains a large number of variants, some of which are extremely significant, not present in the poem as published in 1816 or thereafter (cf Extract 3 nn); secondly, it gives a very different and much shorter account than the 1816 Preface of the date and circumstances of the composition of 'Kubla Khan': 'This fragment with a good deal more, not recoverable, composed, in a sort of Reverie brought on by two grains of Opium, taken to check a dysentery, at a Farm House between Porlock and Linton, a quarter of a mile from Culbone Church, in the fall of the year, 1797.' It needs to be added that this statement appears as a *postscript* to the poem in the Crewe Manuscript and not, as in 1816, as a preface introducing it.

A number of scholars have described and discussed the textual variants in the Crewe Manuscript: see A. D. Snyder, 'The Manuscript of "Kubla Khan"' *TLS* 2 August 1934 541; E. H. W. Meyerstein, 'A Manuscript of "Kubla Khan"' *TLS* 12 January 1951 21; J. Shelton, 'The Autograph Manuscript of "Kubla Khan" and an Interpretation' *REL* 7 (1966) 30–42. Shelton includes a photographic reproduction of the manuscript, which is also available in *BMQ* 26 Nos 3–4 77–83, plates XXX, XXXI.

2. In the 1834 edition of STC's poems the title reads: 'KUBLA KHAN: Or, A Vision in a Dream. A Fragment.'

3. The issue of whether or not 'Kubla Khan' is a fragment has been often raised: see, for example, Lowes (1930) 363, 409; House (1953) 114–16; Beer (1959) 275; Schulz (1963) 114. Since the disclosure of the Crewe Manuscript, the relevance and value of the 1816 Preface have been hotly (sometimes acrimoniously) disputed. Lowes (1930) took the Preface at face value, but he was writing before the Crewe Manuscript came to light. Beer, however, writing in 1959 argues that, although the prefatory account 'has sometimes been criticized, in substance or in detail,' it yet remains true that 'the accumulation of various pieces of evidence has tended to confirm many features of it' (200). Bostetter (1963), on the other hand, sees the Preface as 'one of [STC's] apologies for uncompleted work' (85), and W. U. Ober summarily dismisses it as a 'Coleridgean hoax, albeit a harmless one' ('Southey, Coleridge, and "Kubla Khan"', *JEGP* 58 (1959) 414). In a more positive vein, Chayes (1966) argues that 'the 1816 headnote to "Kubla Khan" is . . . largely a prose imitation of the poem it introduces, also serving in part as argument and gloss' (4).

4. In the spring of 1816 STC had recited 'Kubla Khan' to Lord Byron, who shortly thereafter (through the agency of the publisher John Murray) offered him £80 for 'Christabel' and £20 for 'Kubla Khan'; these two poems, together with 'The Pains of Sleep', were published by Murray towards the end of May 1816.

5. On the date of 'Kubla Khan', see Extract 3, n 1.

6. As we know from the Crewe Manuscript, the *anodyne* was 'two grains of Opium': cf n 1 above. For the possible effects of opium on 'Kubla Khan', see M. H. Abrams, *The Milk of Paradise: The Effect of Opium Visions on the Works of DeQuincey, Crabbe, Francis Thompson, and Coleridge* (London: Milford, Cambridge, Mass.: Harvard University Press, 1934); Schneider (1953) especially 21–109; Hayter (1968) 214–24.

7. For Purchas's exact words, see Extract 3, n 4.

8. The disparity between 'a sort of Reverie' (*Crewe MS*) and a vision occurring during 'a profound sleep' (*1816 Preface*) is an important critical crux, and is discussed by many of the critics listed in nn 3 and 6 above, as well as those critics listed in Extract 3, n 1.

9. Lines 91–100 of STC's 'The Picture; or, The Lover's Resolution' (1802): *CPW* I 372.

10. Σάμερον ἄδιον ᾀσῶ : 'Today I'll sing a sweeter song'. The error was corrected in the 1834 edition, when σάμερον was altered to αὔριον: Αὔριον ἄδιον ᾀσῶ, i.e. 'Tomorrow I'll sing a sweeter song'. (Variant of Theocritus, *Idylls* i 145: χαίρετ' ἐγὼ δ' ὔμμιν καὶ ἐς ὕστερον ἄδιον ᾀσῶ , 'Farewell, and I'll sing you even a sweeter song tomorrow'.)

11. I.e., 'The Pains of Sleep' (cf n 4 above), a poem describing the nightmares brought on by opium.

35. from *THE STATESMAN'S MANUAL* (December 1816)

(A) from the text of *The Statesman's Manual*

And in nothing is Scriptural history more strongly contrasted with the histories of highest note in the present age than in its freedom from the hollowness of abstractions.[1] While the latter present a shadow-fight of Things and Quantities, the former gives us the history of Men, and balances the important influence of individual Minds with the previous state of the national morals and manners, in which, as constituting a specific susceptibility, it presents to us the true cause both of the Influence itself, and of the Weal or Woe that were its Consequents. How should it be otherwise? The histories and political economy of the present and preceding century partake in the general contagion of its mechanic philosophy,[2] and are the *product* of an unenlivened generalizing Understanding.[3] In the Scriptures they are the living *educts*[4] of the Imagination; of that reconciling and mediatory power, which incorporating the Reason in Images of the Sense, and organizing (as it were) the flux of the Senses by the permanence and self-circling energies of the Reason, gives birth to a system of symbols, harmonious in themselves, and consubstantial with the truths, of which they are the *conductors*.[5] These are the Wheels which Ezekiel beheld, when the hand of the Lord was upon him, and he saw visions of God as he sate among the captives by the river of Chebar. *Whithersoever the Spirit was to go, the wheels went, and thither was their spirit to go: for the spirit of the living creature was in the wheels also.*[6] The truths and the symbols that represent them move in conjunction and form the living chariot that bears up (for *us*) the throne of the Divine Humanity. Hence, by a derivative, indeed, but not a divided, influence, and though in a secondary yet in more than a metaphorical sense, the Sacred Book is worthily intitled the WORD OF GOD. Hence too, its contents present to us the stream of time continuous as Life and a symbol of Eternity, inasmuch as the Past and the Future are virtually contained in the Present. According therefore to our relative position on its banks the Sacred History becomes prophetic, the Sacred Prophecies historical, while the power and substance of both inhere in its Laws, its Promises, and its Comminations.[7] In the Scriptures therefore both Facts and Persons must of necessity have a two-fold significance, a past and a future, a temporary and a perpetual, a particular and a universal application. They must be at once Portraits and Ideals.

Eheu! paupertina philosophia in paupertinam religionem ducit:[8]—A hunger-bitten and idea-less philosophy naturally produces a starveling and comfortless religion. It is among the miseries of the present age that it recognizes no medium between *Literal* and *Metaphorical*. Faith is either to be buried in the dead letter, or its name and honors usurped by a counterfeit product of the mechanical understanding, which in the blindness of self-complacency confounds SYMBOLS with ALLEGORIES.[9] Now an Allegory is but a translation of abstract notions into a picture-language which is itself nothing but an abstraction from objects of the senses; the principle being more worthless even than its phantom proxy, both alike unsubstantial, and the former shapeless to boot. On the other hand a Symbol (δ $\xi\sigma\tau\iota\nu$ $\dot{\alpha}\epsilon\dot{\iota}$ $\tau\alpha\upsilon\tau\eta\gamma\acute{o}\rho\iota\kappa\upsilon\nu$)[10] is characterized by a translucence of the Special in the Individual or of the General in the Especial or of the Universal in the General. Above all by the translucence of the Eternal through and in the Temporal. It always partakes of the Reality which it renders intelligible; and while it enunciates the whole, abides itself as a living part in that Unity, of which it is the representative.[11] The other are but empty echoes which the fancy arbitrarily associates with apparitions of matter, less beautiful but not less shadowy than the sloping orchard or hill-side pasture-field seen in the transparent lake below. Alas! for the flocks that are to be led forth to such pastures! '*It shall even be as when the hungry dreameth, and behold! he eateth; but he waketh and his soul is empty: or as when the thirsty dreameth, and behold he drinketh; but he awaketh and is faint!*'[12]

(*CC* VI 28–31)

Notes

1. The 'histories of highest note' were David Hume's *History of Great Britain* (1754–61) and Edward Gibbon's *Decline and Fall of the Roman Empire* (1776–88).
2. I.e., the empirical philosophy of Locke, Hume, Hartley, etc.
3. On Understanding, see Extract 35–B, n 1.
4. The image of streams issuing from a central fountain or spring would seem to be uppermost in STC's mind here. *OED*, which cites this passage from *The Statesman's Manual*, defines *educt* as 'a result of inference or of development'. In James Gillman's copy of *The Statesman's Manual*, STC altered 'educts' to 'Produce' and added the following note: 'Or perhaps these $\mu o\rho\phi\omega\mu\alpha\tau\alpha$ [forms, figures] of the mechanic Understanding as distinguished from the "$\pi o\iota\eta\sigma\epsilon\tilde{\iota}\varsigma$" [makings] of the imaginative Reason might be named *Products* in antithesis to *Produce*—or Growths.'
5. Keppel-Jones (1967) is helpful here: 'Reason, unlike the Understanding which deals with truths derived from the senses, is concerned with truths of a higher kind, that can be defined as truths above sense, and are named *ideas*. . . . In approaching these truths, Reason (unlike the Understanding which remains in contact with the concrete world through the medium of the senses) needs no intermediate organ, for it is itself their source. . . . [Imagination functions as the mediator between Reason and Understanding:] in its peculiar and magical operation, [Imagination] is able to use suitable contradictory images of sense, and produce a synthesis from them (that is, from the concrete world) that corresponds to an idea—the conjunction, in fact, which is the exponent of the idea. In this way the Imagination is able to reconcile "the idea, with the image". . . . What the Imagination is doing, then, is to produce symbols. . . . Thus a synthesis produced from images of sense by the Imagination is a symbol and embodies an idea; but is also itself actually part of the truth of that idea. Through this process the Imagination presents the ideas of Reason in a manageable form to the

Understanding . . . [and] modifies images of the concrete world to embody ideas of Reason' (56—65). Cf also Knights (1965).

For STC on *Idea*, see for example his letter of 10 November 1816 to James Gillman (*CL* IV 690) and Appendix E of *The Statesman's Manual* (*CC* VI 100—14). On *Reason* and *Understanding*, see Extract 35—B, n 1. On *Symbol*, see for example *CN* II 2274 (quoted in Extract 25, n 1); *CN* III 4253; *PL* 193—4; *CL* V 19, 324—7 and VI 611.

6. Ezekiel 1: 20 (*variatim*).

7. *commination*: 'a threatening of divine vengeance'.

8. *Eheu! paupertina philosophia*, etc.: 'Alas! an impoverished philosophy leads toward an impoverished religion'. STC's own free translation follows the Latin sentence.

9. In a note to the ninth of the Aphorisms on Spiritual Religion in *Aids to Reflection*, STC writes: 'Must not of necessity the FIRST MAN [Adam] be a SYMBOL of Mankind, in the fullest force of the word, Symbol, rightly defined—that is, a sign included in the idea, which it represents;—an actual *part* chosen to represent the *whole*, as a lip with a chin prominent is a symbol of a man; or a *lower* form or species used as the representative of a higher in the same *kind*: thus Magnetism is the Symbol of Vegetation, and of the vegetative and reproductive power in animals; the Instinct of the ant-tribe, or the bee, is a symbol of the human understanding. And this definition of the word is of great practical importance, inasmuch as the symbolical is hereby distinguished *toto genere* [in every aspect] from the allegoric and metaphorical' (*AR* 173). Cf also Extract 40—A; and *CN* III 4183 and 4498.

10. ὁ ἔστιν ἀεὶ ταυτηγόρικον: 'which is always tautegorical'. Whalley (1974) translates: 'which is always self-declarative' (16); for another version, see *CC* VI 30, n 3. The word *tautegorical* is STC's coinage; *OED* uses as a definition STC's own explanation in *Aids to Reflection*: 'The *base* of Symbols and symbolical expressions; the nature of which is always *tau*tegorical, that is, expressing the *the same* subject but with a *difference*, in contra-distinction from metaphors and similitudes, that are always *alle*gorical, that is expressing a *different* subject but with a resemblance' (*AR* 136).

11. On STC's organicism—the relation of parts to a whole—see Extract 13—A, n 2 and Extract 28, n 2.

Whalley (1974), having quoted this description of a *symbol*, concludes: 'Symbols, then, are neither distinguishable items nor conventional marks in a denotative system, but centres rather of finely disposed shaping energy that command a wider or narrower field of poetic activity. By partaking of the reality that they render intelligible they are patient of very detailed analogical exploration . . . and this is the delight and duty of critical inquiry. Yet they transcend the abstract parallelism of analogy because they are active in a field where the centrifugal force of recognition is opposed by the centripetal activity of evocation or "association"; and this in itself ensures that interpretation will normally be peripheral to critical inquiry. It is better to ask of a symbolic event, not "What does it mean?" but "What is it doing?" We expect (if our poetic experience has any depth) that a symbol will not be single but manifold—that its true simplicity will disclose an astonishing complexity. It is in symbolic process that the *data* of perception (if there are such things) are transformed into the *données* of poems' (16–17).

12. Isaiah 29: 8 (*variatim*).

(B) from Appendix C

Reason and Religion differ only as a two-fold application of the same power. But if we are obliged to distinguish, we must *ideally* separate. In this sense I affirm, that Reason is the knowledge of the laws of the WHOLE considered as ONE: and as such it is contradistinguished from the Understanding, which concerns itself exclusively with the quantities, qualities, and relations of *particulars* in time and space.[1] The UNDERSTANDING, therefore, is the science of phaenomena, and their subsumption under distinct kinds and sorts, (*genus* and *species*.) Its functions supply the rules and constitute the possibility of EXPERIENCE; but remain mere logical *forms*, except as far as *materials* are given by the senses or sensations. The REASON, on the other hand, is the science of the *universal*, having the ideas of ONENESS and ALLNESS as its two elements or primary factors. In the language of the old schools,

$$\text{Unity} + \text{Omnëity}^2 = \text{Totality.}$$

The Reason first manifests itself in man by the *tendency* to the comprehension of all as one. We can neither rest in an infinite that is not at the same time a whole, nor in a whole that is not infinite. Hence the natural Man is always in a state either of resistance or of captivity to the understanding and the fancy, which cannot represent totality without limit: and he either loses the ONE in the striving after the INFINITE, (i.e. Atheism with or without polytheism) or the INFINITE in the striving after the ONE, (i.e. anthropomorphic monotheism.)[3]

$$[\quad . \quad . \quad . \quad . \quad . \quad]$$

Of this latter faculty [i.e. the Understanding] considered in and of itself the peripatetic[4] aphorism, nihil in intellectu quod non prius in sensu,[5] is strictly true, as well as the legal maxim, de rebus non apparentibus et non existentibus eadem est ratio.[6] The eye is not more inappropriate to sound, than the *mere* understanding to the modes and laws of spiritual existence. In this sense I have used the term; and in this sense I assert that 'the understanding or experiential faculty, unirradiated by the reason and the spirit, has no appropriate object but the material world in relation to our worldly interests. The far-sighted prudence of man, and the more narrow but at the same time far less fallible cunning of the fox, are both no other than a nobler *substitute for salt, in order* that the hog may not putrefy before its destined hour.' FRIEND, p. 80.[7]

It must not, however be overlooked, that this insulation of the understanding is our own act and deed. The man of healthful and undivided intellect uses his understanding in this state of abstraction only as a tool or organ: even as the arithmetician uses numbers, that is, as the means not the end of knowledge. Our Shakespear in agreement both with truth and the philosophy of his age names it '*discourse* of reason,'[8] as an instrumental faculty *belonging* to reason: and Milton opposes the discursive to the intuitive, as the lower to the higher,

'Differing but in degree, in *kind* the same!'[9]

Of the *discursive* understanding, which forms for itself general notions and terms of classification for the purpose of comparing and arranging phaenomena, the Characteristic is Clearness without Depth. It contemplates the unity of things in their *limits* only, and is consequently a knowledge of superficies[10] without substance. So much so indeed, that it entangles itself in contradictions in the very effort of comprehending the *idea* of substance. The completing power which unites clearness with depth, the plenitude of the sense with the comprehensibility of the understanding, is the IMAGINATION, impregnated with which the understanding itself becomes intuitive, and a living power. The REASON, (not the abstract reason, not the reason as a mere *organ* of science, or as the faculty of scientific principles and schemes a priori; but reason) as the integral *spirit* of the regenerated man, reason substantiated and vital, 'one only, yet manifold, overseeing all, and going through all understanding; the breath of the power of God, and a pure influence from the glory of the Almighty; which remaining in itself regenerateth all other powers, and in all ages entering into holy souls maketh them friends of God and prophets;' (Wisdom of Solomon, c. vii.)[11] the REASON without being either the SENSE, the UNDERSTANDING or the IMAGINATION contains all three within itself, even as the mind contains its thoughts, and is present in and through them all; or as the expression pervades the different features of an intelligent countenance. Each individual must bear witness of it to his own mind, even as he describes life and light: and with the silence of light it describes itself, and dwells in *us* only as far as we dwell in *it*. It cannot in strict language be called a faculty, much less a personal property, of any human mind! He, with whom it is present, can as little appropriate it, whether totally or by partition, as he can claim ownership in the breathing air or make an inclosure in the cope of heaven.

The object of the preceding discourse was to recommend the Bible, as the end and center of our reading and meditation.

(*CC* VI 59–60, 67–70)

Notes

1. STC's Reason–Understanding distinction is—for his metaphysical, theological and psychological system—perhaps his most important attempt at *desynonymization*. On Reason and Understanding, see the following: Extract 35–A, n 5 and Extract 41–A and n 3; STC's long marginal note in Gillman's copy of *The Statesman's Manual* (*CC* VI 60–1); 'The Landing Place, Essay 5' in the 1818 *Friend* (*CC* IV i 154–61); letter of 12 February 1821 to C. A. Tulk (*CL* V 136–8); 'On the Difference in Kind of Reason and the Understanding', following the eighth of the Aphorisms on Spiritual Religion in *Aids to Reflection* (*AR* 143–56)—quoted in part in Extract 15–B, n 1; 'Appendix A' in *Aids to Reflection* (*AR* 277–8); *Table Talk* for 15 June 1830 and 15 May 1833.

As early as 1806, STC had written to Thomas Clarkson: 'What is the difference between the Reason, and the Understanding?—I would reply, that the Faculty of the Soul which apprehends and retains the mere notices of Experience, as for instance that such an object has a triangular figure, that it is of such or such a magnitude, and of such and such a color, and consistency, with the anticipation of meeting the same under the same circumstances, in other words, all the mere φαινόμενα* of our nature, we may call the Understanding. But all such notices, as are characterized by UNIVERSALITY and NECESSITY, as that every Triangle *must* in all places and at all times have its two sides greater than it's third—and which are evidently not the effect of any Experience, but the condition of all Experience, & that indeed without which Experience itself would be inconceivable, we may call Reason' (*CL* II 1198). [*φαινόμενα: 'phenomena, appearances'.] R. F. Brinkley brings together a number of important statements (many of them previously unpublished) of the Reason–Understanding distinction: cf *CSC* 109–17, 685–94.

D. Emmet (1952), noting that STC adapted his Reason – Understanding distinction from Kant, continues: 'To Kant, the Understanding orders the phenomenal world; that is, it enables us to explore a world appearing to the senses which we interpret by means of the Categories as a world of substances in Space and Time causally and reciprocally affecting each other. Coleridge accepts this in general. "By the Understanding", he says, "I mean the faculty of thinking and forming judgments on the notices furnished by the senses, according to certain rules existing in itself" (viz., in the Understanding). Reason, on the other hand, for Kant is the kind of thinking which seeks a completeness which can never be found in empirical knowledge. Empirical knowledge is essentially incomplete, both because it proceeds by adding bit to bit in our factual understanding of the phenomenal world, and because it can never tell us the nature of things in themselves, as distinct from their appearances. Reason makes us aware of this essential incompleteness by holding before us ideals, such as the ideal of the world as an intelligible whole, or of the Soul as an active unity behind the succession of states studied by empirical psychology. But these ideals of the Reason are to Kant *regulative* only; they hold before the mind ideals which would give satisfaction, but they are as it were intellectual carrots; they can never be reached by the empirical methods by which alone knowledge (as distinct from postulates of practical reason) is possible. When Coleridge speaks of Reason and of the "Ideas of the Reason" he uses these expressions to mean neither "As If" concepts, nor formal principles of totality, but rather to express something like the dynamic power behind an actual way of thinking; that is to say, something which is not an objective concept at all' (167–8).

For other recent critical examinations of STC's Reason – Understanding distinction, see the following: McKenzie (1939) 6–13; Lovejoy (1940) 341–62; Sanders (1942) 35–48; Willey (1946; repr. 1949) 35–9; Bate (1950) 138–41; A. O. Lovejoy, *The Reason, The Understanding and Time* (Baltimore: Johns Hopkins, 1961) *passim*; Appleyard (1965) 119–22; Keppel-Jones (1967) 61–74; Orsini (1969) 130–48; Barfield (1972) 92–114.

2. *omnëity*: 'the condition of being all; "allness"'. (*OED*, which cites this passage from *The Statesman's Manual*.)

3. *anthropomorphic monotheism*: 'the attribution of personality or human form to (a single) God'.

4. *peripatetic*: 'Aristotelian; of Aristotle or his disciples'.

5. *nihil in intellectu*, etc.: 'there is nothing in the mind that is not first in the senses'. (This phrase, a commonplace in Western philosophy, originated in medieval commentaries on Aristotle's *De Anima*.) Cf *Biographia* Chap ix: 'Assume in its full extent the position, *nihil in intellectu quod non prius in sensu*, without Leibnitz's qualifying *præter ipsum intellectum*[a] ['except the mind itself'], and in the same sense, in which the position was understood by Hartley and Condillac:[b] and what Hume had dem-

onstratively deduced from this concession concerning cause and effect,[c] will apply with equal and crushing force to all the other eleven categorical forms,[d] and the logical functions corresponding to them. How can we make bricks without straw? or build without cement? We learn all things indeed by *occasion* of experience; but the very facts so learnt force us inward on the antecedents, that must be pre-supposed in order to render experience itself possible' (*BL* I 93–4). Cf also Extract 47–A, n 4.

a. Leibnitz, *Nouveaux Essais sur l'Entendement Humain* (1701; pub. 1765: criticism of Locke's *Essay*) LIV ii 1: 'On m'opposera cet axiome reçu parmi les Philosophes: que rien n'est dans l'âme qui ne vienne des sens. Mais il faut excepter l'âme même et ses affections. Nihil est in intellectu, quod non fuerit in sensu, excipe: nisi ipse intellectus'. [*Translation*: The axiom recognised by the Rationalists will be levelled against me: that there is nothing in the mind that does not come from the senses. But the mind itself and its affects must be excluded. There is nothing in the mind that has not been in the senses—except the mind itself.]

b. Etienne Condillac (1715–80), successor of Locke, reduced all the human faculties to a sensory basis. David Hartley (1705–57), founder of associationist school of psychology.

c. The process, that is, 'by which Hume degraded the notion of cause and effect into a blind product of delusion and habit, into the mere sensation of *proceeding* life (nisus vitalis) associated with the images of memory' (*Biographia* Chap vii; *BL* I 83). See David Hume (1711–76), *A Treatise of Human Nature* (1739–40) III xiv–xv; for brief statements of Hume's view of 'cause and effect', see *DP* 132, and *OCEL* 830.

d. I.e. Kant's 'Categories' in Part II of *The Critique of Pure Reason*. For a brief explanation, see *DP* 159.

6. *de rebus non apparentibus*, etc.: 'the rule is the same, both for things which do not appear and those which do not exist'.

7. *The Friend*, No. 5 (14 September 1809): *CC* IV ii 78. The passage (not included in the 1818 *Friend*) is altered slightly in the above quotation from the 1809 *Friend*.

8. *Hamlet* I ii 150.

9. *Paradise Lost* V 490 (*variatim*).

10. *superficies*: 'the outer surface of a body; the outward form or aspect'.

11. A pastiche of verses 22–7 of Chapter 7.

36. from CRABB ROBINSON'S DIARY (21 December 1816)

We found Coleridge at home, and we enjoyed his conversation for an hour and half. He looked ill, and indeed Mr Gillman[1] says he has been very ill. His bowels have been diseased, which he says is a family disease; but Gillman gives the best account of Coleridge's submission to discipline. He drinks only three glasses of wine every day, and takes no spirits nor any opium but when prescribed by Mr Gillman himself. Coleridge has been able to work a great deal of late and with success. His second and third *Lay Sermons*[2] and his *Poems* and Memoirs of his life,[3] etc., in two volumes are to appear. These exertions have been too great, Mr Gillman says. Coleridge talked easily and well, with less than his usual declamation. He explained at our request, and as I anticipated, his idea of fancy, styling it memory without judgment, and, of course, not filling that place in a chart of the mind[4] which imagination holds, and which in his *Lay Sermon* he has admirably described as the 'reconciling and mediatory power which, incorporating the reason in images of the sense, and organizing as it were the flux of the senses by the permanence and self-circling energies of the reason, gives birth to a system of symbols,' etc.[5] . . . Wordsworth's obscure discrimination between fancy and imagination in his last preface[6] is greatly illustrated by what Coleridge has here said and written.

(*HCR* I 200)

Notes

1. On 15 April 1816 STC had moved into the house of James Gillman, the Highgate physician, so that he might be kept under strict medical supervision. Although he expected to remain with the Gillmans for only a month, he stayed with the family in fact until his death in 1834; and, while he was unable to break his opium habit completely, his consumption of the drug certainly did decline—with beneficial results (as Crabb Robinson remarks) for his career as an author.
2. The first Lay Sermon (i.e. *The Statesman's Manual*), which appeared in December 1816, was to have been followed by two others; however, while the second, bearing the title *A Lay Sermon*, was published in March 1817, the third (which was to have been addressed to 'the Lower and Labouring Classes of Society') was in fact never written.
3. *Sibylline Leaves* and *Biographia Literaria* were published in July 1817.
4. Cf Extract 41–A.
5. Cf Extract 35–A.

6. For Wordsworth's Preface to *Poems* (1815), see Appendix. Crabb Robinson refers on several occasions (some well before the 1815 Preface was written) to Wordsworth's 'rather obscure account' of Fancy and Imagination: cf Diary entries for 31 May and 3 June 1812, 16 April 1815 and 11 September 1816 (*HCR* 1 89–90, 93, 165, 190–1).

37. 'FANCY IN NUBIBUS, OR THE POET IN THE CLOUDS' (1817)

O! it is pleasant, with a heart at ease,
Just after sunset, or by moonlight skies,
To make the shifting clouds be what you please,[1]
Or let the easily persuaded eyes[2]
Own each quaint likeness issuing from the mould
Of a friend's fancy; or with head bent low
And cheek aslant see rivers flow of gold
'Twixt crimson banks; and then, a traveller, go
From mount to mount through Cloudland, gorgeous land!
Or list'ning to the tide, with closéd sight,
Be that blind bard,[3] who on the Chian strand
By those deep sounds possessed with inward light,
Beheld the Iliad and the Odyssee[4]
Rise to the swelling of the voiceful sea.

(*CPW* 1 435)

Notes

1. Cf *Hamlet* III ii 390–9.
2. Cf *Biographia* Chap vi: 'Under that despotism of the eye, . . . we are restless because invisible things are not the objects of vision' (*BL* 1 74). Cf Introduction, p. 6.
3. Homer was traditionally supposed to have been born on the Ionian island of Chios.
4. Although this is one of the traditional spellings of *Odyssey*, STC may intend a pun on *sea* and *see*: the blind poet 'possessed with inward light' inspired to compose his epics by the rising sea-tides.

38. from 'Apologetic Preface' to 'FIRE, FAMINE, AND
SLAUGHTER' (1817)

If ever two great men might seem, during their whole lives, to have
moved in direct opposition, though neither of them has at any time
introduced the name of the other, Milton and Jeremy Taylor[1] were
they. [. . .] The same antithesis might be carried on with the
elements of their several intellectual powers. Milton, austere, condensed, imaginative, supporting his truth by direct enunciation of
lofty moral sentiment and by distinct visual representations, and in
the same spirit overwhelming what he deemed falsehood by moral
denuciation and a succession of pictures appalling or repulsive. In his
prose, so many metaphors, so many allegorical miniatures. Taylor,
eminently discursive, accumulative, and (to use one of his own
words) agglomerative; still more rich in images than Milton himself,
but images of fancy, and presented to the common and passive eye,
rather than to the eye of the imagination. Whether supporting or
assailing, he makes his way either by argument or by appeals to the
affections, unsurpassed even by the schoolmen in subtlety, agility,
and logic wit, and unrivalled by the most rhetorical of the fathers in
the copiousness and vividness of his expressions and illustrations. Here
words that convey feelings, and words that flash images, and words of
abstract notion, flow together, and whirl and rush onward like a
stream, at once rapid and full of eddies; and yet still interfused here
and there we see a tongue or islet of smooth water, with some picture
in it of earth or sky, landscape or living group of quiet beauty.

(CPW I 603, 604—5)

Note

1. For Taylor, see Extract 27 and n 1.

39. from *THE FRIEND* (1818)

(A) from 'On the Grounds of Morals and Religion', Essay IV
We have seen that from the confluence of innumerable impressions in
each moment of time the mere passive memory must needs tend to
confusion—a rule, the seeming exceptions to which (the thunder-

bursts in Lear, for instance) are really confirmations of its truth. For, in many instances, the predominance of some mighty Passion takes the place of the guiding Thought, and the result presents the method of Nature, rather than the habit of the Individual. For Thought, Imagination (and we may add, Passion), are, in their very essence, the first, connective, the latter co-adunative. . . .

(*CC* IV i 456)

(B) from 'On the Grounds of Morals and Religion', Essay VI
Such, too, is the case with the assumed indecomponible[1] substances of the LABORATORY. They are the symbols of elementary powers, and the exponents of a law, which, as the root of all these powers, the chemical philosopher, whatever his theory may be, is instinctively labouring to extract. This instinct, again, is itself but the form, in which the idea, the mental Correlative of the law, first announces its incipient germination in his own mind: and hence proceeds the striving after unity of principle through all the diversity of forms, with a feeling resembling that which accompanies our endeavours to recollect a forgotten name;[2] when we seem at once to have and not to have it; which the memory feels but cannot find. Thus, as 'the lunatic, the lover, and the poet,'[3] suggest each other to Shakspeare's Theseus, as soon as his thoughts present him the ONE FORM, of which they are but varieties; so water and flame, the diamond, the charcoal, and the mantling champagne, with its ebullient sparkles, are convoked and fraternized by the theory of the chemist. This is, in truth, the first charm of chemistry, and the secret of the almost universal interest excited by its discoveries. The serious complacency which is afforded by the sense of truth, utility, permanence, and progression, blends with and ennobles the exhilarating surprise and the pleasurable sting of curiosity, which accompany the propounding and the solving of an Enigma. It is the sense of a principle of connection given by the mind, and sanctioned by the correspondency of nature. Hence the strong hold which in all ages chemistry has had on the imagination. If in SHAKSPEARE we find nature idealized into poetry, through the creative power of a profound yet observant meditation, so through the ' meditative observation of a DAVY, a WOOLLASTON, or a HATCHETT;[4]

> By some connatural force,
> Powerful at greatest distance to unite
> With secret amity things of like kind,[5]

we find poetry, as it were, substantiated and realized in nature: yea, nature itself disclosed to us, GEMINAM *istam naturam, quæ fit et facit, et creat et creatur*,[6] as at once the poet and the poem!

(*CC* IV i 470—1)

Notes

1. *indecomponible*: 'not capable of being decomposed'.
2. Cf Extract 33—D.
3. *A Midsummer Night's Dream* v i 7.
4. Sir Humphry Davy (1778—1829), William Hyde Wollaston (1776—1828), and Charles Hatchett (1765—1847)—all chemists and physicists.
5. Milton, *Paradise Lost* x 246—8 (*variatim*).
6. GEMINAM *istam naturam*, etc.: 'that dual nature, which is made and makes, both creates and is created'. Cf Extract 14, n 4(c).

40. from the LECTURES ON LITERATURE (1818)

(A) from Lecture viii (20 February 1818)[1]

The Symbolical cannot, perhaps, be better defined in distinction from the Allegorical,[2] than that it is always itself a part of that, of the whole of which it is the representative.— 'Here comes a sail,'—(that is, a ship) is a symbolical expression. 'Behold our lion!' when we speak of some gallant soldier, is allegorical. Of most importance to our present subject is this point, that the latter (the allegory) cannot be other than spoken consciously;—whereas in the former (the symbol) it is very possible that the general truth represented may be working unconsciously in the writer's mind during the construction of the symbol;—and it proves itself by being produced out of his own mind,—as the Don Quixote out of the perfectly sane mind of Cervantes,[3] and not by outward observation, or historically. The advantage of symbolical writing over allegory is, that it presumes no disjunction of faculties, but simple predominance.

[. . . . . . .]

. . . madness may perhaps be defined as the circling in a stream which should be progressive and adaptive: Don Quixote grows at length to be a man out of his wits; his understanding is deranged; and hence without the least deviation from the truth of nature, without losing the least trait of personal individuality, he becomes a substantial living allegory, or personification of the reason and the moral sense, divested of the judgment and the understanding. Sancho is the converse.[4] He is the common sense without reason or imagination; and Cervantes not only shows the excellence and power of reason in Don Quixote, but in both him and Sancho the mischiefs resulting from a severance of the two main constituents of sound intellectual and moral action. Put him and his master together, and they form a perfect intellect; but they are separated and without cement; and hence each having a need of the other for its own completeness, each has at times a mastery over the other. For the common sense, although it may see the practical inapplicability of the dictates of the imagination or abstract reason, yet cannot help submitting to them. These two characters possess the world, alternately and interchangeably the cheater and the cheated. To impersonate them, and to combine the permanent with the individual, is one of the highest creations of genius, and has been achieved by Cervantes and Shakspeare, almost alone.

(*MC* 99, 102–3)

Notes

1. The manuscript sources which HNC used in preparing these notes for STC's lecture on *Don Quixote* have not survived; Raysor in *MC* simply reprints HNC's version from *LR*. STC also lectured on Cervantes in the lecture series delivered in February–March 1819: cf *CN* III 4503.
2. On the distinction between *symbol* and *allegory*, see Extract 35–A and n 9. Crabb Robinson records in his Diary that 'Coleridge was not in one of his happiest moods to-night. His subject was Cervantes, but he was more than usually prosing, and his tone peculiarly drawling. His digressions on the nature of insanity were carried too far, and his remarks on the book but old and by him often repeated . . .' (*HCR* 1 219).
3. Miguel Cervantes, *Don Quixote de la Mancha* (1605–15).
4. STC also contrasts Don Quixote and Sancho Panza in Extract 51–B. Cf also Extract 51–E.

(B) from Lecture xi (3 March 1818)[1]

The Asiatic supernatural beings are all produced by imagining an excessive magnitude, or an excessive smallness combined with great power; and the broken associations, which must have given rise to such conceptions, are the sources of the interest which they inspire, as exhibiting, through the working of the imagination, the idea of power in the will. This is delightfully exemplified in the Arabian Nights Entertainments,[2] and indeed, more or less, in other works of the same kind. In all these there is the same activity of mind as in dreaming, that is—an exertion of the fancy in the combination and recombination of familiar objects so as to produce novel and wonderful imagery.

[. . . . . .]

In the education of children, love is first to be instilled, and out of love obedience is to be educed. Then impulse and power should be given to the intellect, and the ends of a moral being be exhibited. For this object thus much is effected by works of imagination;—that they carry the mind out of self, and show the possible of the good and the great in the human character. The height, whatever it may be, of the imaginative standard will do no harm; we are commanded to imitate one who is inimitable.[3] We should address ourselves to those faculties in a child's mind, which are first awakened by nature, and consequently first admit of cultivation, that is to say, the memory and the imagination. The comparing power, the judgment, is not at that age active, and ought not to be forcibly excited, as is too frequently and mistakenly done in modern systems of education, which can only lead to selfish views, debtor and creditor principles of virtue, and an inflated sense of merit. In the imagination of man exist the seeds of all moral and scientific improvement;[4] chemistry was first alchemy, and out of astrology sprang astronomy. In the childhood of those sciences the imagination opened a way, and furnished materials, on which the ratiocinative powers in a maturer state operated with success. The imagination is the distinguishing characteristic of man as a progressive being;[5] and I repeat that it ought to be carefully guided and strengthened as the indispensable means and instrument of continued amelioration and refinement.[6] Men of genius and goodness are generally restless in their minds in the present, and this, because they are by a law of their nature unremittingly regarding themselves in the future, and contemplating the possible of moral and intellectual advance towards perfection. Thus we live by hope and faith; thus we are for the most part able to realize what we will, and thus we accomplish the end of our being. The contemplation of futurity inspires humility of soul in our judgment of the present.

I think the memory of children cannot, in reason, be too much stored with the objects and facts of natural history. God opens the images of nature, like the leaves of a book, before the eyes of his creature, Man—and teaches him all that is grand and beautiful in the foaming cataract, the glassy lake, and the floating mist.

The common modern novel, in which there is no imagination, but a miserable struggle to excite and gratify mere curiosity, ought, in my judgment, to be wholly forbidden to children. Novel-reading of this sort is especially injurious to the growth of the imagination, the judgment, and the morals, especially to the latter, because it excites mere feelings without at the same time ministering an impulse to action.[7] Women are good novelists, but indifferent poets; and this because they rarely or never thoroughly distinguish between fact and fiction. In the jumble of the two lies the secret of the modern novel, which is the *medium aliquid*[8] between them, having just so much of fiction as to obscure the fact, and so much of fact as to render the fiction insipid. The perusal of a fashionable lady's novel is to me very much like looking at the scenery and decorations of a theatre by broad daylight. The source of the common fondness for novels of this sort rests in the dislike of vacancy and that love of sloth, which are inherent in the human mind; they afford excitement without producing reaction.[9] By reaction I mean an activity of the intellectual faculties, which shows itself in consequent reasoning and observation, and originates action and conduct according to a principle.[10] Thus, the act of thinking presents two sides for contemplation,—that of external causality, in which the train of thought may be considered as the result of outward impressions, of accidental combinations, of fancy, or the associations of the memory,—and on the other hand, that of internal causality, or of the energy of the will on the mind itself. Thought, therefore, might thus be regarded as passive or active; and the same faculties may in a popular sense be expressed as perception or observation, fancy or imagination, memory or recollection.[11]

(*MC* 193–6)

Notes

1. According to the syllabus the subjects of Lecture xi were to have been as follows: 'On the Arabian Nights Entertainments, and on the *romantic* Use of the Supernatural in Poetry, and in Works of Fiction not poetical. On the Conditions and Regulations under which such Books may be employed advantageously in the earlier Periods of Education.' We are, as Raysor remarks (*MC* 191), 'sadly cheated in hearing nothing of "the *romantic* use of the supernatural in poetry"' in the notes that have

survived.

2. The *Arabian Nights' Entertainments* (or *The Thousand and One Nights*) is a collection of Arabic tales of uncertain provenance and date; these tales were introduced to Europe in Antoine Galland's French translation (1704–17), and were later translated (1739–41) into English by E. W. Lane. According to STC's own account, he had read the tales by the age of six (*CL* I 347); and he referred to them throughout his life (e.g. Extracts 48 and 51–A).

3. In a lecture on education delivered at the Royal Institution in May 1808, STC also stressed the importance of instilling love, morality and imagination in the early stages of education: cf *SC* II 9–12.

4. In Lecture ix (22 February 1819) of his series on the history of philosophy, STC argued that 'Extremes are produced by extremes. The tyranny of Aristotle and the Aristotelian philosophy called forth the visionaries and the mystics. . . . They indulged themselves with [their] imaginings so that certain indulgences became so vivid from hope that they declared they were so, and afterwards many of them, I believe, really believed it. But yet where the whole human faculties were called forth, and with amazing industry, something must come of it; and to the Alchemists we are indebted for chemistry as it now exists, a wonderful science I may call it, for it has transmuted into reality all the dreams of polytheism; and it would be difficult to find in the *Arabian Nights* anything more wonderful than chemistry has presented. So that which began in imagination, (proceeding and wedding with common sense, and finally with science), has ended in the gratification of it' (*PL* 282–3).

On the conjunction of Morality and Imagination, see also Shelley's *Defence of Poetry* (1821): 'The great secret of morals is love; or a going out of our own nature . . . A man, to be greatly good, must imagine intensely and comprehensively. . . . The great instrument of moral good is the imagination; and poetry administers to the effect by acting upon the cause. Poetry enlarges the circumference of the imagination by replenishing it with thoughts of ever new delight, which have the power of attracting and assimilating to their own nature all other thoughts, and which form new intervals and interstices whose void for ever craves fresh food. Poetry strengthens that faculty which is the organ of the moral nature of man, in the same manner as exercise strengthens a limb.' This line of reasoning eventually leads Shelley, in the closing sentence of his essay, to assert that 'Poets are the unacknowledged legislators of the world.'

5. Cf Extract I.

6. Walsh (1959), who quotes the passage thus far, comments: 'Imagination, it will be seen, receives an importance as an educative agency greater than the attenuated respect given it by most modern educators. For these to exercise the imagination is to cultivate a sense of the

aesthetic. And this, in a civilisation which confounds the artist with the aesthete, and confuses the severity and the chastity of the one with the preciousness and frivolity of the other, means a trivial and decorative addition to more seriously important human powers. But imagination is not a garnish of the soul, a mere finish according to a fashionable specific. . . . the duty of the school is to bring before the learner works of imagination of such quality (and science is also a human achievement imaginatively initiated) that "they show the possible of the good and great in the human character". The bleakness of so much schooling and the dehumanising influence of most science teaching come from confining imagination to a cramped parish of aesthetic activity. But imagination is the air in which new knowledge breathes, as it is the salt preserving the savour of the old. "Knowledge", it has been said, "does not keep any better than fish"' (23–4). STC discusses the role of imagination in education in other lectures as well: cf *SC* (1930) II 109–10, 293.

7. In arguing that the function of imaginative literature is to prompt moral action through the agency of delightful fictions, STC is placing himself firmly in the Christian humanist tradition. For Renaissance apologists, as for STC, the high importance of literature (especially poetry) is that it teaches morality and incites men to moral action more efficaciously than any other art or science. Sir Philip Sidney, for example, argues in the *Apologie for Poetrie* (1595) that, 'the ending end of all earthly learning being vertuous action, those skilles that most serue to bring forth that haue a most iust title to bee Princes ouer all the rest'; and he not unexpectedly concludes his argument in this way: 'Nowe therein of all Sciences (I speak still of humane, and according to the humaine conceits) is our Poet the Monarch. For he dooth not only show the way, but giueth so sweete a prospect into the way, as will intice any man to enter into it. . . . and with a tale forsooth he commeth vnto you, with a tale which holdeth children from play, and old men from the chimney corner. And, pretending no more, doth intende the winning of the mind from wickednesse to vertue: euen as the childe is often brought to take most wholsom things by hiding them in such other as haue a pleasant tast. . . . [And,] as vertue is the most excellent resting place for all worldlie learning to make his end of, so Poetrie, beeing the most familiar to teach it, and most princelie to moue towards it, in the most excellent work is the most excellent workman.' (Cf also Extract 13–D, n 2 and Extract 28, n 4.) It may be added that, since the purpose of poetry—indeed, of literature in general—is to teach virtue, it follows that the poet himself must be a virtuous man; and STC (like Shelley after him) here follows firmly in the footsteps of Minturno, Sidney, Ben Jonson and Milton: 'Coleridge', as Crabb Robinson recorded in his Diary (29 May 1812), 'talked of the impossibility of being a good poet

without being a good man' (*HCR* I 89). Ben Jonson had likewise asserted in the Preface to *Volpone* (1607): 'For if men will impartially, and not à-squint, looke toward the offices and functions of a *Poët*, they will easily conclude to themselues the impossibility of any mans being the good *Poët*, without first being a good *Man*'; and Milton in a famous sentence in the *Apology for Smectymnuus* (1642) maintains that 'he who would not be frustrate of his hope to write well hereafter in laudable things, ought him selfe to bee a true Poem, that is, a composition, and patterne of the best and honourablest things . . .'

I have stressed these points at such length, not only to locate STC in the moral tradition of Christian humanist poetics, but also to suggest how it was that he came to treat Imagination as an integral component of education, science, philosophy and theology—as well as literature. 'All Truth', as he told Poole (Extract 4), 'is a species of Revelation'; and the function of Imagination is, through *symbols*, to mediate truth to the Understanding: 'We cannot reason without imagination' (*CN* III 357). By its very nature art, and especially poetry, is admirably—indeed pre-eminently—suited to this task; and while the *immediate* object of poetry may be pleasure, its *ultimate* object is to bring 'the whole soul of man into activity' (Extract 33–G)—that is, to delight in order to teach (*docere cum delectatione*). Thus, we find him objecting to trivial fictions (as in the present Extract) and castigating the morals of Gessner's 'Der erste Schiffer' (Extract 7), but praising Wordsworth's achievement in *The Prelude* (Extract 30) and discoursing on the relationship between poetry and religion in a lecture on *Romeo and Juliet* (Extract 20).

8. *medium aliquid*: 'middle term'.

9. In *Biographia* Chap iii the 'devotees of the circulating libraries', who treat reading as 'their *pass-time*, or rather *kill-time*,' are characterised 'by the power of reconciling the two contrary yet co-existing propensities of human nature, namely, indulgence of sloth, and hatred of vacancy. In addition to novels and tales of chivalry in prose or rhyme . . . this genus comprises as its species, gaming, swinging, or swaying on a chair or gate; spitting over a bridge; smoking; snuff-taking; tête-à-tête quarrels after dinner between husband and wife; conning word by word all the advertisements of a daily newspaper in a public house on a rainy day, &c. &c. &c.' (*BL* I 34 n). Cf also the following statement in the 1818 *Friend*: 'It cannot but be injurious to the human mind never to be called into effort: the habit of receiving pleasure without any exertion of thought, by the mere excitement of curiosity and sensibility, may be justly ranked among the worst effects of habitual novel reading' (*CC* IV i 20).

10. In the opening number of *The Friend* (June 1809), STC gave succinct expression to a life-long conviction: 'It is my object to refer men to PRINCIPLES in all things; in Literature, in the Fine Arts, in Morals, in Legislation, in Religion' (*CC* IV ii 13). Cf also *Biographia* Chap xviii:

'The ultimate end of criticism is much more to establish the principles of writing, than to furnish *rules* how to pass judgement on what has been written by others; if indeed it were possible that the two could be separated' (*BL* II 63).

11. These are, of course, standard Coleridgean polarities: passive perception *versus* active observation; aggregative fancy *versus* coadunative imagination; mechanical, empirical memory *versus* intuitive, Platonic recollection. (On *recollection*, see Extract 40–C, n 20.)

(C) Lecture xiii (10 March 1818)[1]

Man communicates by articulation of Sounds, and paramountly by the memory in the Ear—Nature by the impressions of Surfaces and Bounds on the Eye, and thro' the Eye gives significance and appropriation, and thus the conditions of Memory (or the capability of being remembered) to Sounds, smells, &c. Now *Art* (I use the word collectively for Music, Painting, Statuary and Architecture) is the Mediatress, the reconciliator of Man and Nature.—

The primary Art is *Writing*, primary if we regard the purpose, abstracted from the different modes of realizing it—the *steps*, of which the instances are still presented to us in the lower degrees of civilization—gesticulation and rosaries or Wampum,[2] in the lowest—picture Language—Hieroglyphics—and finally, Alphabetic/ These all alike consist in the *translation*, as it were, of Man into Nature—the use of the visible in place of the Audible. The (so called) Music of Savage Tribes as little deserves the name of Art to the Understanding, as the Ear warrants it for Music—. Its lowest step is a mere expression of Passion by the sounds which the Passion itself necessitates—its highest, a voluntary re-production of those Sounds, in the absence of the occasioning Causes, so as to give the pleasure of *Contrast*—ex. gr. the various outcries of Battle in the song of Triumph, & Security.

Poetry likewise is purely *human*—all its materials are *from* the mind, and all the products are *for* the mind. It is the Apotheosis of the former state—viz. Order and Passion—*N.b.* how by excitement of the Associative Power Passion itself imitates Order, and the *order* resulting produces a pleasurable *Passion* (whence Metre) and thus elevates the Mind by making its feelings the Objects of its reflection/ and how recalling the Sights and Sounds that had accompanied the occasions of the original passion it impregnates them with an interest not their own by means of the Passions, and yet tempers the passion by the calming power which all *distinct* images exert on the human soul. (This *illustrated*.)

In this way Poetry is the Preparation for Art: inasmuch as it avails itself of the forms of Nature to recall, to express, and to modify the thoughts and feelings of the mind—still however thro' the medium of *articulate Speech*, which is so peculiarly human that in all languages it is the ordinary phrase by which Man and Nature are contra-distinguished—it is the original force of the word *brute*—and even now mute, and dumb do not convey the absence of sound, but the absence of articulate Sounds.

As soon as the human mind is intelligibly addressed by any outward medium, exclusive of articulate Speech, so soon does *Art* commence. But please to observe, that I have layed stress on the words, *human mind*—excluding thereby all results common to Man and all sentient creatures—and consequently, confining it to the effect produced by the congruity of the animal impression with the reflective Powers of the mind—so that not the Thing presented, but that which is *re*-presented, by the Thing, is the source of the Pleasure.— In this sense Nature itself is to a religious Observer the Art of God—and for the same cause Art itself might be defined, as of a middle nature between a Thought and a Thing,[3] or, as before, the union and reconciliation of that which is Nature with that which is exclusively Human.— Exemplify this by a good Portrait, which becomes more and more like in proportion to its excellence as a Work of Art—While a real *Copy*, a Fac Simile, ends in shocking us.—

Taking therefore *mute* as opposed not to sound but to articulate Speech, the oldest definition of Painting is in fact the true and the best definition of the Fine Arts in general—*muta Poesis*[4]— mute Poesy—and of course, *Poesy*—/—(and as all Languages perfect themselves by a gradual process of desynonymizing words originally equivalent, as Propriety, Property—I, Me—Mister, Master—&c/ I have cherished the wish, to use the word, Poesy, as the generic or common term, distinguishing that species of Poesy, which is not *muta* Poesis, by its usual name, *Poetry*/)[5] while of all the other species, which collectively form the *Fine Arts*, there would remain this as the common definition—that they all, like Poetry, are to express intellectual purposes, Thoughts, Conceptions, Sentiments that have their origin in the human Mind, but not, as Poetry, by means of articulate Speech, but as Nature, or the divine Art, does, by form color, magnitude, Sound, and proportion, silently or musically.—

Well—it may be said—but who has ever thought otherwise. We all know, that Art is the imitatress of Nature.—And doubtless, the Truths, I hope to convey, would be barren Truisms, if all men meant the same by the words, *imitate* and *nature*. But is would be flattering mankind at large, to presume that this is the Fact./ First, imitate—The impression on the wax is not an imitation but *a Copy* of the Seal—the Seal itself is an Imitation./ But farther—in order to form a philosophic conception, we must seek for the *kind*—as the *heat* in Ice—invisible Light—&c—but for practical purposes, we must have reference to the degree.

It is sufficient that philosophically we understand that in all Imitation two elements must exist, and not only exist but must be perceived as existing—Likeness and unlikeness, or Sameness and Difference.[6] All Imitation in the Fine Arts is the union of Disparate Things.—Wax Images—Statues—Bronze—Pictures—the Artist may take his point where he likes—provided that the effect desired is produced—namely, that there should be a Likeness in Difference & a union of the two—*Tragic Dance*.[7]

So Nature—346.[8]—i.e. natura naturata[9]—& hence the natural Question/ What *all* and every thing?— No, but the Beautiful.—And what is the Beautiful?[10]—The definition is at once undermined.—/ If the Artist painfully *copies* nature, what an idle rivalry! If he proceeds from a Form, that answers to the notion of Beauty, namely, the many seen as one—what an emptiness, an unreality—as in Cypriani[11]—The *essence* must be mastered—the natura naturans,[9] & this presupposes *a bond* between *Nature* in this higher sense and the soul of Man—.—

Sir Joshua Reynolds—/ 350—[12]

Far be it from me, to intend a censure—Sacred be his memory as that of a Benefactor of the Race in that which is its highest destination— &c—

The wisdom in Nature distinguished from Man by the coinstantaneity[13] of the Plan & the Execution, the Thought and the Production—In Nature there is no reflex act[14]—but the same powers without reflection, and consequently without Morality. (Hence *Man* the *Head* of the visible Creation—*Genesis*.[15]) Every step antecedent to full consciousness found in Nature—so to place them as for some one effect, totalized & fitted to the limits of a human Mind, as to elicit and as it were superinduce *into* the forms the reflection, to which they approximate—this is the Mystery of Genius in the Fine Arts—Dare I say that the Genius must act on the feeling, that *Body* is but a striving to become Mind—that it is *mind*, in its essence——?

As in every work of *Art* the Conscious is so impressed on the Unconscious, as to appear *in* it (ex. gr. Letters on a Tomb compared with Figures constituting a Tomb)—so is the Man of Genius the Link that combines the two—but for that reason, he must partake of both—Hence, there is in Genius itself an unconscious activity[16]—nay, that is *the* Genius in the man of Genius.—

This the true Exposition of the Rule, that the Artist must first *eloign*[17] himself from Nature in order to return to her with full effect.—Why this?—Because—if he began by mere painful copying, he would produce Masks only, not forms breathing Life—he must out of his own mind create forms according to the several Laws of the Intellect, in order to produce in himself that co-ordination of Freedom & Law, that involution of the Obedience in the Prescript,[18] and of the Prescript in the impulse to obey, which assimilates him to Nature—enables him to understand her—. He absents himself from her only in his own Spirit, which has the same ground with Nature, to learn her unspoken language, in its main radicals,[19] before he approaches to her endless compositions of those radicals—Not to acquire cold notions, lifeless technical Rules, but living and life-producing Ideas, which contain their own evidence/ and in that evidence the certainty that they are essentially one with the germinal causes in Nature, his Consciousness being the focus and mirror of both—for this does he for a time abandon the external *real*, in order to return to it with a full sympathy with its internal & actual—. Of all, we see, hear, or touch, the substance is and must be in ourselves—and therefore there is no alternative *in reason* between the dreary (& thank heaven! almost impossible) belief that everything around us is but a phantom, or that the Life which is in us is in them likewise—and that to know is to *resemble*. When we speak of Objects out of ourselves, even as within ourselves to learn is, according to Plato, only to *recollect*.[20]—The only effective Answer to which (that I have been fortunate enough to meet with) is that which Mr Pope has consecrated for future use in the Line—

And Coxcombs vanquish Berkley with a *Grin*.[21]

To that within the thing, active thro' Form and Figure as by symbols[?discoursing][22] *Natur-geist*[23] must the Artist imitate, as we unconsciously imitate those we love—So only can he produce any work truly *natural*, in the Object, and truly *human* in the Effect.—The Idea that puts the forms together, can not be itself form—It is above Form, is its Essence, the Universal in the Individual, Individuality itself—the Glance and the Exponent of the indwelling Power—[24]

Each thing, that lives, has its moment of *self-exposition*, and each period of *each* thing—if we remove the disturbing forces of accident—and this is the business of ideal Art.—Child-hood—Youth—Age—Man—Woman/—And each thing, that appears not to live, has its possible position & relation to Life/ & so it is in Nature—where she cannot *be*, she *prophecies*—in the tree-like forms of ores &c/

Difference of Form as proceeding and Shape as superinduced—the latter either the Death or the imprisonment of the Thing; the former, its self-witnessing, and self-effected sphere of agency—

Art would or should be the abridgment of Nature. Now the Fullness of Nature is without character as Water is purest when without taste, smell or color—but this is the Highest, the Apex, not the whole—& Art is to give *the whole* ad hominem/[25] hence each step of Nature has its Ideal, & hence too the possibility of a climax up to the perfect Form, of harmonized Chaos—

To the idea of Life Victory or Strife is necessary—As Virtue not in the absence of vicious Impulses but in the overcoming of them/[26] so Beauty not in the absence of the Passions, but on the contrary—it is heightened by the sight of what is conquered—this *in* the [?figure/fugue], or *out* by contrast—

(*CN* III 4397)

Notes

1. *CN* III 4397 n: 'The entry is a series of fragmentary notes, some of them condensed transcriptions of the main headings of the first part of Schelling's lecture "Über das Verhältniss der bildenden Künste zu der Natur" (1807). . . . Like some of his other lecture notes, these look less like planned notes for a lecture and more like desultory notes from reading.' Shawcross prints an expanded version of this Notebook entry under the title 'On Poesy or Art': *BL* II 253–63. Both Coburn's and Shawcross's footnotes to this entry should be consulted; they are, unfortunately, too long to be reprinted here. An English translation of Schelling's essay ('Concerning the Relation of the Plastic Arts to Nature') is available in Read (1957) 323–64. See also *CN* III 4066 n.

2. *Wampum*: 'Cylindrical beads made from the ends of shells rubbed down, polished, and threaded on strings; used among North American Indians as currency, for ornament, and (as a substitute for writing) for mnemonic and symbolic purposes, according to the arrangement of the beads.'

3. Cf Extract 33–B, n 3.

4. *muta Poesis*: In the Introduction to *Laokoon* (1766), Gotthold Ephraim Lessing (with whose works STC was intimately familiar) 'undertook to undo the confusion in theory and practice between poetry and the graphic and plastic arts which, he believed, resulted from an uninquisitive acceptance of Simonides' maxim that "painting is dumb poetry and poetry a speaking painting"': Abrams (1953) 13. Simonides of Ceos (*c.* 556–468 BC) was a Greek lyric poet.

5. In MS Egerton 2800 (British Museum) there is a fragment in STC's hand containing the following sentence: 'It were perhaps to be wished, that we should desynonymize the two words, Poetry and Poesy, by using the latter, as the generic name of all the fine Arts: for every work of Genius, containing the End in the Means, is a ποιησις [making], as distinguished from a mere συνταξις [arrangement, ordering], or collocation for an external and conventional End' (*CC* IV i 465, n 2).

6. Cf *Table Talk* (3 July 1833): 'Imitation is the mesothesis of likeness and difference. The difference is as essential to it as the likeness; for without the difference, it would be copy or fac-simile. But to borrow a term from astronomy, it is a librating* mesothesis: for it may verge more to likeness as in painting, or more to difference, as in sculpture.' [* In astronomy *libration* is 'a real or apparent motion of an oscillating kind'. A *mesothesis* is 'a middle term or thing, serving to connect or reconcile antagonistic agencies or principles'.] Cf also Extracts 25 and 33–I, and *AR* 3–4.

7. On the 'reconciliation of opposites', see Extracts 21, 33–G, 35–A and n 5.

8. A page reference to Schelling's *Verhältniss*: n 1 above.

9. *natura naturata* (*lit.* 'nature natured'): 'created nature'; *natura naturans* (*lit.* 'nature naturing'): 'creating nature'. (Cf Extract 17–A.) Miss Coburn cites Schelling's *Naturphilosophie* (1799): '*Nature* as mere *product* (natura naturata) we call Nature as *Object*. . . . *Nature* as *productivity* (natura *naturans*) we call *Nature as Subject*.' The distinction between *natura naturata* and *natura naturans* is integral not only to STC's aesthetic and philosophic theory but also to his theology—for instance, in a letter to C. A. Tulk (the Swedenborgian) of September 1817 he develops the distinction in these terms: 'True Philosophy begins with the τὸ θεῖον ['God's handiwork'] in order to end in the ὉΘεός ['God']; takes it's root in Science in order to blossom into Religion' (*CL* IV 768). For a helpful modern commentary on STC's use of *naturata* and *naturans*, see Barfield (1972) 22–5.

10. Cf Extract 26.

11. Giovanni Battista Cipriani (1727–85) is an Italian painter whose 'decorative, highly-artificial subjects—nymphs, amorini, and mythical figures—were much too Della Cruscan in spirit to be acceptable' to STC (Coburn).

12. Sir Joshua Reynolds (1723–92) was a portrait painter and the author of fifteen *Discourses* delivered before the Royal Academy (1769 to 1790) on the subject of mimesis.

    350: another page reference to Schelling's *Verhältniss*.

13. *coinstantaneity*: 'occuring or existing at the same instant'.

14. I.e., 'no turning back of the mind upon itself' (Coburn).

15. Genesis 1: 26–30.

16. On the role of the unconscious in STC's aesthetic theory, see Baker (1957). Cf also Extract 33–B.

17. *eloign*: in *CN* III 3624 STC defines the word as meaning 'withdraw, absent &c.'; and in *CN* III 4166 he provides a fanciful etymology and jocular series of definitions for the word: '. . . in the imperative eloign thee! = make thyself distant/ off with thee to moldary! Go to Hell & to the farthest end of it! &c &c'.

18. *prescript*: 'that which is laid down as a rule; an ordinance, law; a regulation'.

19. *radicals*: 'qualities inherent in the nature or essence of a thing'.

20. Plato, *Phaedo* 75e: 'And if it is true that we acquired our knowledge before our birth, and lost it at the moment of birth, but afterward, by the exercise of our senses upon sensible objects, recover the knowledge which we had once before, I suppose that what we call learning will be the recovery of our own knowledge, and surely we should be right in calling this recollection' (Tredennick translation). Cf *Meno* 81c–d.

21. Here, as in *Biographia* Chap x (*BL* I 93), STC ascribes the line to Alexander Pope; in fact, however, it comes from John Brown's *Essay on Satire, Occasioned by the Death of Mr Pope* II 224 (*variatim*). Brown's tribute was published in Warburton's edition of Pope's *Works* (1751).

    Berkley: George Berkeley (1685–1753), pluralistic idealist.

22. The word is illegible. Miss Coburn, however, who suggests three possibilities—*discoursing, discovering, discerning*—concludes that 'the correct reading. . . . is probably *discoursing*' (*CN* III 4397 n).

23. *Natur-geist*: 'Nature-spirit'. The term is from Schelling's *Verhältniss*: n 1 above.

24. In connection with this paragraph, see STC's discussion of *symbol* in Extract 35–A.

25. *ad hominem: lit.* 'to the human being', i.e., so as to appeal to an individual's circumstances, or to speak to his condition.

26. Cf Milton, *Areopágitica* (1644): 'And perhaps this is that doom which Adam fell into of knowing good and evil, that is to say of knowing good by evil. As therefore the state of man now is; what wisdom can there be to choose, what continence to forbear without the knowledge of evil? He that can apprehend and consider vice with all her baits and seeming pleasures, and yet abstain, and yet distinguish, and yet prefer that which is truly better, he is the true warfaring Christian. I cannot praise a

fugitive and cloistered virtue, unexercised and unbreathed, that never sallies out and sees her adversary, but slinks out of the race, where that immortal garland is to be run for, not without dust and heat. Assuredly we bring not innocence into the world, we bring impurity much rather; that which purifies us is trial, and trial is by what is contrary. . . . Wherefore did ˙[God] create passions within us, pleasures round about us, but that these rightly tempered are the very ingredients of virtue?'

41. MARGINALIA in Tennemann's *Geschichte der Philosophie*[1]

(A) from Vol.VIII, Pt. ii, back paste-down[2]
The simplest yet practically sufficient order of the Mental Powers is, beginning from the

lowest	highest	
Sense	Reason	Fancy and Imagination are
Fancy	Imagination	Oscillations, *this* connecting
Understanding	Understanding	R[eason] and U[nder-
		standing]; *that* connect-
Understanding	Understanding	ing Sense and Understanding.
Imagination	Fancy,	
Reason	Sense[3]	

(CSC 693–4)

Notes

1. W. G. Tennemann, *Geschichte der Philosophie*, 11 vols (1798–1812). For a general assessment of STC's marginalia in Tennemann, see *PL* 18.
2. Jackson (1969) writes: 'This note can be dated with some confidence as belonging to the period between the beginning of July, 1818, and the end of March, 1819. The set of Tennemann belonged to J. H. Green: Coleridge sent him a letter on 3 July 1818 asking if he might borrow it "two Volumes at a time" (*CL* IV 870), and used it when he was preparing for his series of philosophical lectures which ended on 29 March 1819' (190–1).
3. The importance of this marginal note and its place in STC's theory of Imagination (both philosophic and aesthetic) are examined by Jackson

(1969) 113–21; Barfield (1972) 96–103; Boulger (1973) 13–24; Pradhan (1974) 235–54.

On STC's Reason–Understanding distinction, see Extract 35–B, n 1. In a famous essay on Coleridge published in *The Westminster Review* (1840), John Stuart Mill summarised STC's view of Reason and Understanding in this way: STC 'claims for the human mind a capacity, within certain limits, of perceiving the nature and properties of "Things in themselves". He distinguishes in the human intellect two faculties, which, in the technical language common to him with the Germans, he calls Understanding and Reason. The former faculty judges of phenomena, or the appearances of things, and forms generalizations from these: to the latter it belongs, by direct intuition, to perceive things, and recognize truths, not cognizable by our senses. These perceptions are not indeed innate, nor could ever have been awakened in us without experience; but they are not copies of it: experience is not their prototype, it is only the occasion by which they are irresistibly suggested. The appearances in nature excite in us, by an inherent law, ideas of those invisible things which are the causes of the visible appearances, and on whose laws those appearances depend: and we then perceive that these things must have pre-existed to render the appearances possible; just as (to use a frequent illustration of Coleridge's) we see, before we know that we have eyes; but when once this is known to us, we perceive that eyes must have pre-existed to enable us to see. Among the truths which are thus known *à priori*, by occasion of experience, but not themselves the subjects of experience, Coleridge includes the fundamental doctrines of religion and morals, the principles of mathematics, and the ultimate laws even of physical nature; which he contends cannot be proved by experience, though they must necessarily be consistent with it, and would, if we knew them perfectly, enable us to account for all observed facts, and to predict all those which are as yet unobserved': from *Mill on Bentham and Coleridge*, ed. F. R. Leavis (London: Chatto & Windus, 1950) 109–10.

(B) from Vol. X, pp. 183–97[1]

The imaginative power (a multiform power, which acting with its permeative modifying unifying might on the Thought and Images specificates[2] the Poet, the swimming Crimson of eve in mountain Lake, River, Vale, Village and Village Church, the flashing or sleeping Moonshine in Nature's Poesy—and which exercising the same power in moral intuitions & the representations of worth or baseness in action is the essential constituent of what is called *a Good heart*—this power cannot be given or bought. It is always an Indigena of the Soil. Therefore I ought not to wonder—& yet from the sincere respect and *good liking* I bear to Tennemann I cannot help wondering—that he could give even the meagre and gritty account, that he has given, of poor Böhmen[3] without some sympathy with the strivings and ferment of a genius so compressed and distorted by strait circumstances and the want of all the aids and organs of Speculative Thought, as that of the Visionary Sutor,[4] or some admiration of the occasional Auroras[5] & Streaming Lights in his dark Heaven.

(*PL* 452–3, n 25)[6]

Notes

1. On the date of this extract, see Extract 41–A, n 2.
2. *specificate*: 'to distinguish as belonging to a particular species, group, kind, etc.' (*OED*)
3. Jacob Boehme (1575–1624) was a German peasant and mystic, by vocation a shoemaker in Görlitz. STC owned—and from February 1808 onward annotated copiously—a copy of *The Works of Jacob Behmen, the Teutonic Theosopher*, ed. W. Law, 4 vols (London, 1764–81). STC's interest in Boehme was life-long; he read the *Aurora* as a schoolboy and, in an early Notebook entry of 1795 or 1796 (*CN* I 174), he placed Boehme's name fourth in a list of projected works; for a later assessment, see *BL* I 95–8. The nature of Boehme's influence is discussed by A. D. Snyder, 'Coleridge on Böhme' *PMLA* 45 (1930) 616–18—where Miss Snyder quotes from STC's marginalia on Boehme; Stallknecht (1958) 51–3, 105–8; McFarland (1969) 248–51, 325–32. Cf also Extract 47–B, nn 1 and 7.
4. *Sutor* is Latin for shoemaker; Boehme was a cobbler.
5. A punning reference to Boehme's *Aurora*: cf n 3 above.
6. Revised text supplied by George Whalley.

42. from the *LECTURES ON THE HISTORY OF PHILOSOPHY*

(A) from Lecture iii (4 January 1819)

In my last address I understand that that part of the lecture which referred to the peculiar arithmetical metaphysics of Pythagoras[1] was not fully understood and as it will lead me immediately to the purpose of the present I will take the opportunity of attempting to explain myself. There is no one among us who feels the least inclination to call a cudgel a bruise or a sword a wound or the pain. The reason is evidently this, because a cudgel and a sword are separate and distinct images to the senses. But we all of us and in all languages call the sensation heat or cold and the outward cause of it by the same names; and inevitable as this is, it has produced a great confusion of thought, not indeed in the palpable instance which I have now mentioned, but in many others; and yet as common to all nations and arising out of the nature of the human mind it may well be believed to refer to some important truth. We know that chemistry found itself soon compelled to frame a different word for the *cause*, to distinguish it from the *sensation* it was produced to effect: and hence we have the word 'calorif' or 'calorific'.[2] We know, too, that in the first edition of Newton's *Optics* he had spoken of *radii colorati*, colored rays, which he altered afterwards to *radii colorati formati*, color-making rays.[3] Now it appears that Pythagoras had proceeded upon this opinion, that those unknown somethings, powers or whatever you may call them, that manifest themselves in the intellect of man, or what in the language of the old philosophy would be called the intelligible world, as numbers, and the essential power of numbers, these same manifest themselves to us and are the objects of our senses, I mean as creative and organizing powers: in short, that the very powers which in men reflect and contemplate, are in their essence the same as those powers which in nature produce the objects contemplated. This position did indeed appear to be deducible from that of the Ionic school, I mean that of Thales,[4] that there is no action but from like on like, that no substances or beings essentially dissimilar could possibly be made sensible of each other's existence or in any way act thereon.

This involves an essential—I know not how I can avoid using a pedantic word—HOMOGENEITY—a sameness of the conceiver *and the conception*, of the idea and the law corresponding to the idea. In the language of the old philosophy they would say that the eye could not possibly perceive light but by having in its own essence something luciferous,[5] that the ear could not have been the organ of hearing but by having in its essence, and not by mechanism, something conformed to the air. The obstacle to the acceptance of this position is to be found in the [sensuous][6] fancy and imagination, as far as they take their materials from the senses, which constantly present the soul, the percipient, as a sort of inner more subtle body, a kind of under waistcoat, as it were, to the bodily garment, and the mind itself as a vessel or at best a MOULD, sometimes even as a blank tablet,[7] in short, to take the meaning of all inclusively, as a passive receiver, A

SUBSTANCE which in fact, however, as we may convince ourselves by a little self-examination, is nothing more than the craving for AN INNER SURFACE, an image SUPPORTING. We have been accustomed by all our affections, by all our wants, to seek after outward images; and by the love of association, therefore, to whole truth we attach that particular condition of truth which belongs to sensible bodies or to bodies which can be touched. [8] The first education which we receive, that from our mothers, is given to us by touch; the whole of its process is nothing more than, to express myself boldly, an extended touch by promise. [9] The sense itself, the sense of vision itself, is only acquired by a continued recollection of touch. No wonder therefore, that beginning in the animal state, we should carry this onward through the whole of our being however remote it may be from the true purposes of it. Therefore an image supporting something (which in itself is a contradiction, for an image always supposes a superficies [10] and a something supported, and is asked for under the name of a substance) is construed into an agent when we can no longer boldly bring forward a thing for it; and this agent is contradistinguished from an act as if these oppositions of our human language and thoughts were really the true conditions and the very essence of our being. But to comprehend the philosophy of Pythagoras the mind itself must be conceived of AS AN ACT; and the numbers of Pythagoras and the Cabalists [11] with the equivalent Ideas of the Platonists, ARE not so properly acts of the Reason, in their sense I mean, as they are THE Reason itself in act. [12]

[. . . . .]

. . . in this age was Socrates born, whose whole life was one contest against the sophists, [13] but who yet marked the necessity of revelation by an intermixture of weakness, nay even of sophistry, in his own mode of contending against them. He did the best it was *possible* for unassisted man to do. He lived holily and died magnanimously. . . .

He was a man (if I may speak of him as a man and as far as we can learn of his biographer Xenophon [14] or the more suspicious representations of Plato, who however is very faithful in his portraits) one who generally appears to have possessed a fine and active but yet not very powerful imagination—an imagination instrumental and illustrative rather than predominant and creative; but beyond all doubt what characterized him was—pardon the play on words, the UNCOMMON excellence of common sense. Naturally and by observation he excelled in this and cultivated it. There was in his character an exquisite balance, an equilibrium and harmony of all the various faculties, so that everywhere his mind acted by a sort of tact, as it were, rather than arithmetically or by examining the process. This without genius would have been the character of a wise, natural, unaffected man; but Socrates doubtless possessed genius in a high degree, a peculiar turn for contemplation, not for the purposes of physical truth, but in aid of prior truths or anticipations found in his own nature by meditation. He meditated, observed the goings on of his mind, started questions to himself; as far as by himself he could decide them he did, but then modestly went forth among mankind and still questioned everywhere how far general experience authorized him to generalize those truths.[15]

(*PL* 113–15, 136–7)

Notes

1. Pythagoras was a Greek philosopher of the sixth century BC who 'discovered the numerical relation between the length of strings and the musical notes which they produce when vibrating, and evolved the idea that the explanation of the universe is to be sought, not in matter, but in numbers and their relations, of which the objects of sense are the representations' (*OCCL* 356). For a more detailed examination of Pythagorean numerology, see *OCD* 904.

2. *calorific*: 'producing heat'. According to *OED*, the word was first used in 1682.

3. Sir Isaac Newton (1642–1727) first communicated his theory of light and colours to the Royal Society in 1672; later, his researches were summed up in his *Optics* (1704).

4. Thales of Miletus (seventh century BC) founded the first Greek school of philosophy. According to Aristotle (*Metaphysics* 983b20–984a3), Thales posited that everything in the universe is a modification of a single imperishable substance, which he held to be water.

5. The 'old philosophy' in this instance is the Alexandrian Neoplatonism of Plotinus and his school; see, for example, *Enneads* IV v 4 and V v 7. Cf *CN* II 2164.

6. Notebook 25 has the word 'sensuous' (as Miss Coburn notes in her list of variants: *PL* 114).

7. The empiricist view that the mind is initially like a blank tablet (or a block of wax) on which experience leaves impressions goes back to classical philosophy: e.g., Plato, *Theaetetus* 191c–200c *passim* (where the theory is posited but then rejected), and Aristotle, *De Anima* 424a16–23 where it is argued that sensory experience 'must be conceived of as taking place in the way in which a piece of wax takes on the impress of a

signet-ring without the iron or gold . . .' (Smith translation). This idea passed in due course to the British empiricists and, largely through the influence of John Locke's *Essay Concerning Human Understanding* (1690), became the stereotyped view of the mind in the eighteenth century. In an early draft of his *Essay*, Locke asserted that the soul 'at first is perfectly *rasa tabula*', i.e. a *scraped slate*; in the 1690 version the image, but not the idea, changes: 'Let us then suppose the mind to be, as we say, white paper void of all characters, without any *ideas*. How comes it to be furnished? . . . Whence has it all the materials of reason and knowledge? To this I answer, in one word, from *experience*; in that all our knowledge is founded, and from that it ultimately derives itself' (II i 2). In such systems the mind is merely a passive receiver and recorder of external impressions; and it is against this 'philosophy of death' that STC asserts, with Pythagoras *et al.*, that 'the mind itself must be conceived of AS AN ACT'. Cf also Introduction, p. 1, and Extracts 4 and 17–A.

8. Cf Introduction, p. 6. In a marginal comment in his copy of Erigena's *De Divisione Naturae*, STC deplored 'that Slavery of the Mind to the Eye and the visual Imagination or Fancy under the influence of which the Reasoner must have a *picture* and mistakes surface for substance' (*PL* 434).

9. 'Another example of Coleridge's pre-Freudian insights': Coburn's note (*PL* 405, n 5).

10. *superficies*: 'the outer surface of a body; the surface layer'.

11. Originally the Kabbalah (or Cabbala) referred to the oral tradition handed down from Moses to the Rabbis of the Mishnah and the Talmud; however, 'since the 11th or 12th century . . . Kabbalah has become the exclusive appellation for the renowned system of theosophy which claims to have been transmitted uninterruptedly by the mouths of the patriarchs and prophets ever since the creation of the first man' (*Encyclopædia Britannica* 9th ed. s.v.). On the number system of the Kabbalah, see either the *Britannica* article cited above, or the *Encyclopædia of Religion and Ethics*, ed. J. Hastings *et al.* (Edinburgh: T. Clark, 1914) VII 624.

12. For STC on Reason, see Extract 35–B, n 1.

13. In ancient Greece a *sophist* was one who gave lessons in the various arts and sciences—for a fee. As time passed the sophists began to concentrate on rhetoric, that is, to stress the *form* rather than the *substance* of knowledge, and the term came to denote a 'quibbler'. Cf Socrates' biting definition in Plato's *Sophist* 223b: 'his art may be traced as a branch of the appropriative, acquisitive family—which hunts animals, living, land, tame animals—which hunts man, privately, for hire, taking money in exchange, having the semblance of education—and this is termed Sophistry, and is a hunt after young men of wealth and rank—such is the conclusion.'

14. Xenophon, the famous Athenian commander who led the 'Ten Thousand' safely out of Persia, had been from boyhood a friend and student of Socrates; he set down later in life his recollections of his old master in three treatises: *Memorabilia, Symposium* and *Apology*. Plato seems less trustworthy as a biographer because of a tendency to put his own ideas into Socrates' mouth; however, it may be that Xenophon, not being a philosopher, does less than proper justice to these doctrines.

15. STC also discussed the Socratic method of instruction in Lecture iv: see *PL* 148–54.

(B) from Lecture xi (8 March 1819)

But that there is potentially, if not actually, in every rational being a somewhat, call it what you will, the purest reason, the spirit, true light, intellectual intuition, etc. etc.; and that in this are to be found the indispensable conditions of all science, and scientific research, whether meditative, contemplative, or experimental; is often expressed and everywhere supposed by Lord Bacon.[1] And that this is not only the right but the possible nature of the human mind, to which it is capable of being restored, is implied in the various remedies prescribed by him for its diseases, and in the various means of neutralizing or converting into useful instrumentality the imperfections which cannot be removed. There is a sublime truth contained in his favourite phrase—*Idola intellectus*.[2] He tells us that the mind of man is an edifice not built with human hands, which needs only to be purged of its idols and idolatrous services to become the temple of the true and living light. Nay, he has shown and established the true criterion between the ideas of the mind and the idols, namely that the former are manifested by their adequacy to those ideas in nature which in and through them are contemplated.

This therefore is the true Baconic philosophy. It consists in this, in a profound meditation on those laws which the pure reason[3] in man reveals to him, with the confident anticipation and faith that to this will be found to correspond certain laws in nature. If there be aught that can be said to be purely in the human mind, it is surely those acts of its own imagination which the mathematician avails himself of, for I need not I am sure tell you that a line upon a slate is but a picture of that act of the imagination which the mathematician alone consults. That it is the picture only is evident, for never could we learn the art of the imagination, or form an idea of a line in the mathematical sense, from that picture of it which we draw beforehand. Otherwise how could we draw it without depth or breadth? It becomes, evidently, too, an act of the imagination. Out of these simple acts the mind, still proceeding, raises that wonderful superstructure of geometry and then looking abroad into nature finds that in its own nature it has been fathoming nature, and that nature itself is but the greater mirror in which he beholds his own present and his own past being in the law, and learns to reverence while he feels the necessity of that one great Being whose eternal reason is the ground and absolute condition of the ideas in the mind, [4] and no less the ground and the absolute cause of all the correspondent realities in nature—the reality of nature for ever consisting in the law by which each thing is that which it is.

Hence, and so has Lord Bacon told us, all science approaches to its perfection in proportion as it immaterializes objects. . . .

(PL 333–4)

Notes

1. Francis Bacon (1561–1626), whom STC elsewhere calls 'the British Plato' (CC IV i 488), was an English anti-Aristotelian philosopher.

2. *Idola intellectus*: 'intellectual idols *or* spectres' (cf n 4 c below). 'Inspired by the Renaissance, and in revolt against Aristotelianism and Scholastic logic, [Bacon] proposed an *inductive* method of discovering truth, founded upon empirical observation, analysis of observed data, inference resulting in hypotheses, and verification of hypotheses through continued observation and experiment. The impediments to the use of this method are preconceptions and prejudices, grouped by Bacon under four headings, or *Idols*: (a) *The Idols of the Tribe*, or racially "wishful", anthropocentric ways of thinking, e.g. explanation by final causes, (b) *The Idols of the Cave* or personal prejudices, (c) *The Idols of the Market Place*, or failure to define terms, (d) *The Idols of the Theatre*, or blind acceptance of tradition and authority' (DP 34). For a more detailed account of this aspect of Baconian thought, see Chapter VIII ('Idols or False Phantoms') of F. H. Anderson's *The Philosophy of Francis Bacon* (Chicago: University of Chicago Press, 1948; New York: Octagon Books, 1971, repr. 1975).

3. For STC on Reason, see Extract 35–B, n 1.

4. In the 1818 *Friend* STC draws an explicit parallel between Bacon and Plato's views of *idea* in a discussion which throws considerable light on the passage from Lecture xi: 'Thus the difference, or rather distinction between Plato and Lord Bacon is simply this: that philosophy being necessarily bi-polar, Plato treats principally of the truth, as it manifests itself at the *ideal* pole, as the science of intellect (i.e. de mundo intelligibili[a]); while Bacon confines himself, for the most part, to the same truth, as it is manifested at the other, or material pole, as the science of nature (i.e. de mundo sensibili[b]). . . . Hence too, it will not surprise us, that Plato so often calls ideas LIVING LAWS, in which the mind has its

whole true being and permanence; or that Bacon, vicè versâ, names the laws of nature, *ideas*; and represents what we have, in a former part of this disquisition, called *facts of science* and *central phænomena*, as signatures, impressions, and symbols of ideas. A distinguishable power self-affirmed, and seen in its unity with the Eternal Essence, is, according to Plato, an IDEA: and the disipline, by which the human mind is purified from its idols (εἰδῶλα),[c] and raised to the contemplation of Ideas, and thence to the secure and ever-progressive, though never-ending, investigation of truth and reality by scientific method, comprehends what the same philosopher so highly extols under the title of Dialectic.[d] According to Lord Bacon, as describing the same truth seen from the opposite point, and applied to natural philosophy, an idea would be defined as—Intuitio sive inventio, quæ in perceptione sensûs non est (ut quæ puræ et sicci luminis Intellectioni est propria) idearum divinæ mentis, prout in creaturis per signaturas suas sese patefaciant'[e] (*CC* IV i 492–3).

a. 'concerning the intelligible world'.

b. 'concerning the world of sense'.

c. εἴδωλον : '1. shape, spectre, phantom; 2. an image in the mind: vision, fancy; 3. a portrait, esp. of a god: idol, false god' (Liddell and Scott, *Greek Lexicon*). Cf n 2 above.

d. *Republic* 532a–33d.

e. Despite the Baconian ring (e.g. *lumen siccum*), the Latin is STC's. Miss Rooke translates as follows: 'An intuition or discovery of ideas of the divine mind, in the same way that they disclose themselves in things by their own signatures, and this (as is proper to the dry light's Intellection) is not in [the field of] sense perception' (*CC* IV i 493, n 2).

43. from the *NOTEBOOKS* (March 1819)[1]

Spenser's great character of mind. Fancy under the conditions of Imagination, with a feminine tenderness & almost a maidenly purity—above all, deep moral earnestness—.[2] The conception of Talus[3] is, perhaps, the boldest effort of imaginative Power—as if no substance so untractable to which the Poet could not give Life, as in a Swedenborg[4] World.—

(*CN* III 4501)

Notes

1. From notes for a lecture on Edmund Spenser (1552?–99). HNC (*LR* 197), followed by Raysor (*MC* 38), erroneously assigns a version of this note to the literary lectures of 1818.
2. Cf Extract 40–B, n 7.
3. Talus, the 'yron man', is Artegall's attendant in Book v of Spenser's *Faerie Queene* (1589–96).
4. Emanuel Swedenborg (1688–1772), Swedish scientist, philosopher, and mystic. After experiencing a number of visions (culminating in a revelation in 1745), Swedenborg turned from philosophy and science to theosophy and psychical subjects. He came to believe that Scripture, of which he had been appointed official interpreter, was the testimony of how God had descended to earth to restore the connection (broken by evil spirits) between Himself and the world of man and nature. STC's interest in Swedenborg dates back to about 1796: cf *CN* i 165 n. He annotated a number of Swedenborg's works—both scientific and mystical—in his later years; his interest in Swedenborg was revived as a result of his friendship with C. A. Tulk (whom he met in 1817).

44. Letter TO AN UNKNOWN CORRESPONDENT (November 1819?)[1]

My dear Sir

In a Copy of Verses entitled, 'a Hymn before Sunrise in the Vale of Chamouny', I described myself under the influence of strong devotional feelings gazing on the Mountain till as if it had been a Shape emanating from and sensibly representing her own essence, my Soul had become diffused thro' 'the mighty Vision'; and there

As in her natural Form, swell'd vast to Heaven.[2]

Mr Wordsworth, I remember, censured the passage as strained and unnatural, and condemned the Hymn in toto (which nevertheless I ventured to publish in my 'Sibylline Leaves') as a specimen of the Mock Sublime. It may be so for others; but it is impossible that I should myself find it unnatural, being conscious that it was the image and utterance of Thoughts and Emotions in which there was no Mockery. Yet on the other hand I could readily believe that the mood and Habit of mind out of which the Hymn rose—that differs from Milton's and Thomson's[3] and from the Psalms, the source of all three, in the Author's addressing himself to *individual* objects actually present to his Senses, while his great predecessors apostrophize *classes* of Things, presented by the Memory and generalized by the understanding—I can readily believe, I say, that in this there may be too much of what our learned Med'ciners call the *Idiosyncratic* for true Poetry. For from my very childhood I have been accustomed to *abstract* and as it were unrealize whatever of more than common interest my eyes dwelt on;[4] and then by a sort of transfusion and transmission of my consciousness to identify myself with the Object—and I have often thought, within the last five or six years, that if ever I should feel once again the genial warmth and stir of the poetic impulse,[5] and refer to my own experiences, I should venture on a yet stranger & wilder Allegory than of yore—that I would *allegorize* myself, as a Rock with it's summit just raised above the surface of some Bay or Strait in the Arctic Sea,

> While yet the stern and solitary Night
> Brook'd no alternate Sway—[6]

all around me fixed and firm, methought as my own Substance, and near me lofty Masses, that might have seemed to 'hold the Moon and Stars in fee'[7] and often in such wild play with meteoric lights, or with the quiet Shine from above which they made rebound in sparkles or dispand in off-shoots and splinters and iridescent Needle-shafts of keenest Glitter, that it was a pride and a place of Healing to lie, as in an Apostle's Shadow, within the Eclipse and deep substance-seeming Gloom of 'these dread Ambassadors from Earth to Heaven, Great Hierarchs'![8] and tho' obscured yet to think myself obscured by consubstantial Forms, based in the same Foundation as my own. I grieved not to serve them—yea, lovingly and with gladsomeness I abased myself in their presence: for they are my Brothers, I said, and the Mastery is their's by right of elder birth and by right of the mightier strivings of the hidden Fire that uplifted them above me.[9]

(*CL* IV 974–5)

Notes

1. Griggs (*CL* IV 974) dates the letter 'November 1819?' and suggests that it may have been written to 'Peter Morris', the pseudonym of John

Gibson Lockhart (1794–1854) who was one of the chief contributors of reviews to *Blackwood's Magazine* and later (1825–53) editor of the *Quarterly Review*.

2. Lines 13–28 of 'Hymn before Sun-Rise', in the version printed in STC's *Sibylline Leaves* (1817), read as follows:

> O dread and silent Mount! I gazed upon thee,
> Till thou, still present to the bodily sense,
> Didst vanish from my thought: entranced in prayer
> I worshipped the Invisible alone.
> Yet, like some sweet beguiling melody,
> So sweet, we know not we are listening to it,
> Thou, the meanwhile, wast blending with my Thought,
> Yea, with my Life and Life's own secret joy:
> Till the dilating Soul, enrapt, transfused,
> Into the mighty vision passing—there
> As in her natural form, swelled vast to Heaven!
>   Awake, my soul! not only passive praise
> Thou owest! not alone these swelling tears,
> Mute thanks and secret ecstasy! Awake!
> Voice of sweet song! Awake, my heart, awake!
> Green vales and icy cliffs, all join my Hymn.

For an earlier version of these lines, see Extract 10.

3. James Thomson (1700–48), author of 'The Seasons', a long poem challenging poetic artificiality in descriptions of nature.
4. Cf Introduction, pp. 5–7.
5. Cf Extracts 3, 5, 6, 8, 48 and 50.
6. STC, 'Destiny of Nations' 67–8.
7. Milton, 'Sonnet XII' 7 (*variatim*).
8. STC, 'Hymn before Sun-Rise' 82–3 (*variatim*).
9. The Manuscript breaks off at this point.

45. 'TO NATURE' (1820?)

> It may indeed be phantasy, when I
>   Essay to draw from all created things
>   Deep, heartfelt, inward joy[1] that closely clings;
> And trace in leaves and flowers that round me lie
> Lessons of love and earnest piety.[2]   5

So let it be; and if the wide world rings
   In mock of this belief, it brings
Nor fear, nor grief, nor vain perplexity.
So will I build my altar in the fields,
   And the blue sky my fretted dome shall be,   10
And the sweet fragrance that the wild flower yields
   Shall be the incense I will yield to Thee,
Thee only God! and thou shalt not despise
Even me, the priest of this poor scarifice. [3]

(*CPW* I 429)

Notes

1. Cf Extract 6, n 7.
2. Although the idea here expressed almost invariably calls
   Wordsworth to mind (especially the closing stanza of 'Ode:
   Intimations of Immortality'), the conjunction of religious faith and
   natural beauty seems to me closer to certain of Henry Vaughan's lyrics
   in *Silex Scintillans* (1650, 1655).
3. A sense of priestly unworthiness coupled with the knowledge of God's
   willingness (*gratia gratis*) to accept the prayers of even so unworthy a
   servant is a prominent theme in George Herbert's *The Temple* (1633);
   see especially the lyrics 'Aaron' and 'The Priesthood'.

46. from a LETTER TO JOHN MURRAY (18 January 1822)

Leighton [1] had by nature a quick and pregnant Fancy: and the august
Objects of his habitual Contemplation, and their remoteness from the
outward senses; his constant endeavour to see or to bring all things
under some point of Unity; but above all, the rare and vital Union of
Head and Heart, of Light and Love, in his own character;—all these
working conjointly could not fail to form and nourish in him the
higher power, and more akin to Reason—the power, I mean, of
Imagination.

(*CL* V 198–9)

Note

1. Robert Leighton (1611–84), Archbishop of Glasgow, who 'laboured

hard for the restoration of Church unity in Scotland, but being neither a
consistent Presbyterian nor a typical Episcopalian, he failed in his hopes
of accomodating the two systems' (*ODCC* 810). STC's *Aids to Reflection*
(Extract 47), which he expected Murray to publish, was 'at first intended
only for a Selection of Passages from Leighton's Works but in the course
of printing has become an original work almost' (Letter to John Anster,
18 February 1824; *CL* v 336). *Aids to Reflection* was eventually
published by Taylor and Hessey in May 1825. Three copies of
Leighton's *Works* with marginalia by STC have survived.

47. from AIDS TO REFLECTION (May 1825)

(A) Moral and Religious Aphorisms, Comment on Aphorism VI
If any reflecting mind be surprised that the aids of the Divine Spirit
should be deeper than our Consciousness can reach, it must arise from
the not having attended sufficiently to the nature and necessary limits
of human Consciousness. For the same impossibility exists as to the
first acts and movements of our own will—the farthest distance our
recollection can follow back the traces, never leads us to the first foot-
mark—the lowest depth that the light of our Consciousness can visit
even with a doubtful glimmering, is still at an unknown distance
from the ground:[1] and so, indeed, must it be with all Truths, and all
modes of Being that can neither be counted, coloured, or delineated.[2]
Before and After, when applied to such Subjects, are but allegories,
which the Sense or Imagination supplies to the Understanding.[3] The
Position of the Aristotelians, *nihil in intellectu quod non prius in sensu*, on
which Mr Locke's Essay is grounded, is irrefragable:[4] Locke erred
only in taking half the Truth for a whole Truth. Conception is
consequent on Perception.[5] What we cannot *imagine*, we cannot, in
the proper sense of the word, conceive.

(*AR* 43—4)

Notes

1. Cf STC's extended metaphor on 'the first range of hills' in Extract
   33—E.
2. Cf Introduction, pp. 5—6.
3. For STC's use of the terms *allegory* and *understanding*, see Extracts 35—A
   and 35—B.

4. In his section on the 'Difference in Kind of Reason and the Understanding', STC has the following helpful note: 'But if we think on some one thing, the length of our own foot, or of our hand and arm from the elbow joint, it is evident that in *order* to do this, we must have the conception of measure. Now these antecedent and most general conceptions are what is meant by the constituent *forms* of the Understanding: we call them *constituent* because they are not *acquired* by the Understanding, but are implied in its constitution. . . .This is what Leibnitz meant, when to the old adage of the Peripatetics, *Nihil in intellectu quod non prius in sensu* (There is nothing in the Understanding not derived from the Senses, or—There is nothing *conceived* that was not previously *perceived*;) he replied—*præter intellectum ipsum* (except the Understanding itself)' (*AR* 150). Cf also Extract 35–B and nn 4 and 5; on Locke, see Extract 42–A, n 7. George Whalley has also kindly supplied me with the following marginal note on William Fitzwilliam Owen, *Narrative of Voyages to . . . Africa, Arabia, and Madagascar* (1833): '. . . the *diversity*, the more than difference, of reason and understanding, as first taught explicitly in Coleridge's Aids to Reflection'.

5. For a gloss on the terms *Conception* and *Perception*, see Appendix E of *The Statesman's Manual: CC* VI 113.

(B) Conclusion: 'Mystics and Mysticism'[1]

We will return to the harmless species—the enthusiastic Mystics;[2]—a species that may again be subdivided into two ranks. And it will not be other than germane to the subject, if I endeavour to describe them in a sort of allegory, or parable. Let us imagine a poor pilgrim benighted in a wilderness or desert, and pursuing his way in the starless dark with a lantern in his hand. Chance or his happy genius leads him to an Oasis or natural Garden, such as in the creations of my youthful fancy I supposed Enos the Child of Cain to have found.[3] And here, hungry and thirsty, the way-wearied man rests at a fountain; and the taper of his lantern throws its light on an overshadowing tree, a boss of snow-white blossoms, through which the green and growing fruits peeped, and the ripe golden fruitage glowed. Deep, vivid, and faithful are the impressions, which the lovely Imagery comprised within the scanty circle of light, makes and leaves on his memory! But scarcely has he eaten of the fruits and drunk of the fountain, ere scared by the roar and howl from the desert he hurries forward: and as he passes with hasty steps through grove and glade, shadows and imperfect beholdings and vivid fragments of things distinctly seen blend with the past and present shapings of his brain. Fancy modifies sight. His dreams transfer their forms to real objects;[4] and these lend a substance and an *outness*[5] to his dreams. Apparitions greet him; and when at a distance from this enchanted land, and on a different track, the dawn of day discloses to him a caravan, a troop of his fellow-men, his memory, which is itself half fancy,[6] is interpolated afresh by every attempt to recall, connect, and *piece out* his recollections. His narration is received as a madman's tale. He shrinks from the rude laugh and contemptuous sneer, and retires into himself. Yet the craving for sympathy, strong in proportion to the intensity of his convictions, impels him to unbosom himself to abstract auditors; and the poor Quietist becomes a Penman, and, all too poorly stocked for the writer's trade, he borrows his phrases and figures from the only writings to which he has had access, the sacred books of his religion. And thus I shadow out the enthusiast Mystic of the first sort; at the head of which stands the illuminated Teutonic theosopher and shoemaker, honest Jacob Behmen,[7] born near Gorlitz, in Upper Lusatia, in the 17th of our Elizabeth's reign, and who died in the 22nd of her successor's.

To delineate a Mystic of the second and higher order, we need only endow our pilgrim with equal gifts of nature, but these developed and displayed by all the aids and arts of education and favourable fortune. *He* is on his way to the Mecca of his ancestral and national faith, with a well-guarded and numerous procession of merchants and fellow-pilgrims, on the established track. At the close of day the caravan has halted: the full moon[8] rises on the desert: and he strays forth alone, out of sight but to no unsafe distance; and chance leads *him* too, to the same oasis or Islet of Verdure on the Sea of Sand. He wanders at leisure in its maze of beauty and sweetness, and thrids[9] his way through the odorous and flowering thickets into open spots of greenery,[10] and discovers statues and memorial characters, grottos, and refreshing caves. But the moonshine, the imaginative poesy of nature, spreads its soft shadowy charm over all, conceals distances, and magnifies heights, and modifies relations: and fills up vacuities with its own whiteness, counterfeiting substance; and where the dense shadows lie, makes solidity imitate hollowness; and gives to all objects a tender visionary hue and softening. Interpret the moonlight and the shadows as the peculiar genius and sensibility of the individual's own spirit: and here you have the other sort: a Mystic, an Enthusiast of a nobler breed—a Fenelon.[11] But the residentiary, or the frequent visitor of the favoured spot, who has scanned its beauties by steady day-light, and mastered its true proportions and lineaments, he will discover that both pilgrims have indeed been there. *He* will know, that the delightful dream, which the latter tells, is a dream of truth; and that even in the bewildered tale of the former there is truth mingled with the dream.

(*AR* 262–4)

Notes

1. Foreseeing the possibility that some 'suborner of anonymous criticism [might] have engaged some literary bravo or buffoon' to vilify *Aids to Reflection* as a work of 'mysticism', STC takes the occasion of this postscript to state his views on mystics and mysticism. In *Biographia* Chap ix STC notes that 'the writings of these mystics [George Fox, Jacob Boehme and William Law] acted in no slight degree to prevent my mind from being imprisoned within the outline of any single dogmatic system. They contributed to keep alive the *heart* in the *head*; gave me an indistinct, yet stirring and working presentiment, that all the products of the mere *reflective* faculty partook of DEATH, and were as the rattling twigs and sprays in winter, into which a sap was yet to be propelled from some root to which I had not penetrated, if they were to afford my soul either food or shelter. If they were too often a moving cloud of smoke to me by day, yet they were always a pillar of fire throughout the night, during my wanderings through the wilderness of doubt, and enabled me to skirt, without crossing, the sandy deserts of utter unbelief' (*BL* 1 98). Cf also Appendix D of *The Statesman's Manual*: *CC* VI 96.

2. In the preceding paragraph STC distinguishes between the *Enthusiastic Mystic* whose 'error consists simply in the Mystic's attaching to these anomalies [i.e. '*inward feelings* and *experiences*'] of his individual temperament the character of *reality*, and in receiving them as permanent truths, having a subsistence in the Divine Mind, though revealed to himself alone; but entertains this persuasion without demanding or expecting the same faith in his neighbours', and the *Fanatical Mystic* who 'is led ['by ambition or still meaner passions'] to impose his faith, as a duty, on mankind generally.' On the distinction between fanatic and enthusiast, see *The Statesman's Manual* (*CC* VI 56 and n 2).

3. In a footnote STC quotes the seventeen 'specimen' lines of an incomplete poem on Cain which he later published (1828) in the Prefatory Note to 'The Wanderings of Cain': *CPW* 1 287.

4. Beer (1959) quotes an important marginal comment of STC's: 'The idea that "fears will set the fancy at work, and haply, for a time, transform the mists of dim and imperfect knowledge into determinate superstitions" [*AR* (1825) 22] is basic with Coleridge. In a copy of *Aids to Reflection* now in the British Museum, he wrote, "When the Invisible

is sought for by means of the Fancy in the world *without*, and the Awe is transferred to imaginary Powers (Dæmons, Genii, &c) or to sensible Objects (*Fetisches, Gri gris*, Saints' Images, Relics, &c) the Man becomes a Phantast in the one case and superstitious in the other.—The *Idea* of God is contained in the Reason: and the *Reality* of this Idea is a Command of the Conscience. Yet by placing even this *out of* ourselves, as if it existed in Space, we change it into an *Idol*" ' (325–6, n 67). On *idol*, see Extract 42–B, n 2; on *phantast*, see STC's Glossary in Part II of *On the Constitution of Church and State* (December 1829): 'Where a person mistakes the anomalous misgrowths of his own individuality for ideas, or truths of universal reason, he may, without impropriety, be called a *Mystic*, in the abusive sense of the term; though pseudo-mystic, or phantast, would be the more proper designation' (*CC* x 165).

5. For STC on *outness*, see Barfield (1972) 59–68.
6. In *Biographia* Chap xxiv STC writes of those 'mystic theologians, whose delusions we may more confidently hope to separate from their actual intuitions, when we condescend to read their works without the presumption that whatever our fancy (always the ape, and too often the adulterator and counterfeit of our memory) has not made or cannot make a picture of, must be nonsense' (*BL* II 208).
7. On Boehme, see Extract 41–B, n 3. Cf also STC's assessment of Boehme in *PL* 327.
8. Beer (1959) writes: 'Generally speaking, though not always, [STC] tends to speak of "moonlight" when he is showing some sympathy with the idea of natural revelation, and "moonshine" to display his contempt for the concept when held only in isolation. His final position in relation to the symbol is to be found in his conclusion to the *Aids to Reflection*, where he limits the moonlight image to describe the natural mystic within a religious faith. The natural mystic outside religion, on the other hand, is merely a man with a lantern: he illuminates the scene but is totally incapable of interpreting it to others' (118).
9. *thrids*: dialectal form of 'threads'.
10. Cf 'Kubla Khan', 11: 'Enfolding sunny spots of greenery' (Extract 3). The moon, shadows, and caves of 'Kubla Khan' all resurface in this passage from *Aids to Reflection*.
11. François de Salignac de la Mothe-Fénelon (1651–1715), French theologian and Archbishop of Cambrai. Fénelon came under the influence of Mme Guyon and was captivated by the doctrine of Quietism which she advocated. The mystic theology of Quietism, consisting in passive devotional contemplation with extinction of the will and a complete abandonment to the Divine Presence, was supported by Fénelon in his *Explication des Maximes des Saints* (1697); the doctrine was condemned by Pope Innocent XII in 1699. Fénelon was subsequently deprived of his court appointments and relegated to

his diocese where he died, still unpardoned, fifteen years later.

48. from a LETTER TO JAMES GILLMAN (9 October 1825)

My dear Friend

It is a flat'ning Thought, that the more we have seen, the less we have to say. In Youth and early Manhood the Mind and Nature are, as it were, two rival Artists, both potent Magicians, and engaged, like the King's Daughter and the rebel Genie in the Arabian Nights' Enternts., in sharp conflict of Conjuration—[1] each having for it's object to turn the other into Canvas to paint on, Clay to mould, or Cabinet to contain. For a while the Mind seems to have the better in the contest, and makes of Nature what it likes; takes her Lichens and Weather-stains for Types & Printer's Ink and prints Maps & Fac Similes of Arabic and Sanscrit Mss. on her rocks; composes Country-Dances on her moon-shiny Ripples, Fandangos[2] on her Waves and Walzes on her Eddy-pools; transforms her Summer Gales into Harps and Harpers,[3] Lovers' Sighs and sighing Lovers, and her Winter Blasts into Pindaric Odes,[4] Christabels & Ancient Mariners set to music by Beethoven, and in the insolence of triumph conjures her Clouds into Whales[5] and Walrusses with Palanquins[6] on their Backs, and chaces the dodging Stars in a Sky-hunt!—But alas! alas! that Nature is a wary wily long-breathed old Witch, tough-lived as a Turtle and divisible as the Polyp, repullulative[7] in a thousand Snips and Cuttings, integra et in toto![8] She is sure to get the better of Lady MIND in the long run, and to take her revenge too—transforms our To Day into a Canvass dead-colored to receive the dull featureless Portrait of Yesterday; not alone turns the mimic Mind, the ci-devant[9] Sculptress with all her kaleidoscopic freaks and symmetries! into clay, but *leaves* it such a *clay*, to cast dumps[10] or bullets in; and lastly (to end with that which suggested the beginning—) she mocks the mind with it's own metaphors, metamorphosing the Memory into a lignum vitae[11] Escrutoire to keep unpaid Bills & Dun's[12] Letters in, with Outlines that had never been filled up, MSS that never went farther than the Title-pages, and Proof-Sheets & Foul Copies[13] of Watchmen, Friends, Aids to Reflection & other *Stationary* Wares that have kissed the Publisher's Shelf with gluey Lips with all the tender intimacy of inosculation![14]—Finis!—And what is all this about?

Why, verily, my dear Friend! the thought forced itself on me, as I was beginning to put down the first sentence of this letter, how impossible it would have been 15 or even ten years ago for me to have travelled & voyaged by Land, River, and Sea a hundred and twenty miles,[15] with fire and water blending their souls for my propulsion, as if I had been riding on a Centaur[16] with a Sopha for a Saddle—& yet to have nothing more to tell of it than that we had a very fine day, and ran aside the steps in Ramsgate Pier at ½ past 4 exactly, all having been well except poor Harriet, who during the middle Third of the Voyage fell into a reflecting melancholy, in the contemplation of successive specimens of her inner woman in a Wash-hand Basin. She looked pathetic. . . .

(*CL* V 496–7)

Notes

1. On the *Arabian Nights*, see Extract 40–B, n 2.
2. *fandango*: 'a lively dance in 3/4 time'.
3. E.g. 'The Eolian Harp', and 'Dejection: An Ode' 96–125.
4. E.g. 'Ode to the Departing Year' (1796).
5. Cf *Hamlet* III ii 389–90.
6. *palanquin*: 'a covered litter, carried by several men by means of poles projecting before and behind'.
7. *repullulate*: 'bud or sprout again'. Cf the quotation from *CN* II 2431 which appears, as second epigraph, at the beginning of this book.
8. *integra et in toto*: 'unimpaired and whole'.
9. *ci-devant*: 'former'.
10. *dump*: 'A familiar term for objects of a dumpy shape: (a) a leaden counter, used by boys in games; (b) a name of certain small coins; (c) a bolt or nail used in ship-building' (*OED*). *Cast* here, of course, means 'form into shape, by pouring (molten lead) into a mould'.
11. *lignum vitae*: 'a hard and heavy wood from the West Indies and tropical America; called *lignum vitae* ('wood of life') because of its use in medicines'. An *escritoire* is a writing desk.
12. *dun*: 'an importunate creditor'. .
13. *Foul Copies*, i.e. STC's own manuscript copies of *The Watchman*, *The Friend*, etc.
14. *inosculation*: 'anastomosis: the action of joining or uniting so as to become continuous'. A pun is intended with *osculation* ('a kiss'): the books have kissed the shelf so firmly that they have become a part of it. There is also a pun on *stationary*, i.e. *stationery*.
    Beer (1959), commenting on the letter thus far, writes: 'It might seem from this stream of pessimism that all was lost—until one notices how

imaginatively the case [for a loss of Imagination] is presented. Something at the centre had gone, some essential shaping and organizing power, but apart from that his mind ranged as vividly as before' (290). On STC's 'loss' of Imagination, see also Extracts 3, 5 and n 3, 7, 8 and 50; also Introduction, pp. 23–4.

15. During the last years of his life while he was living with the Gillmans, STC often accompanied them on vacations to Ramsgate; business pressures often kept Gillman himself at Highgate. On this occasion STC and Mrs Gillman have come to Ramsgate by steamer and Harriet Macklin, Mrs Gillman's maidservant, has succumbed to seasickness.

16. There seems to be another pun here: a *centaur* is both a mythological grotesque (half man, half horse) and a kind of ship. The same pun was further developed in STC's next letter to Gillman (16 October 1825): *CL* v 498–9.

49. from A MARGINAL NOTE (21 June 1829)[1]

And then the thorough apathy of the so called Public, and the cowardly dread of War./ What is to come of it? What are the real Prospects of the World? I only know, that Mammon and Belial are the Gods of the Age—and that neither Individual nor Nation can serve both God and Mammon.[2] Even in France I see more to *hope*, than in Britain. It is wonderful, how closely Reason and Imagination are connected, and Religion the union of the two.[3] Now the Present is the Epoch of the Understanding and the Senses.

(*CC* IV i 203)

Notes

1. This handwritten note, dated 21 June 1829, appears on the fly-leaf of the second volume of Derwent Coleridge's copy of *The Friend* (1818). STC wrote the comment to express how 'sick at heart' he was made by the Tory Government's apathy in its *de facto* recognition of the government of the Portuguese usurper, Dom Miguel.

2. Belial (*lit.* 'worthlessness') is the personification of wickedness and, in 2 Corinthians 6: 15, is denominated Christ's opposite. Mammon is the usual New Testament personification of riches; STC's allusion is to Matthew 6: 24 (cp Luke 16: 13): 'No man can serve two masters. . . . Ye cannot serve God and Mammon.'

3. Cf Extracts 35–A and 35–B.

50. 'COELI ENARRANT' (1830?)[1]

The stars that wont to start, as on a chace,
Mid twinkling insult on Heaven's darken'd face,
Like a conven'd conspiracy of spies
Wink at each other with confiding eyes!
Turn from the portent—all is blank on high,[2]   5
No constellations alphabet the sky:[3]
The Heavens one large Black Letter only shew,
And as a child beneath its master's blow
Shrills out at once its task and its affright—[4]
The groaning world now learns to read aright,   10
And with its Voice of Voices cries out, O!

(*CPW* I 486)

Notes

1. *STC's note*: 'I wrote these lines in imitation of Du Bartas as translated by our Sylvester.' Guillaume du Bartas (1544–90) published *La Semaine*, an epic poem on the creation of the world, in 1578; the work was translated into English in 1592–9 by Joshua Sylvester.

   The ironic title 'Coeli Enarrant' (supplied by EHC, *not* by STC) is taken from the opening words of Psalm 18 in the Vulgate: *Caeli enarrant gloriam Dei et opera manuum eius adnuntiat firmamentum*, 'The heavens declare the glory of God; and the firmament sheweth his handywork'. (It is Psalm 19 in Protestant Bibles.)

2. Cf 'Dejection: An Ode', 25–38—for an early version of these lines, see Extract 6, lines 30–43. On STC's loss of Imagination, see Extract 48, n 14. Cf also STC's letter of 25 March 1823 to Mrs Aders: 'But if Mr R[ees *or* Reece] could give me *time*, unused as for so many many years I have been to versifying of any kind, and dried up as, I fear, my poetic Spring will be found by the *severities* of austere Metaphysics, I will *attempt* it [the translation of an unnamed poem of Schiller] for him' (*CL* v 271); here, as in the years 1800–3 (Extract 5, n 3), STC connects loss of Imagination with his intense philosophical studies.

3. Cf Extract 2.

4. *EHC's note* (*CPW* I 486): Compare Leigh Hunt's story of Boyer's reading-lesson at Christ's Hospital: '*Pupil.*—(. . . never remembering the stop at the word "Missionary"). "*Missionary* Can you see the wind?" (Master gives him a slap on the cheek.) *Pupil.*—(Raising his voice to a cry, and still forgetting to stop.) "*Indian* No."' *Autobiography of Leigh Hunt* (1860) 68.

   On Boyer, see Extract 33–A and n 1. STC's Notebooks contain

accounts of several nightmares connected with Boyer and Christ's Hospital.

51. from *TABLE TALK*[1]

(A) 31 May 1830

Mrs Barbauld[2] once told me that she admired *The Ancient Mariner* very much, but that there were two faults in it—it was improbable, and had no moral. As for the probability, I owned that that might admit some question; but as to the want of a moral, I told her that in my own judgement the poem had too much; and that the only, or chief fault, if I might say so, was the obtrusion of the moral sentiment so openly on the reader as a principle or cause of action in a work of such pure imagination.[3] It ought to have had no more moral than the *Arabian Nights'* tale of the merchant's sitting down to eat dates by the side of a well, and throwing the shells aside, and lo! a genie starts up, and says he *must* kill the aforesaid merchant, *because* one of the date shells had, it seems, put out the eye of the genie's son.[4]

(*TT* 106)

Notes

1. STC's *Table Talk*, compiled and edited by his nephew and son-in-law HNC, appeared in 1835; a revised edition was published in 1836. Crabb Robinson, who read the book shortly after its first appearance, wrote of it: 'I . . . concluded the evening by going to the Athenaeum where I read a third of volume one of Coleridge's *Table Talk*. This book will be harshly and unjustly estimated I think. A more difficult book, not original, I cannot well imagine. Coleridge's sayings were curious as well as wise in their connection, but without their connection they may to the ordinary reader seem merely odd. His puns and strong sayings are recollectable and repeatable; not so the wiser and deeper words that fell from him. I have seen nothing yet in this book at all equal to what I recollect' (Diary, 25 May 1835).

2. Anna Letitia Barbauld (1743–1825), whom Crabb Robinson described in 1816 as a lady who could still 'keep up a lively argumentative conversation as well as any one I know, and at her advanced age (she is turned of seventy) . . . is certainly the best specimen of female Presbyterian society in the country' (Diary, 11 February 1816), was a

zealous Unitarian and a minor poetess.

The strained relations between STC and Mrs Barbauld—cf *CL* II 1039; *CN* II 2303, and III 3965 and 4035; *HCR* (27 January 1812); *CT* 217—should alert us to the necessity of approaching the celebrated anecdote in *Table Talk* with circumspection. The printed page does not give us STC's intonation (serious? jocular? sarcastic?); and in the absence of stage-directions, it seems wisest not to build too elaborate an edifice of poetic interpretation upon a foundation so unsure.

3. Robert Penn Warren (1946) argues that 'The Ancient Mariner' is a poem of 'pure imagination' in the sense that its subject is the poetic, or Secondary, Imagination itself. Whalley (1946–7) believes that 'whether consciously or unconsciously' the albatross is 'the symbol of Coleridge's creative imagination'. House (1953) opposes the rigidity of Penn Warren's symbolic analysis and argues that the poem is 'part of the exploration . . . part of the experience which led Coleridge into his later theoretic statements (as of the theory of the Imagination) rather than a symbolic adumbration of the theoretic statements themselves' (84, 113). See also Beer (1959) 170–2, and Brett (1960) 78–107.

4. *The Arabian Nights' Entertainments*, 4 vols (London, 1778) I 18–19. HNC (*TT* 106–7) quotes part of the tale; see also House (1953) 90. STC uses this same tale from the *Arabian Nights* in *CN* III 4317 (which Miss Coburn tentatively assigns to 1816). Since in the *Table Talk* entry STC 'was relating a conversation that had taken place apparently some considerable time earlier' (Coburn), it may be that both the Notebook entry and the original conversation with Mrs Barbauld belong to 1816.

(B) 11 August 1832

Don Quixote[1] is not a man out of his senses, but a man in whom the imagination and the pure reason are so powerful as to make him disregard the evidence of sense when it opposed their conclusions. Sancho is the common sense of the social man-animal, unenlightened and unsanctified by the reason. You see how he reverences his master at the very time he is cheating him.

(*TT* 197)

Note

1. Don Quixote and Sancho Panza are the central characters in Miguel Cervantes' *Don Quixote de la Mancha*, a satirical romance published in 1605–15. STC devoted a lecture to the work in March 1819, in which he contrasted 'the Madness of Imagination and that of Passion': *CN* III 4504. Cf also Extract 40–A.

(C) 1 May 1833

'Great wits are sure to madness near allied,' says Dryden,[1] and true so far as this, that genius of the highest kind implies an unusual intensity of the modifying power, which detached from the discriminative and reproductive power, might conjure a platted straw into a royal diadem: but it would be at least as true, that great genius is most alien from madness,—yea, divided from it by an impassable mountain,—namely, the activity of thought and vivacity of the accumulative memory, which are no less essential constituents of 'great wit'.

(TT 233)

Note

1. 'Absalom and Achitophel' (1681) 1 163. There is a similar statement in a letter of STC's of 20 February 1828 (CL vi 729) and, even earlier, in Biographia Chap ii (BL 1 30 n).

(D) 1 January 1834

What is it that Mr Landor[1] wants, to make him a Poet? His powers are certainly very considerable, but he seems to be totally deficient in that modifying faculty, which compresses several units into one whole. The truth is, he does not possess imagination in its highest form—that of stamping *il più nell' uno*.[2] Hence his poems, taken as wholes, are unintelligible; you have eminences excessively bright, and all the ground around and between them in darkness. Besides which, he has never learned, with all his energy, how to write simple and lucid English.

(TT 286)

Notes

1. Walter Savage Landor (1775–1864), better remembered today for his *Imaginary Conversations* (1824–9 and 1853); his early poetry includes the epic *Gebir* (1798) and a tragedy *Count Julian* (1812).
2. *il più nell' uno*: 'the many in the one'. Cf STC's use of the phrase 'Multëity in unity' in Extract 26 and n 4.

(E) 23 June 1834

You may conceive the difference in kind between the Fancy and the Imagination in this way, that if the check of the senses and the reason were withdrawn, the first would become delirium, and the last mania.[1] The Fancy brings together images which have no connexion natural or moral, but are yoked together by the poet by means of some accidental coincidence;[2] as in the well-known passage in *Hudibras*:

> The sun had long since in the lap
> Of Thetis taken out his nap,
> And like a lobster boyl'd, the morn
> From black to red began to turn.[3]

The Imagination modifies images, and gives unity to variety; it sees all things in one, *il piu nell' uno*.[4] There is the epic imagination, the perfection of which is in Milton; and the dramatic, of· which Shakespeare is the absolute master.[5] The first gives unity by throwing back into the distance; as after the magnificient approach of the Messiah to battle, the poet, by one touch from himself—

> . . . far off their coming shone—

makes the whole one image.[6] And so at the conclusion of the description of the appearance of the entranced angels, in which every sort of image from all the regions of earth and air is introduced to diversify and illustrate, the reader is brought back to the single image by:

> He call'd so loud, that all the hollow deep
> Of Hell resounded.[7]

The dramatic imagination does not throw back, but brings close; it stamps all nature with one, and that its own, meaning, as in *Lear* throughout.

$$(TT\ 309\text{–}10)$$

Notes

1. Cf Extracts 16 and 23. Willey (1946) comments: 'In delirium the mind pours forth its contents incoherently, that is, with no unifying principle to order its sequences save the law of association; in mania, the mind, obsessed by a fixed idea, sees and interprets all things in relation to that idea, and so has (though in a morbid form) a coordinating power. If we translate disease into health, delirium becomes Fancy, and mania

Imagination: Fancy assembling and juxtaposing images without fusing them; Imagination moulding them into a new whole in the heat of a predominant passion' (1964 edition, 21).

2. Cf Extract 16, n 13.
3. Samuel Butler, *Hudibras* (1663–78) II ii 29–32. Cf also Extract 13–C.
4. Cf Extract 51–D, n 2.
5. A Common distinction in STC's writings: see Extracts 7, 13–B, 13–M, 13–N, 17–B and 33–H.
6. Cf the description of Christ moving in his chariot to meet the rebellious Satan in battle, *Paradise Lost* VI 749–79:

> forth rushed with whirlwind sound
> The chariot of paternal deity,
> Flashing thick flames, wheel within wheel undrawn,
> It self instinct with spirit, but convoyed
> By four cherubic shapes, four faces each
> Had wondrous, as with stars their bodies all
> And wings were set with eyes, with eyes the wheels
> Of beryl, and careering fires between;
> Over their heads a crystal firmament,
> Whereon a sapphire throne, inlaid with pure
> Amber, and colours of the showery arch.
> He in celestial panoply all armed
> Of radiant urim, work divinely wrought,
> Ascended, at his right hand Victory
> Sat, eagle-winged, beside him hung his bow
> And quiver with three-bolted thunder stored,
> And from about him fierce effusion rolled
> Of smoke and bickering flame, and sparkles dire;
> Attended with ten thousand thousand saints,
> He onward came, *far off his coming shone*,
> And twenty thousand (I their number heard)
> Chariots of God, half on each hand were seen:
> He on the wings of cherub rode sublime
> On the crystalline sky, in sapphire throned.
> Illustrious far and wide, but by his own
> First seen, them unexpected joy surprised,
> When the great ensign of Messiah blazed
> Aloft by angels borne, his sign in heaven:
> Under whose conduct Michael soon reduced
> His army, circumfused on either wing,
> Under their head embodied all in one.

7. Cf *Paradise Lost* I 300–15—Milton's description of the fallen angels

lying insensate on the 'burning marl' who are roused by Satan, their
leader:

> he stood and called
> His legions, angel forms, who lay entranced
> Thick as autumnal leaves that strew the brooks
> In Vallombrosa, where the Etrurian shades
> High overarched imbower; or scattered sedge
> Afloat, when with fierce winds Orion armed
> Hath vexed the Red Sea coast, whose waves o'erthrew
> Busiris and his Memphian chivalry,
> While with perfidious hatred they pursued
> The sojourners of Goshen, who beheld
> From the safe shore their floating carcasses
> And broken chariot wheels, so thick bestrewn
> Abject and lost lay these, covering the flood,
> Under amazement of their hideous change.
> *He called so loud, that all the hollow deep*
> *Of hell resounded.*

Appendix

From Wordsworth's Preface to *Poems* (1815)
Let us come now to the consideration of the words Fancy and
Imagination, as employed in the classification of the following
Poems.[1] 'A man,' says an intelligent author, 'has imagination in
proportion as he can distinctly copy in idea the impressions of sense: it
is the faculty which *images* within the mind the phenomena of
sensation. A man has fancy in proportion as he can call up, connect, or
associate, at pleasure, those internal images (φαντάζειν is to cause to
appear) so as to complete ideal representations of absent objects.
Imagination is the power of depicting, and fancy of evoking and
combining. The imagination is formed by patient observation; the
fancy by a voluntary activity in shifting the scenery of the mind. The
more accurate the imagination, the more safely may a painter, or a
poet, undertake a delineation, or a description, without the presence
of the objects to be characterized. The more versatile the fancy,
the more original and striking will be the decorations produced.'—*British Synonyms discriminated, by W. Taylor.*

Is not this as if a man should undertake to supply an account of a
building, and be so intent upon what he had discovered of the
foundation, as to conclude his task without once looking up at the
superstructure? Here, as in other instances throughout the volume,
the judicious Author's mind is enthralled by Etymology; he takes up
the original word as his guide and escort, and too often does not
perceive how soon he becomes its prisoner, without liberty to tread in
any path but that to which it confines him. It is not easy to find out
how imagination, thus explained, differs from distinct remembrance
of images; or fancy from quick and vivid recollection of them: each is
nothing more than a mode of memory. If the two words bear the
above meaning, and no other, what term is left to designate that
faculty of which the Poet is 'all compact;'[2] he whose eye glances from
earth to heaven, whose spiritual attributes body forth what his pen is

prompt in turning to shape; or what is left to characterise Fancy, as insinuating herself into the heart of objects with creative activity?—Imagination, in the sense of the word as giving title to a class of the following Poems, has no reference to images that are merely a faithful copy, existing in the mind, of absent external objects; but is a word of higher import, denoting operations of the mind upon those objects, and processes of creation or of composition, governed by certain fixed laws. I proceed to illustrate my meaning by instances. A parrot *hangs* from the wires of his cage by his beak or by his claws; or a monkey from the bough of a tree by his paws or his tail. Each creature does so literally and actually. In the first Eclogue of Virgil, the shepherd, thinking of the time when he is to take leave of his farm, thus addresses his goats:—

> 'Non ego vos posthac viridi projectus in antro
> Dumosa *pendere* procul de rupe videbo.'[3]

> ——'half way down
> *Hangs* one who gathers samphire,'[4]

is the well-known expression of Shakespeare, delineating an ordinary image upon the cliffs of Dover. In these two instances is a slight exertion of the faculty which I denominate imagination, in the use of one word: neither the goats nor the samphire-gatherer do literally hang, as does the parrot or the monkey; but, presenting to the senses something of such an appearance, the mind in its activity, for its own gratification, contemplates them as hanging.

> 'As when far off at sea a fleet descried
> *Hangs* in the clouds, by equinoctial winds
> Close sailing from Bengala, or the isles
> Of Ternate or Tidore, whence merchants bring
> Their spicy drugs; they on the trading flood
> Through the wide Ethiopian to the Cape
> Ply, stemming nightly toward the Pole: so seemed
> Far off the flying Fiend.'[5]

Here is the full strength of the imagination involved in the word *hangs*, and exerted upon the whole image: First, the fleet, an aggregate of many ships, is represented as one mighty person, whose track, we know and feel, is upon the waters; but, taking advantage of its appearance to the senses, the Poet dares to represent it as *hanging in the clouds*, both for the gratification of the mind in contemplating the image itself, and in reference to the motion and appearance of the sublime object to which it is compared.

From impressions of sight we will pass to those of sound; which, as they must necessarily be of a less definite character, shall be selected from these volumes:

'Over his own sweet voice the Stock-dove *broods*;'[6]

of the same bird,

'His voice was *buried* among trees,
Yet to be come at by the breeze;'

'O, Cuckoo! shall I call thee *Bird*,
Or but a wandering *Voice?*'[7]

The stock-dove is said to *coo*, a sound well imitating the note of the bird; but, by the intervention of the metaphor *broods*, the affections are called in by the imagination to assist in marking the manner in which the bird reiterates and prolongs her soft note, as if herself delighting to listen to it, and participating of a still and quiet satisfaction, like that which may be supposed inseparable from the continuous process of incubation. 'His voice was buried among trees,' a metaphor expressing the love of *seclusion* by which this Bird is marked; and characterising its note as not partaking of the shrill and the piercing, and therefore more easily deadened by the intervening shade; yet a note so peculiar and withal so pleasing, that the breeze, gifted with that love of the sound which the Poet feels, penetrates the shades in which it is entombed, and conveys it to the ear of the listener.

'Shall I call thee Bird,
Or but a wandering Voice?'

This concise interrogation characterises the seeming ubiquity of the voice of the cuckoo, and dispossesses the creature almost of a corporeal existence; the Imagination being tempted to this exertion of her power by a consciousness in the memory that the cuckoo is almost perpetually heard throughout the season of spring, but seldom becomes an object of sight.

Thus far of images independent of each other, and immediately endowed by the mind with properties that do not inhere in them, upon an incitement from properties and qualities the existence of which is inherent and obvious. These processes of imagination are carried on either by conferring additional properties upon an object, or abstracting from it some of those which it actually possesses, and thus enabling it to re-act upon the mind which hath performed the process, like a new existence.

I pass from the Imagination acting upon an individual image to a consideration of the same faculty employed upon images in a conjunction by which they modify each other. The Reader has already had a fine instance before him in the passage quoted from Virgil, where the apparently perilous situation of the goat, hanging upon the shaggy precipice, is contrasted with that of the shepherd contemplating it from the seclusion of the cavern in which he lies stretched at ease and in security. Take these images separately, and how unaffecting the picture compared with that produced by their being thus connected with, and opposed to, each other!

> 'As a huge stone is sometimes seen to lie
> Couched on the bald top of an eminence,
> Wonder to all who do the same espy
> By what means it could thither come, and whence,
> So that it seems a thing endued with sense,
> Like a sea-beast crawled forth, which on a shelf
> Of rock or sand reposeth, there to sun himself.
>
> Such seemed this Man; not all alive or dead
> Nor all asleep, in his extreme old age.
>   *   *   *   *   *
> Motionless as a cloud the old Man stood,
> That heareth not the loud winds when they call,
> And moveth altogether if it move at all.'[8]

In these images, the conferring, the abstracting, and the modifying powers of the Imagination, immediately and mediately acting, are all brought into conjunction. The stone is endowed with something of the power of life to approximate it to the sea-beast; and the sea-beast stripped of some of its vital qualities to assimilate it to the stone; which intermediate image is thus treated for the purpose of bringing the original image, that of the stone, to a nearer resemblance to the figure and condition of the aged Man; who is divested of so much of the indications of life and motion as to bring him to the point where the two objects unite and coalesce in just comparison. After what has been said, the image of the cloud need not be commented upon.

Thus far of an endowing or modifying power: but the Imagination also shapes and *creates*; and how? By innumerable processes; and in none does it more delight than in that of consolidating numbers into unity, and dissolving and separating unity into number,—alternations proceeding from, and governed by, a sublime consciousness of the soul in her own mighty and almost divine powers. Recur to the passage already cited from Milton. When the compact Fleet, as one Person, has been introduced 'Sailing from Bengala,' 'They,' *i.e.* the 'merchants,' representing the fleet resolved into a multitude of ships, 'ply' their voyage towards the extremities of the earth: 'So,' (referring to the word 'As' in the commencement) 'seemed the flying Fiend;' the image of his Person acting to recombine the multitude of ships into one body,—the point from which the comparison set out. 'So seemed,' and to whom seemed? To the heavenly Muse who dictates the poem, to the eye of the Poet's mind, and to that of the Reader, present at one moment in the wide Ethiopian, and the next in the solitudes, then first broken in upon, of the infernal regions!

'Modo me Thebis, modo ponit Athenis.'⁹

Hear again this mighty Poet,—speaking of the Messiah going forth to expel from heaven the rebellious angels,

'Attended by ten thousand thousand Saints,
He onward came: far off his coming shone,'—¹⁰

the retinue of Saints, and the Person of the Messiah himself, lost almost and merged in the splendour of that indefinite abstraction 'His coming!'

As I do not mean here to treat this subject further than to throw some light upon the present Volumes, and especially upon one division of them, I shall spare myself and the Reader the trouble of considering the Imagination as it deals with thoughts and sentiments, as it regulates the composition of characters, and determines the course of actions: I will not consider it (more than I have already done by implication) as that power which, in the language of one of my most esteemed Friends, 'draws all things to one; which makes things animate or inanimate, beings with their attributes, subjects with their accessaries, take one colour and serve to one effect.'[11] The grand store-houses of enthusiastic and meditative Imagination, of poetical, as contradistinguished from human and dramatic Imagination, are the prophetic and lyrical parts of the Holy Scriptures, and the works of Milton; to which I cannot forbear to add those of Spenser. I select these writers in preference to those of ancient Greece and Rome, because the anthropomorphitism of the Pagan religion subjected the minds of the greatest poets in those countries too much to the bondage of definite form; from which the Hebrews were preserved by their abhorrence of idolatry.[12] This abhorrence was almost as strong in our great epic Poet, both from circumstances of his life, and from the constitution of his mind. However imbued the surface might be with classical literature, he was a Hebrew in soul; and all things tended in him towards the sublime. Spenser, of a gentler nature, maintained his freedom by aid of his allegorical spirit, at one time inciting him to create persons out of abstractions; and, at another, by a superior effort of genius, to give the universality and permanence of abstractions to his human beings, by means of attributes and emblems that belong to the highest moral truths and the purest sensations,—of which his character of Una is a glorious example. Of the human and dramatic Imagination the works of Shakspeare are an inexhaustible source.

'I tax not you, ye Elements, with unkindness,
I never gave you kingdoms, call'd you Daughters!'[13]

And if, bearing in mind the many Poets distinguished by this prime quality, whose names I omit to mention; yet justified by recollection of the insults which the ignorant, the incapable, and the presumptuous, have heaped upon these and my other writings, I may be permitted to anticipate the judgment of posterity upon myself, I shall declare (censurable, I grant, if the notoriety of the fact above stated does not justify me) that I have given in these unfavourable times, evidence of exertions of this faculty upon its worthiest objects, the external universe, the moral and religious sentiments of Man, his natural affections, and his acquired passions; which have the same ennobling tendency as the productions of men, in this kind, worthy to be holden in undying remembrance.

To the mode in which Fancy has already been characterised as the power of evoking and combining, or, as my friend Mr Coleridge has styled it, 'the aggregative and associative power,' my objection is only that the definition is too general. To aggregate and to associate, to evoke and to combine, belong as well to the Imagination as to the Fancy; but either the materials evoked and combined are different; or they are brought together under a different law, and for a different purpose. Fancy does not require that the materials which she makes use of should be susceptible of change in their constitution, from her touch; and, where they admit of modification, it is enough for her purpose if it be slight, limited, and evanescent. Directly the reverse of these, are the desires and demands of the Imagination. She recoils from every thing but the plastic, the pliant, and the indefinite. She leaves it to Fancy to describe Queen Mab as coming,

> 'In shape no bigger than an agate-stone
> On the fore-finger of an alderman.'[14]

Having to speak of stature, she does not tell you that her gigantic Angel was as tall as Pompey's Pillar; much less that he was twelve cubits, or twelve hundred cubits high; or that his dimensions equalled those of Teneriffe or Atlas;—because these, and if they were a million times as high it would be the same, are bounded: The expression is, 'His stature reached the sky!' the illimitable firmament!—When the Imagination frames a comparison, if it does not strike on the first presentation, a sense of the truth of the likeness, from the moment that it is perceived, grows—and continues to grow—upon the mind; the resemblance depending less upon outline of form and feature, than upon expression and effect; less upon casual and outstanding, than upon inherent and internal, properties: moreover, the images invariably modify each other.—The law under which the processes of Fancy are carried on is as capricious as the accidents of things, and the effects are surprising, playful, ludicrous, amusing, tender, or pathetic, as the objects happen to be appositely produced or fortunately combined. Fancy depends upon the rapidity and pro-fusion with which she scatters her thoughts and images; trusting that their number, and the felicity with which they are linked together, will make amends for the want of individual value: or she prides herself upon the curious subtilty and the successful elaboration with which she can detect their lurking affinities. If she can win you over to her purpose, and impart to you her feelings, she cares not how unstable or transitory may be her influence, knowing that it will not be out of her power to resume it upon an apt occasion. But the Imagination is conscious of an indestructible dominion;—the Soul may fall away from it, not being able to sustain its grandeur; but, if once felt and acknowledged, by no act of any other faculty of the mind can it be relaxed, impaired, or diminished.— Fancy is given to quicken and to beguile the temporal part of our nature, Imagination to incite and to support the eternal.— Yet is it not the less true that Fancy, as she is an active, is also, under her own laws and in her own spirit, a creative faculty. In what manner Fancy ambitiously aims at a rivalship with Imagination, and Imagination stoops to work with the materials of Fancy, might be illustrated from the compositions of all eloquent writers, whether in prose or verse; and chiefly from those of our own Country. Scarcely a page of the impassioned parts of Bishop Taylor's[15] Works can be opened that shall not afford examples.— Referring the Reader to those inestimable volumes, I will content myself with placing a conceit (ascribed to Lord Chesterfield) in contrast with a passage from the Paradise Lost:—

'The dews of the evening most carefully shun,
    They are the tears of the sky for the loss of the sun.'[16]

After the transgression of Adam, Milton, with other appearances of sympathising Nature, thus marks the immediate consequence,

'Sky lowered, and, muttering thunder, some sad drops
    Wept at completion of the mortal sin.'[17]

The associating link is the same in each instance: Dew and rain, not distinguishable from the liquid substance of tears, are employed as indications of sorrow. A flash of surprise is the effect in the former case; a flash of surprise, and nothing more; for the nature of things does not sustain the combination. In the latter, the effects from the act, of which there is this immediate consequence and visible sign, are so momentous, that the mind acknowledges the justice and reasonableness of the sympathy in nature so manifested; and the sky weeps drops of water as if with human eyes, as 'Earth had before trembled from her entrails, and Nature given a second groan.'[18]

(Text: *The Prose Works of William Wordsworth*,
ed. W. J. B. Owen and J. W. Smyser, 3 vols
(Oxford: Clarendon Press, 1974) III 30–7)

Notes

1. In the 1815 edition of his poems, Wordsworth undertook to classify them according to subject-matter and the psychology of literary creation; the result was that the poems were grouped together under 'appropriate' subtitles: e.g. 'Naming of Places', 'Old Age', 'Fancy' and 'Imagination'. It is clear that the purpose of the 1815 Preface is to define 'the words Fancy and Imagination, as employed in the classification of the . . . Poems' in this edition.

2. *A Midsummer Night's Dream* v i 7ff.

3. Virgil, *Eclogue 1* 75–6. Translation: 'Never again shall I, stretched out in some green glen, see you far away *hanging* on the rocky hillside covered with thorny brambles.'

4. *King Lear* IV vi 15–16.

5. *Paradise Lost* II 636–43.

6. 'Resolution and Independence' 5.

7. 'O Nightingale' 13–14; 'To the Cuckoo' 3–4.

8. 'Resolution and Independence' 57–65, 75–7.

9. Horace, *Epistles* II i 213. Translation: 'Sets me down now in Thebes, now in Athens'.

10. *Paradise Lost* VI 767–8.

11. *Wordsworth's note*: 'Charles Lamb upon the genius of Hogarth.'

12. Cf Extract 9.

13. *King Lear* III ii 16–17.

14. *Romeo and Juliet* I iv 55–6.

15. Cf Extracts 27 and 38.

16. 'Advice to a Lady in Autumn', in *The Life of the Late Earl of Chesterfield* (1774) ii 248–9.

17. *Paradise Lost* IX 1002–3.

18. Ibid. 1000–1.

Bibliography

Abercrombie, L., *The Idea of Great Poetry* (London: Martin Secker, 1925) esp. 25.

Abrams, M. H., 'Coleridge's "A Light in Sound": Science, Meta-science, and Poetic Imagination', *Proceedings of the American Philosophical Society* 116 (1972) 458–76.

—— *The Mirror and the Lamp: Romantic Theory and the Critical Tradition* (London and New York: O.U.P., 1953; New York: Norton, 1958; New York: O.U.P., 1971) esp. 68, 119, 156–83, 282–3.

Appleyard, J. A., 'Coleridge and Criticism: I. Critical Theory', in *S. T. Coleridge* (Writers and their Background), ed. R. L. Brett (London: Bell, 1971) 123–46.

—— *Coleridge's Philosophy of Literature: The Development of a Concept of Poetry, 1791–1819* (London: O.U.P., Cambridge, Mass.: Harvard University Press, 1965) esp. 93–100, 197–208.

Babbitt, I., 'Coleridge and Imagination', *The Nineteenth Century and After*, 106 (1929) 383–98. Reprinted in Babbitt's *On Being Creative and Other Essays* (London: Constable, Boston and New York: Houghton Mifflin, 1932) 97–133.

Badawi, M. M., *Coleridge: Critic of Shakespeare* (London and New York: C.U.P., 1973) esp. 43–8.

Baker, J. V., *The Sacred River: Coleridge's Theory of the Imagination* (London: O.U.P., Baton Rouge: Louisiana State University Press, 1957; New York: Greenwood Press, 1969).

Barfield, O., 'Either: Or', in *Imagination and the Spirit: Essays in Literature and the Christian Faith Presented to Clyde S. Kilby*, ed. C. A. Huttar (Grand Rapids: Eerdmans, 1971) 25–42.

—— *What Coleridge Thought* (London: O.U.P., Middletown, Conn.: Wesleyan University Press, 1972) esp. 69–91.

Bate, W. J., *Coleridge* (New York: Macmillan, 1968; London: Weidenfeld and Nicolson, 1969) esp. 157–69.

—— 'Coleridge on the Function of Art', in *Perspectives of Criticism*, ed. H. Levin (Cambridge, Mass.: Harvard University Press, London: Cumberlege, 1950) 125—59.

—— and J. Bullitt, 'Distinctions between Fancy and Imagination in Eighteenth-Century English Criticism', *MLN* 60 (1945) 8—15.

Beer, J. B., *Coleridge the Visionary* (London: Chatto & Windus, 1959; New York: Collier Books, 1962).

—— *Coleridge's Poetic Intelligence* (London: Macmillan, 1977).

—— 'Ice and Spring: Coleridge's Imaginative Education', in *Coleridge's Variety*, ed. J. Beer (London: Macmillan, 1974) 54—80.

—— 'A Stream by Glimpses: Coleridge's later Imagination', in *Coleridge's Variety*, ed. J. Beer (London: Macmillan, 1974) 219—42.

Belden, H. M., 'Observation and Imagination in Coleridge and Poe: A Contrast', in *Papers, Essays, and Stories . . . in Honor . . . of Charles Frederick Johnson*, ed. O. Shepard and A. Adams (Hartford, Conn.: Trinity College, 1928) 131—75.

Bloom, H., *The Visionary Company: A Reading of English Romantic Poetry* (New York: Doubleday, 1961; London: Faber, 1962; New York: Doubleday, 1963; 2nd ed., revised and enlarged, Ithaca and London: Cornell University Press, 1971).

Bodkin, M., *Archetypal Patterns in Poetry. Psychological Studies of Imagination* (Oxford: O.U.P., London: Milford, 1934; New York: Random House, 1958) esp. 25—58, 'The Ancient Mariner' and 87—93, 'Kubla Khan'.

Bostetter, E. E., *The Romantic Ventriloquists: Wordsworth, Coleridge, Keats, Shelley, Byron* (Seattle: University of Washington Press, 1963) esp. 4, 98—9.

Boulger, J. D., *Coleridge as Religious Thinker* (New Haven and London: Yale University Press, 1961).

—— 'Coleridge on Imagination Revisited', *TWC* 4 (1973) 13—24.

—— 'Imagination and Speculation in Coleridge's Conversation Poems', *JEGP* 64 (1965) 691—711.

Bouslog, C. S., 'Structure and Theme in Coleridge's "Dejection: An Ode"', *MLQ* 24 (1963) 42—52.

Bowra, C. M., *The Romantic Imagination* (Cambridge, Mass.: Harvard University Press, 1949; London and New York: O.U.P., 1961).

Brett, R. L., 'Coleridge's Theory of the Imagination', *ES* 20 (1949) 75—90.

—— *Fancy and Imagination* (Critical Idiom series) (London: Methuen,

New York: Harper & Row, 1969; repr. 1973).

—— *Reason and Imagination: A Study of Form and Meaning in Four Poems* (Oxford: O.U.P., for Hull University, 1960) esp. 78–107, 'The Ancient Mariner'.

Brisman, L., 'Coleridge and the Ancestral Voices', *Georgia Review* 29 (1975) 469–98.

Brooke, N., 'Coleridge's "True and Original Realism"', *Durham University Journal*, n.s., 22 (1960) 58–69.

Carver, P. L., 'Coleridge and the Theory of Imagination', *UTQ* 9 (1940) 452–65.

—— 'The Evolution of the Term "Esemplastic"', *Modern Language Review* 24 (1929) 329–31.

Chayes, I. H., '"Kubla Khan" and the Creative Process', *SIR* 6 (1966) 1–21.

Chinol, E., *Il Pensiero di S. T. Coleridge* (Collezione di varia critica, vol. 10) (Venice: Neri Pozza, 1953).

Coburn, K., *The Self Conscious Imagination: A Study of Coleridge's notebooks in celebration of the bi-centenary of his birth, 21 October 1772*, Riddell Memorial Lectures at the University of Newcastle upon Tyne, 1973 (London, New York and Toronto: O.U.P., 1974).

Creed, H. H., 'Coleridge's Metacriticism', *PMLA* 69 (1954) 1160–80.

Deschamps, P., *La formation de la pensée de Coleridge (1772–1804)* (Paris: Didier, 1964) esp. 128–58, 511–27.

Dodds, E. R., *The Romantic Theory of Poetry: An examination in the light of Croce's Æsthetic* (New York: Russell & Russell, 1926; repr. 1962) esp. 104–9.

Eiseley, L., 'Darwin, Coleridge, and the Theory of Unconscious Creation', *Library Chronicle of the University of Pennsylvania* 31 (1965) 7–22. Revised version in *Daedalus* 94 (1965) 588–602.

Eliot, T. S., *The Use of Poetry and the Use of Criticism. Studies in the Relation of Criticism to Poetry in England* (London: Faber, Cambridge, Mass.: Harvard University Press, 1933; Faber reprints 1964, 1967, 1970, 1975) esp. 28–9, 58.

Elliott, J. W., Jr, 'A Critical Index to the Letters of Samuel Taylor Coleridge from 1785 to 1801 on the Subjects of *Philosophy and Religion* and *Literature and Literary Theory*: A Presentation of his Thought', unpub. dissertation, Columbia University, 1974.

Emmet, D. M., 'Coleridge on the Growth of the Mind', *Bulletin of the John Rylands Library* 34 No. 2 (Mar 1952). Reprinted in *Coleridge* (Twentieth Century Views), ed. K. Coburn (Englewood Cliffs:

Prentice-Hall, 1967) 161—78.

Fogle, R. H., 'The Dejection of Coleridge's Ode', *ELH* 17 (1950) 71—7.

——— *The Idea of Coleridge's Criticism* (London: C.U.P., Berkeley: University of California Press, 1962) esp. 1—17, 52—61.

Fruman, N., *Coleridge, The Damaged Archangel* (New York: Braziller, 1971; London: Allen & Unwin, 1972) esp. 180—9.

Gérard, A. S., 'Counterfeiting Infinity: "The Eolian Harp" and the Growth of Coleridge's Mind', *JEGP* 60 (1961) 411—22. Reprinted in Gérard's *English Romantic Poetry: Ethos, Structure, and Symbol in Coleridge, Wordsworth, Shelley, and Keats* (London: C.U.P., Berkeley and Los Angeles: University of California Press, 1968) 40—63.

——— *L'Idée romantique de la poésie en Angleterre: Etudes sur la théorie de la poésie chez Coleridge, Wordsworth, Keats et Shelley* (Paris: Les Belles Lettres, 1955) esp. 163—216, 324—34.

Gokak, V. K., *Coleridge's Aesthetics* (New Delhi: Abhinav Publications, 1975).

Greiner, W., 'Deutsche Einflüsse auf die Dichtungstheorie von Samuel Taylor Coleridge. Eine neue Untersuchung über den Einfluß von Tetens, Kant, und Schelling auf Coleridge', unpub. dissertation, Tubingen, 1957.

Hardy, B., 'Distinction Without Difference: Coleridge's Fancy and Imagination', *EIC* 1 (1951) 336—44.

Harold, E., 'Shipwreck in Infinity: Leopardi, Coleridge, and Wordsworth on the Imagination', in *Proceeding of the Pacific Northwest Conference on Foreign Languages*, ed. R. W. Baldner (Victoria, B.C.: University of Victoria Press, 1970) 93—101.

Hayter, A., *Opium and the Romantic Imagination* (London: Faber, Berkeley: University of California Press, 1968) esp. 214—24, 'Kubla Khan'.

Hough, G., *The Romantic Poets* (London: Hutchinson, New York: Longmans, 1953; 3rd ed., 1967) esp. 79—85.

House, H., *Coleridge* (Clark Lectures, 1951—2) (London: Hart-Davis, Toronto: Clarke, Irwin, 1953; repr. 1969).

Hume, R. D., 'Coleridge's Retention of the Primary Imagination', *N&Q*, n.s., 16 (1969) 55—6.

——— 'Kant and Coleridge on Imagination', *JAAC* 28 (1969—70) 485—96.

Hutchings, P. Æ., 'Imagination: "as the Sun paints in the camera obscura"', *JAAC* 29 (1970—1) 63—76.

Isaacs, J., 'Coleridge's Critical Terminology', *E&S* 21 (1935) 86–104.

Jackson, J. R. de J., *Method and Imagination in Coleridge's Criticism* (London: Routledge & Kegan Paul, 1969) esp. 109–21.

James, D. G., *The Romantic Comedy* (London, New York, and Toronto: O.U.P., 1948) esp. 155–212.

—— *Scepticism and Poetry: An Essay on the Poetic Imagination* (London: Allen & Unwin, 1937; repr. 1960) esp. 15–18, 44–74.

Kato, R., *Coleridge's Literary Criticism* (Tokyo: Kenkyusha, 1961).

Katsurada, R., 'The Tradition of Coleridge's Theory of Imagination' [in Japanese], *SEL* (Tokyo) 14 (1934) 325–54.

Kennedy, W. L., *The English Heritage of Coleridge of Bristol, 1798. The Basis in Eighteenth-Century English Thought for His Distinction between Imagination and Fancy* (London: Cumberlege, New Haven: Yale University Press, 1947; New York: Archon Books, 1969).

Keppel-Jones, D., 'Coleridge's Scheme of Reason', *Literary Monographs* (Wisconsin) 1 (1967) 49–100, esp. 61–74.

Knights, L. C., *Further Explorations: Essays in Criticism* (London: Chatto & Windus, Stanford: Stanford University Press, 1965) esp. 155–68, STC on *Symbol*.

Knoepfmacher, U. C., 'A Nineteenth-Century Touchstone: Chapter XV of *Biographia Literaria*', in *Nineteenth-Century Literary Perspectives: Essays in Honor of Lionel Stevenson*, ed. C. de L. Ryals (Durham, N.C.: Duke University Press, 1974) 3–16.

Lang, D. B., 'Point Counterpoint: The Emergence of Fancy and Imagination in Coleridge', *JAAC* 16 (1957–8) 384–97.

Leavis, F. R., 'Coleridge in Criticism', *Scrutiny*, 9 (1940) 57–69. Reprinted in *A Selection from Scrutiny*, ed. F. R. Leavis, 2 vols (London: C.U.P., 1968) 1 268–78.

Lefcowitz, B. F., 'Omnipotence of Thought and the Poetic Imagination: Blake, Coleridge, and Rilke', *Psychoanalytic Review* 59 (1972) 417–32.

Lentricchia, F., 'Coleridge and Emerson: Prophets of Silence, Prophets of Language', *JAAC* 32 (1973–4) 37–46.

Lenz, G. H., *Die Dichtungstheorie S. T. Coleridges: Die Konzeption der Imagination als Paradigma der romantischen Poetologie* (Frankfurt: Athenäum, 1971).

Lowes, J. L., *The Road to Xanadu: A Study in the Ways of the Imagination* (London: Constable, Boston: Houghton Mifflin, 1927; revised and enlarged, Boston: Houghton Mifflin, 1930; New York: Randon House, 1959, London: Constable, 1961; repr.

1966).

Lovejoy, A. O., 'Coleridge and Kant's Two Worlds', *ELH* 7 (1940) 341–62.

Lucas, F. L., *The Decline and Fall of the Romantic Ideal* (Cambridge: C.U.P., New York: Macmillan, 1936; repr. 1963).

Mackenzie, N., ' "Kubla Khan": A Poem of Creative Agony and Loss', *English Miscellany* 20 (1969) 229–40.

McFarland, T., *Coleridge and the Pantheist Tradition* (Oxford: Clarendon Press, 1969) esp. 33–7, 156–8, 306–10, 330–1.

—— 'The Origin and Significance of Coleridge's Theory of Secondary Imagination', in *New Perspectives on Coleridge and Wordsworth*, ed. G. H. Hartman (New York: Columbia University Press, 1972) 195–246.

McKenzie, G., *Organic Unity in Coleridge*, University of California Publications in English Vol. VII No. 1 (Berkeley: University of California Press, 1939) esp. 14–29.

Miller, C. W., 'An Examination of the Key Terms in Coleridge's Prose Writings', unpub. dissertation, University of Washington, 1956.

Muirhead, J. H., *Coleridge as Philosopher* (London: Allen & Unwin, New York: Macmillan, 1930) esp. 198–211.

Munday, M., 'John Wilson and the Distinction between Fancy and Imagination', *SIR* 13 (1974) 313–22.

Okamoto, M., 'Coleridge and his Theory of Imagination', *Doshisha Literature* (Kyoto) 24 (1966) 1–22.

Orsini, G. N. G., *Coleridge and German Idealism. A Study in the History of Philosophy, with Unpublished Materials from Coleridge's Manuscripts* (Carbondale and Edwardsville: Southern Illinois University Press, London and Amsterdam: Feffer & Simons, 1969).

Park, R., 'Coleridge and Kant: Poetic Imagination and Practical Reason', *BJA* 8 (1968) 335–46.

—— 'Coleridge: Philosopher and Theologian as Literary Critic', *UTQ* 38 (1968–9) 17–33.

Piper, H. W., *The Active Universe: Pantheism and the Concept of Imagination in the English Romantic Poets* (London: Athlone Press, New York: O.U.P., 1962) esp. 29–59, 85–105, 139–44.

Potts, L. J., and B. Hardy, 'Imagination and Fancy', *EIC* 2 (1952) 345–9.

Powell, G., 'Coleridge's "Imagination" and the Infinite Regress of Consciousness', *ELH* 39 (1972) 266–78.

Pradhan, S. V., 'Coleridge's "Philocrisy" and His Theory of Fancy and Secondary Imagination', *SIR* 13 (1974) 235—54.

—— 'Fancy and Imagination: Coleridge Versus Wordsworth', *PQ* 54 (1975) 604—23.

Prickett, S., *Coleridge and Wordsworth: The Poetry of Growth* (London: C.U.P., 1970) esp. 71—94, 95—102, 154—62.

—— 'The Living Educts of the Imagination: Coleridge on Religious Language', *TWC* 4 (1973) 99—110.

Rainsberry, F. B., 'Coleridge and the Paradox of the Poetic Imperative', *ELH* 21 (1954) 114—45.

Read, H., *The True Voice of Feeling: Studies in English Romantic Poetry* (London: Faber, New York: Pantheon Books, Toronto: McClelland, 1957; Faber reprint 1968) esp. 172—7.

Richards, I. A. *Coleridge on Imagination* (London: Routledge, New York: Harcourt, 1934; 3rd ed., 1962).

—— *The Portable Coleridge* (New York: Viking Press, 1950; repr. often) esp. 44—54.

Sanders, C. R., *Coleridge and the Broad Church Movement* (Durham, N.C.: Duke University Press, 1942).

Schneider, E., *Coleridge, Opium and Kubla Khan* (London: C.U.P., Chicago: University of Chicago Press, 1953).

Schrickx, W., 'Coleridge, Ernst Platner and the Imagination', *ES* 40 (1959) 157—62.

Schulz, M. F., 'Oneness and Multeity in Coleridge's Poems', *Tulane Studies in English* 9 (1959) 53—60.

—— *The Poetic Voices of Coleridge. A Study of his Desire for Spontaneity and Passion for Order* (Detroit: Wayne State University Press, 1963) esp. 201—6, 'Dejection: An Ode'.

Sen, R. K., 'Imagination in Coleridge and Abhinavagupta: A Critical Analysis of Christian and Saiva Standpoints', *JAAC* 24 (1965—6) 97—107.

Shaffer, E. S., 'Studies in Coleridge's Aesthetics', unpub. dissertation, Columbia University, 1966.

Sherwood, M. P., *Coleridge's Imaginative Conception of the Imagination* (Wellesley, Mass.: Hathaway House, 1937; repr. 1960).

Simmons, J. L., 'Coleridge's "Dejection: An Ode": a Poet's Re-generation', *University Review* (Kansas) 33 (1966—7) 212—18.

Stallknecht, N. P., *Strange Seas of Thought: Studies in William Wordsworth's Philosophy of Man and Nature* (London: Mark Paterson, Bloomington: University of Indiana Press, 1958; repr. 1966) esp. 166—7, 258—67.

Stempel, D., 'Revelation on Mount Snowdon: Wordsworth, Coleridge, and the Fichtean Imagination', *JAAC* 29 (1970–1) 371–84.

Thorpe, C. D., 'Coleridge as Aesthetician and Critic', *JHI* 5 (1944) 387–414.

—— 'The Imagination: Coleridge *versus* Wordsworth', *PQ* 18 (1939) 1–18.

Walsh, W., *Coleridge: The Work and the Relevance* (London: Chatto & Windus, Toronto: Clarke, Irwin, 1967).

—— *The Use of Imagination: Educational Thought and the Literary Mind* (London: Chatto & Windus, Toronto: Clarke, Irwin, 1959).

Warren, A. H., Jr, *English Poetic Theory, 1825–1865* (London: O.U.P., 1951; Princeton: Princeton University Press, 1950) esp. 18–20.

Warren, R. P., 'A Poem of Pure Imagination: An Experiment in Reading', *Kenyon Review* 8 (1946) 391–427. Reprinted in Warren's *Selected Essays* (New York: Random House, 1958; London: Eyre & Spottiswoode, 1964) 222–61; and in *The Rime of the Ancient Mariner*, ed. R. P. Warren (New York: Reynal & Hitchcock, 1946) 61–148. Abridged version available in *The Rime of the Ancient Mariner* (Twentieth Century Interpretations), ed. J. D. Boulger (Englewood Cliffs: Prentice-Hall, 1969) 21–47.

Wasserman, E. R., 'Another Eighteenth-Century Distinction between Fancy and Imagination', *MLN* 64 (1949) 23–5.

Watson, G. G., *Coleridge the Poet* (London: Routledge & Kegan Paul, 1966; repr. 1970) esp. 117–30, 'Kubla Khan'. The chapter on 'Kubla Khan' is reprinted in *Coleridge: The Ancient Mariner and Other Poems* (A Casebook), ed. A. R. Jones and W. Tydeman (London: Macmillan, 1973) 221–34.

—— 'Contributions to a Dictionary of Critical Terms: *Imagination* and *Fancy*', *EIC* 3 (1953) 201–14.

Wellek, R., *A History of Modern Criticism, 1750–1950*, 4 vols (London: Jonathan Cape, New Haven: Yale University Press, Toronto: Burns and MacEachern, 1955) esp. II 151–87.

—— *Immanuel Kant in England, 1793–1838* (London: Milford, Princeton: Princeton University Press, 1931).

Whalley, G., 'Coleridge Unlabyrinthed', *UTQ* 32 (1962–3) 325–45, esp. 340.

—— 'Coleridge's Poetic Sensibility', in *Coleridge's Variety*, ed. J. B. Beer (London: Macmillan, 1974) 1–30.

—— 'The Integrity of *Biographia Literaria*', *E&S*, n.s., 6 (1953) 87–101.

—— 'The Mariner and the Albatross', *UTQ* 16 (1946–7) 381–98. Reprinted (slightly abridged) in *Coleridge* (Twentieth Century Views), ed. K. Coburn (Englewood Cliffs: Prentice-Hall, 1967) 32–50; and also in *The Rime of the Ancient Mariner* (Twentieth Century Interpretations), ed. J. D. Boulger (Englewood Cliffs: Prentice-Hall, 1969) 73–91.

Willey, B., 'Coleridge on Imagination and Fancy' (Warton Lecture on English Poetry), *Proceedings of the British Academy* 32 (1946) 173–87. Reprinted, with modifications, as Part 3 of Willey's essay 'Samuel Taylor Coleridge' in his *Nineteenth-Century Studies. Coleridge to Matthew Arnold* (London: Chatto & Windus, New York: Columbia University Press, Toronto: Clarke, Irwin, 1949; London: Penquin Books, 1964).

—— *Samuel Taylor Coleridge* (London: Chatto & Windus, Toronto: Clarke, Irwin, 1972) esp. 188–205.

Wimsatt, W. K., Jr, and C. Brooks, *Literary Criticism: A Short History* (New York: Knopf, 1957; London: Routledge & Kegan Paul, 1958 repr. often) esp. Part III Chap 18 384–411.

Index

An asterisk indicates that the author or work is quoted.